The Martian Named Smith

"Who said I wanted to be *kind* to them? They won't starve; their commissary is by the Kilkenny Cats method. It should please them; they are used to human flesh and enjoy drinking blood—some I suspect of eating their young. But, Jubal, there is an easy way out...for any critic who is even half as smart as he *thinks* he is."

—Lazarus Long
The Number of the Beast

The Martian Named Smith

—

Critical Perspectives on Robert A. Heinlein's *Stranger in a Strange Land*

William H. Patterson Jr.
&
Andrew Thornton

Nitrosyncretic Press   nitrosyncretic
press   Sacramento

Nitrosyncretic Press
PO Box 4313
Citrus Heights, CA 95611
www.nitrosyncretic.com

First Edition

First Printing, 7 July 2001

Printed in the United States of America

Library of Congress Catalog Number: 2001090869

ISBN: 0-9679874–2–3 (Softcover)

Table of Contents

Introduction

Share Water!

Heinlein famously wrote "to entertain his readers"—true, as far as it goes, but it does not go far enough. Asking what it was Heinlein found entertaining opens up just the can of worms Heinlein tried, during his lifetime, to keep sealed. It is quite obvious there is more to his writing than "mere entertainment," particularly in *Stranger*. Heinlein is a writer "who deals with his own time as a reformer as well as an entertainer—as Shaw and H.G. Wells (who, after all, formed a climate of opinion for many years), the later Zola, and Upton Sinclair." (Tarrant, 221).

Tarrant is here speaking of James Branch Cabell,* but he might well be speaking of Heinlein. Like Mark Twain before him (whom Heinlein may consciously have used as a role model)—and Emerson before Twain—Heinlein took on the role of "public moralist"—a description he would, no doubt, have vigorously resisted if anyone leveled such a scurrilous accusation at him during his lifetime. His specific task seems particularly adapted to science fiction: he appears to relate the findings of twentieth century science to the perennial values he held and presented for the reader.

Heinlein did not confine himself to well-traveled pathways of knowledge or discourse. Tracing his ideas is a complex and sometimes difficult process which often leaves us stranded in unfamiliar territory, unrecognizably distant from the

---

* James Branch Cabell (1879–1957) was, during the 1920s, the most famous or infamous writer in the English language. His 1919 *Jurgen: A Comedy of Justice* was suppressed under the censorship laws, and the resulting trial marshalled literary opinion around the world in his favor and resulted in the abandonment of the attempt to censor literature. He was also one of Heinlein's most revered literary influences.

familiar pattern of academic citations and in an intellectual landscape lush with diversity. Or we find ourselves with a familiar roadmap that, unaccountably, has led us far from our usual haunts. We are lost in our own home, astray in our own backyard—a stranger, in fact, in a strange land.

Confusing this may be, but it is a rewarding confusion. Heinlein's layering of complexity upon complexity gives his work an unusual, even remarkable, depth. Twain combines with Cabell combines with Wells combines with Shaw combines with Korzybski—and on and on and on. *Stranger* is unusually rich, even for Heinlein, in terms of extra-textual material referenced in the fiction. Some of the references are to familiar scientific, cultural, or historical notions that make up Heinlein's personal intellectual "toolkit." Others are unique in this book, which is the most NeoPlatonic* of any of his writings. This richness may be due in part to the encyclopedic tendency of the satire form, but it was also always a personal tendency of Heinlein to load in understanding in great gobbets. There is little doubt that the mix is characteristically Heinleinian.

In sorting through this embarrassment of riches, we find that some critical approaches help rather more than do others—Eliade, for example, on myth (rather than Cassirer or Malinowsky). We need an apparatus for dealing with the archetypes we find, and who is better on archetypes than Carl Jung? And for satire, Northrup Frye, supplemented with Mikhail Bakhtin's deep ruminations on parody and on Rabelais. Fashion in contemporary criticism has turned away from the materials Heinlein most relied upon in *Stranger*. Rhetorical analysis is important—and, indeed, consideration of *texte*** has a very special dimension in analysis of *Stranger*—but some of the materials particularly significant in *Stranger* are simply invisible to structural analysis and Deconstruction. It is a book that invites us to peel back layers of references and their associations, revealing still more laminations of references and associations.

Writers ordinarily use extra-textual references to associate a set of ideas which either fill out the thematic development, or add a parallel point of view, or provide resonances and intellectual overtones. Heinlein made a regular practice—here brought to a high state of finish—of using the overt reference to carry a second or third layer of reference of associated ideas. One of the most obvious of

---

* NeoPlatonism is a highly influential philosophy derived from the writings of Plato (a contemporary of Aristotle and Socrates). NeoPlatonism is discussed in greater detail in Chapter 18.

** In talking about the concerns of Deconstruction, it is sometimes necessary to revert to Derrida's or Foucault's original French terms, simply because the words don't say the same thing in English as they do in French. For example, the important term *l'invention de l'autre* does not translate into English at all. It is sometimes rendered by transliteration as "incoming of the other," but the phrase is not, as linguists say, "productive" in English and requires extensive explanation. A Deconstructionist by "text" (*texte*) means, not the published words, but the interplay of a reader's unique subset of the language with the published words and the author's intent.

these multi-layered references is Heinlein's persistent use of elites. These have been theologically referred to the Elect of Calvinism (Slusser, 1975; Stover, 1987). But the full range of uses to which Heinlein puts this figure do not fit within the narrow confines of the Calvinist interpretation. While it is entirely possible that Heinlein begins with the theological Elect as a recognizable symbol suitable to "front" for the entirety of his conception, he then associates other idea-complexes: his elect all have gone through a special process, an initiation, acquiring hidden knowledge, and they associate together in secret or semi-secret societies working for the betterment of humankind. This is not an accidental or incidental figure: Heinlein is here referencing a very ancient tradition among occult and esoteric religions and philosophies of enlightened masters (the "Mahatmas" in the Hindu traditions) who come together in secret societies (called by Theosophists the "White Brotherhood") to work for the spiritual advancement or protection of the human race. Heinlein's "Competent Men" (Panshin) are not merely gung-ho, New Frontier types, "the best and the brightest." They are illuminated. They are enlightened. They belong also to the occult and esoteric tradition of the White Brotherhood. The Nest, the highest circle in the Church of All Worlds, is just one in a long series of these miniature White Brotherhoods, and Heinlein has studied this phenomenon in all stages—including such a secret society in decay, in *Friday*.

The Calvinist elect, which is publicly familiar as a front for the other, less familiar ideas, introduces the reader to them. Heinlein made particular use of this notion in *Stranger* as he builds his Messianic myth.

Again and again, what seems a simple reference on the surface unfolds in layer after layer of complexity, wonder, and delight. Common ideas "front" for or camouflage much deeper and less obvious ideas, adding great depth and dimensionality to his overall treatment. The various propositions on which this layering turns come from many and diverse sources, and whatever their factual or scientific "truth," they go to make up a literary truth of very high order.

Scientific truth needs to be true-to-facts—or, at a minimum, true to *some* dimensions of *some* facts: scientifically, the Sun *is* a gaseous mass undergoing internal nuclear fusion. It *is not*, scientifically, a golden chariot pulled by four horses. This is a metaphor—a poetic, or literary, truth. In psychological terms, "Love" *is* "an emotional interaction leading to pair bonding." But very few writers of Harlequin romances would have a character remark, "Oh, my darling! I'm emotionally interacted with you. Let us pair-bond!"

Literary truth is necessarily true to peoples' experience, including emotional, intellectual, and—occasionally, but not necessarily—factual experience. But it cannot restrict itself to the narrow dimension of the *merely* factual. It engages the *Zeitgeist*; it engages the world-outlook (*Weltanschauung*); it engages the patterns of myth, of genre, of story, of character—and so on. A simply linear description of the factual dimension cannot engage all these other dimensions of experience. That is why we have art.

The test of literary truth is how these various dimensions are chosen, staffed, and played out in order to affect the reader. The literary truth is multi-layered and multi-dimensioned, though a reader may focus on only one or a few of its possible dimensions and lose track of the totality. To help, there is even a summary in the book of its important points, in the "Garden of Gethsemane" talk* Mike has with Jubal when Jubal first comes to visit Mike's Nest. Heinlein has often put these summaries into his books, but *Stranger's* is extremely important, because it sums up and reiterates the most important lines of thought Heinlein has been developing for hundreds of pages. It is very possible, for example, for someone to read *Stranger* without noticing, or caring, how various elements of Western culture are artfully arranged, figure by figure, note by note, as it were, to give resonance, depth, and overtones to the work. This is the "background music" (to continue the musical metaphor) Heinlein used with great skill to pose his questions so that his readers would be forced to think. This is his primary purpose, and he uses all the considerable technique at his command to break through the boundaries of conventional thought patterns.

There seems to be an innate tendency for people to think the social customs and institutions with which they grew up are "the way things have always been" and the only natural and proper way of going about things. One of the themes most personally important to Heinlein throughout his long career was to break through this mental rigidity and develop in his readers flexibility of mind. *Stranger* is a blow struck in this particular campaign, as Heinlein remarked to his agent at the time of publication, and to "A Fan" in 1973, by which time *Stranger* had become a social icon of remarkable status. Heinlein was himself certainly startled by the rise in popularity of this book, nearly a decade after its initial publication, and somewhat startled by the number of people who formed "Nests." Certainly there is nothing *wrong* with doing so—but taking *Stranger* as a social bluepoint misses the essential purpose of the book—which is, to ask yourself the hard questions and come up with your own answers, not copy the fictional "answers" Heinlein posed for purposes of his satire.

"I was *not* giving answers. I was trying to shake the reader loose from some preconception and induce him to think for himself, along new and fresh lines. In consequence each reader gets something different out of that book *because he himself supplies the answers.*

"If I managed to shake him loose from some prejudice, preconception, or unexamined assumption that was all I intended to do. A rational human being does not need answers, spoon-fed to him on 'faith'; he needs questions to worry over—seri-

---

* That is, this talk with Jubal has the same place in *Stranger* that Christ's prayer in the Garden of Gethsemane has in the biblical passion-story. But it also summarizes the entire argument of the satire.

ous ones…But I would never undertake to be a 'Prophet,' handing out neatly pack-aged answers for lazy minds." (*Grumbles*, 245–6)

Heinlein loved science fiction and thought well of its "carrying capacity" for important ideas. His work is replete with interesting technological ideas, but it is also full of important philosophical ideas, derived, many of them, from the American Freethinking heritage. Freethought was a vital intellectual movement current at the time of Heinlein's birth; textual evidence suggests that, as a young man he absorbed important ideas from nineteenth century and early twentieth century thinkers as varied as John Humphrey Noyes, George Bernard Shaw, T.H. Huxley, Walt Whitman, Col. Robert Ingersoll, H.L. Mencken, and Ralph Waldo Emerson. At the time Heinlein was being educated, Friedrich Wilhelm Nietzsche—who also had admired and praised Emerson—was a leading intellectual influence in European and American culture. Heinlein deeply absorbed and transmuted what Nietzsche had to say. The spirit of Nietzsche hovers over *Stranger*, and it is apparent that Heinlein was quite conscious of this: his remarks above quoted in the 1973 letter to "A Fan" echo Nietzsche's deliberate rejection of "disciples" or followers.

Heinlein's individual "take" on Freethinking seems to include some very American Transcendentalist notions. These ideas, which Emerson inherited from the NeoPlatonic movement of the nineteenth century, are deeply embedded in *Stranger*. The book's master message, "Thou Art God," is one of them. The twentieth century and modernism have "forgotten" these important matters, but Heinlein has kept them alive and transmitted them to future generations, and this broadcasting of intellectual seed then slowly found fertile ground. The most immediate and obvious effect was the startling acceptance of *Stranger* by the counterculture of the Sixties, but the Good Word he brings will always be important, so long as hypocrisy remains a thorn in the side of the body politic and a source of personal pain.

A Note about Citations to *Stranger*

Because of the nearly unique fact that *Stranger in a Strange Land* is widely available in two very different editions (the 166,000 word version published in 1961 and the 220,000 "uncut" version published in 1990), references in this book to passages in *Stranger* are given as dual page cites, to the two most widely available editions, in the form: (nnn/nnn). The first number refers to a page in the paperback edition of the 1961 version; and the second number refers to a page in the Ace trade (large size) paperback edition of the "uncut" version. In a few cases, where we are talking about material which appears only in the "cut" version, a single page number is cited, and this refers to the paperback edition of 1961.

Acknowledgements

The authors wish to extend their heartfelt thanks to the Gang of Five for reading and commenting on the penultimate draft of this book:

Rita Bottoms, Archivist, UC Santa Cruz
Virginia Heinlein
Robert James, Ph.D.
Brad Linaweaver
David Silver

Their suggestions and reactions made a major impact on the shape of the final draft (though, of course, the errors and the opinions, and particularly the opinions which are errors, are those of the authors).

The authors wish particularly to thank Mrs. Heinlein for her careful attention in her reading to the correctness of its historical detail and for permission to quote from manuscripts not yet part of the public record.

Dr. James' close and critical reading of the manuscript was of inestimable benefit—most particularly in challenging the assumptions and conclusions of the text. His scholarship and willingness to be put upon were exceptional even in a field of exceptional contributors.

Finally, it is a rare privilege to work with a publisher whose knowledge of the subject matter is authoritative enough to make the errors he catches (which we should have) really, really sting. The authors wish to extend their special thanks to Jim Gifford for this invaluable service—as well as for accommodating the whims and eccentricities of the authors beyond any possible rational tolerance.

PART ONE
"His Maculate Conception"

—

"Jubal shuddered. '*Read* it? Good God!
It's bad enough to write such a thing.'"

— I —

Stranger in Context

Stranger in a Strange Land is unique in Heinlein's *corpus* in that it was written in several widely-separated sessions over a twelve-year period from 1948 to 1960—a period in which American culture underwent a drastic evolution. Heinlein's typical method was to spend a long time—as much as several months—planning a book in his head and then to write it straight through in a period of weeks or a few months. In the case of *Stranger*, however, he had a conception that was much bigger than his other books—a satire that would have had a very strained reception when it was first conceived, if it could be published at all. By the time it was finished, however, the post-war cultural developments Heinlein was concerned with were far enough advanced that the book was only slightly ahead of its time—just enough to help shape the social revolution that took place in the 1960s.

Before World War I science fiction was published only in the adventure magazines. These magazines represented a deliberate new "democratization" of literature pioneered in 1895 by Frank Munsey's *Argosy*. In his efforts to make reading material available to the non-aristocratic classes, he typically printed the magazines on the cheapest grade of rough pulp paper, so that he could reduce the price to ten cents, with garish cover art aimed at sophisticated ten-year olds. Thus the magazines were, and are, affectionately known as "pulps." The pulps grew up around the turn of the century as the "low rent district" of the world of commercial fiction, with the prestige fiction magazines like *Colliers* and the *Atlantic Monthly*, printed on glazed paper (hence called the "slicks") defining the high end of commercial fiction. Many imitators soon followed the commercial success of *Argosy*, and the pulp industry proliferated into many different kinds of magazines, each serving a small audience of specialty readers: detective stories, flying stories, romances, western stories, military stories, and the hero pulps.

Science fiction and fantasy were relatively late in getting their own specialized magazines: the speculative fiction magazine period begins in 1923 with the publication of *Weird Tales*, a magazine devoted to Dunsany and Bierce knockoffs. Belgian emigre-inventor Hugo Gernsback had been publishing science-invention stories in his radio and electric popular science magazines since about 1911; an "all scientific fiction" issue of *Electrical Experimenter* in 1923 had convinced him the market was ready for a genre[1] magazine, and he launched *Amazing Stories* in 1926, followed a few years later by *Air Wonder Stories* and *Thrilling Wonder Stories*. At first the magazines were filled with reprints from Poe, Verne, and Wells, but rapidly a stable of specialist writers began turning out original fiction. Gernsback ran a competition to name the new genre of pulp fiction, which went by such awkward circumlocutions as "scientific romances" and "extraordinary voyages." "Scientific-tion" won the competition, and Gernsback continued to use that term until the 1950s, but most people adopted "science fiction" as the preferred term.

The successful Clayton chain in 1930 launched *Astounding Stories of Super-Science*. *Astounding* was to be the most successful of all the science fiction magazines; it continues to exist under its successor name of *Analog Science Fact–Science Fiction*.

The 1930s were the heyday of the pulps as a publishing phenomenon. Some of the pulp characters migrated into radio series starting as early as the 1930s (e.g., Orson Welles' popular *The Shadow*) or comic books or even book publications as the pulp magazine industry slowly died out by about 1954. Most of the writing in these magazines was of frankly dreadful quality—submarginal by even the most lenient literary standards. But in these magazines generations of novice writers were able to make a living, of a sort, while learning the basics of the craft of writing. And occasionally a writer of genuine genius got his start in the pulps—Upton Sinclair, Dashiell Hammett, Raymond Chandler, Ray Bradbury, and Robert Heinlein.

Science fiction had undergone a peculiar evolution during the 1930s. Its devoted readership had formed local clubs and exchanged amateur magazines ("fanzines") devoted to science fiction. Unlike the other pulp readerships, science fiction fans found that they shared progressive and often technocratic visions of a

---

1. The term *genre* is confusingly used in many different senses in literary criticism. The word literally means "kind" or "type," in the sense of belonging to a family (i.e., *gens*) of like examples. In the sense in which pulp magazines represent "genres," a common style, form, or content is meant. Thus all the "flying ace" stories commonly deal with World War I pilots and their air battles, in terms of content. In terms of style, there are common conventions of language that belong to the pulp magazines, regarded as primitive, crude, and over-written by the standards of the slick magazines, but also there are conventions unique to each genre about what qualities are portrayed in the characters and what typical situations are appropriate for the stories. The science fiction pulps, until about 1939, had only two major conventions of story form (the adventure story and the gadget story), with an occasional sprinkling of utopias.

future increasingly dominated by technology. By the end of the 1930s, a generation of young writers who had grown up with their genre conventions firmly in mind no longer felt it necessary to explain or justify every commonplace invention or novation, so devices such as the manlike robot or faster-than-light travel or ray guns or rocketships could conventionally be treated as "furniture" of the fiction, their validity assumed as a premise of the story. The fictional focus could then be placed on matters other than the wonderful inventions. In the years immediately before World War II, the readership of the science fiction magazines had begun to demand in the letter columns expansion of the permissible story forms away from the simple adventure story (exemplified by the Tarzan and Mars stories of Edgar Rice Burroughs) and the Gernsbackian gadget story. The new stories were to be "sociological"—that is, concerned with human societies interacting with technological change. In short, the readership was trying to take the genre of science fiction writing outside of genre conventions, to make it into a literary form in its own right, within the conventions of the romance genre.

Popular fiction has been called "subliterary" in the sense that it provides a pool of "primitive" sources, out of which the mainstream of literature draws its dominant forms at any given period—highly conventionalized, and highly restricted in emotional scope by comparison to the main body of world literature. The movement within science fiction, led by John W. Campbell Jr. in both his roles as a writer and as a highly influential editor, sought to expand the base of conventional story types permitted in the genre. At the same time, the gulf between "art" literature and commercial fiction in general was widening, commercial fiction containing a mix of romance and "realistic" conventions, while art fiction became more restricted to realistic,[2] even "journalistic" conventions.

Around the turn of the century, a series of books appeared, codifying the conventions of romance fiction into a set of "rules" for story construction—a sure sign that the romance was dead as a living literary movement. These rules produced the recognizable "plot" of commercial fiction, with a defined story arc,

---

2. It should also be noted that "realism" is not particularly descriptive, in the sense that these writers were writing more accurate mimesis than their predecessors (though that seems to be what they thought they were doing). One set of conventions of diction and of subject matter cannot be more or less "accurate" than any other set of conventions, because a literary convention is an agreement between author and reader that a certain symbol represents a certain referent. The communication between author and reader is in the agreement, not in the convention. But it is just as much a matter of the conventions of one's day for O'Neill in *Long Day's Journey Into Night* to focus on a drug addiction that makes a family life a nightmare as it was for Trollope in the middle of the nineteenth century to focus in *The Warden* on the honorable, sweet-natured and eminently respectable Warden of an orphanage. Both sets of convention prescribe subject matter suitable for their practitioners, and good art results in both cases.

development of the story line, and specified resolution of conflict.[3] The important area of integration of plot with theme was neglected, because it cannot be specified by rules of construction. By way of the "well-made story," these conventions of story construction entered film and were perpetuated long after other areas even of commercial fiction had abandoned those rules.

The conventions of the well-made play came to dominate the short story form in commercial fiction during the first decades of the twentieth century, though art fiction and novels somewhat escaped the pressure for writers to conform to the rules.

When Campbell assumed editorship of *Astounding* in 1938, it was with a revolutionary program for science fiction in mind: he wanted to establish a new and wider set of literary conventions as the base for science fiction. With startling energy he began shaping the new writing, talking over story concepts and philosophy with a new stable of writers, all thoroughly versed in the conventional furniture of science fiction. Within a year, what was to be called the "Golden Age of Science Fiction" was clearly taking shape. The familiar writers—Jack Williamson, Nat Schachner, Malcolm Jameson—took on new story forms, and the new writers of the new age began to appear one by one—L. Sprague de Camp, Alfred Bester, Lester del Rey, Theodore Sturgeon, Isaac Asimov, Robert Heinlein.

The before-and-after of the Campbellian revolution was caught in a single issue of *Astounding*—January 1940. In this issue, E.E. "Doc" Smith's *Gray Lensman* serial concluded, and the Heinlein story "Requiem" appeared. *Gray Lensman* is a thundering good read, full of sound and fury, vast armadas of space ships (and planets!) locked in epic battle, meter-thick busbars carrying unimaginable power, ultimate good destroying ultimate evil, and signifying not a whole lot. The economics, sociology, anthropology—all the "fuzzy studies"—are not so much laughable as non-existent.[4] "Requiem," by contrast, is nothing but "fuzzy." It is a story entirely subordinated to a mood of *triste* and transcendence.

A voracious and catholic reader, Heinlein had been reading science fiction ever since there was such a thing—he had encountered Gernsback's "all scientific fiction" issue of *Electrical Experimenter* while on a hiking trip at age 15, in 1923 (Patterson, "Biographical Sketch," 9)—so he was thoroughly familiar with the conventions of the genre. Campbell never had to "train" Heinlein the way he

3. The most highly developed generic rules were for a type of theatrical play called the "well-made play" (the term is taken over from the French *bien fait*), which dominated stages in Europe and the U.S. from about 1880 to about 1920. These rules sought to duplicate the forms of the most successful play of the age: *Bertha, the Sewing Machine Girl*, which had thousands of performances worldwide during its thirty-year run. The plays of Ibsen and Strindberg, which were to be influential on twentieth century literature, were never reduced to a set of structural rules.

4. To be fair to Smith, he did include a view of the psychology and economics of drugs and drug-addiction and of the economics and psychology of grubstake mining.

trained Asimov or others of the *Astounding* stable. Heinlein was also philosophically fully formed in the direction Golden Age science fiction was to go: sociological and "process" fiction was as natural to him as breathing. Instead, Heinlein led the way and the entire field followed his example. Heinlein did not look to the rule-bound area of commercial fiction for his prosodic models; he learned more from "art" writers like H.G. Wells, Mark Twain, Anatole France, and James Branch Cabell. From the first, Heinlein did not look at his material as a writer of popular fiction, but as a writer of literature would—with much more than accustomed flexibility about the conventions he would use for any given story. Indeed, his early stories are remarkable because he often used different sets of conventions for each story, in some cases even inventing new scene forms.

In the early 1940s, Campbell spoke of Heinlein stories as if they were *Post* or *Colliers* stories of the era in which they were set; in the late 1940s, Campbell was to speak of this as the ideal for all *Astounding* stories.

Questions for Discussion

1. Popular literature always reflects the culture it is written for. What social forces or topical events of the period when science fiction was coming into existence (roughly 1910 through 1930) are reflected in the pulp fiction phenomenon?

2. What does the distinction between "art literature" and "commercial fiction" mean? Has this distinction changed since the early twentieth century?

3. Discuss the difference between nineteenth century romance conventions and literary realism. Name some examples of each.

4. Since about 1970, some writers—such as Robert Silverberg and Michael Moorcock—have tried to bring conventions of realism into science fiction. Has this movement been successful in integrating science fiction and realism? Is science fiction naturally a romance literature?

5. Some critics and writers refer to "Campbellian science fiction" as a set of conventions against which they are reacting. John Campbell defined a historically middle ground between the nineteenth century gadget/adventure story and contemporary science fiction. Heinlein's early writing was an important part of this process of definition. What was Campbell doing?

For Further Reading

Aldiss, Brian. *The Trillion Year Spree*. New York: Atheneum Press, 1986

Amis, Kinglsey. *New Maps of Hell*. New York: Ballantine Books, 1960.

Kondo, Yoji, ed. *"Requiem": New Collected Works by Robert A. Heinlein and Tributes to the Grand Master*. New York: Tor Books, 1992. See especially Robert Silverberg's "Heinlein."

Heinlein, Robert A. "Requiem." *The Past Through Tomorrow*. New York: G.P. Putnam's Sons, 1967

Moskowitz, Samuel J. *Seekers of Tomorrow: Masters of Modern Science Fiction*. Cleveland, Ohio: The World Publishing Company, 1966

Smith, Edward E. *Gray Lensman*. Reading, Penn.: Fantasy Press, 1951

Wells, H.G. *The War of the Worlds: A Critical Text of the 1898 London First Edition, with an Introduction, Illustrations and Appendices*. Ed., Leon Stover. Jefferson, North Carolina: McFarland & Company, Inc., 2001

— 2 —

Heinlein and the
Culture of Science Fiction

In a sense, America did not truly enter the twentieth century until World War II. The social power of Victorian sensibilities lingered through the early part of the century, though badly shaken by the first wave of popular feminism and the opening up of the work force to women, the traumas of World War I, and the first age of sexual liberation, the 1920s (the period of Heinlein's youth). The Depression of the "Red" 1930s jolted nineteenth century economic certainties, even as the worst prophecies of Progressives about the death of capitalism seemed to be coming true.

World War II put the tombstone on the grave of nineteenth century sensibilities. Twentieth century technology—both the technology of gadgetry and the technology of social and industrial organization—had an important part in this transition: millions of citizen-soldiers were put directly in contact with technological warfare, and they got a direct sense of the overwhelming importance of the machine to their personal lives, for good and for evil. Rationing at home of the matériel of technological warfare re-ordered peoples' priorities, and the sudden re-opening of the manufacturing workforce to women, on a scale never before dreamed of, jolted the ordered certainties of pre-war world outlooks. On the leading edge of intellectual life, the explosions of the atomic bomb at Alamagordo and at Hiroshima and Nagasaki altered the old world forever. One group, the pessimists, saw the obliteration of cities as evidence of the horror-to-come, while optimists viewed the rapid technological expansion as the basis of a new world order of prosperity. Both optimists and pessimists turned to science fiction to help them interpret the new world, though they wanted their "answers" in simple and easily digested forms. People recognized that they were living in a new world and wanted a vocabulary for discourse, a sense of what it all meant, a means of understanding. Ultimately, it was not information they were seeking, it was a myth, in the exact, anthropological sense of the term.

Science fiction had been exploring process and organization as well as development of science and technology. Campbell's *Astounding* had made great transforming strides in opening up a narrow genre to wider reaches of possibility, but it was not and could never be a truly mass medium for interpretation. People needed a new way of looking at the new world—a new paradigm, a new *Weltanschauung*—but the highly-developed shorthand and jargon of the intellectual discourse going on in the pages of *Astounding* were too far outside the frame of reference of the general public. *Astounding*'s intense background of conventional assumptions, utterly necessary to support the wider range of story possibilities, militated against widespread public acceptance.[5]

Heinlein's personal agenda, however, fell into exactly this public need to interpret the new technological world. He had given up writing to work as a civilian aeronautical engineer for the Navy Aircraft Materials Center in Philadelphia soon after the outbreak of World War II; at the end of the war he was galvanized by an urgent need to communicate the terms of the new world to his fellow citizens. Within a week of V–J day, he resigned and headed back to Los Angeles, to resume his career as a writer, but at a new level of seriousness. He wrote a series of articles about the coming cold war, but the market was resistant and none was ever published contemporaneously. Perhaps he was just too far in advance of demand at the time.

He was also interested in breaking out of the pulp ghetto, and in this he was more successful. He gave considerable thought to what genre conventions had to be kept and what could be dispensed with. Gradually he created a methodology for interpreting the new world for general fiction readers: move the "conventional" stories of perennial conflicts—a man having to choose between his work and his marriage, for example—into the coming age of the industrial exploitation of space. The man's job could be rocket pilot instead of an airline pilot, and that would give a good example to visualize the coming world. This was in fact, "Space Jockey," one of the four stories he sold to the highest-paying of the slick magazines, the *Saturday Evening Post*, in 1947. Similar stories were to sell to *Colliers*, *Blue Book*, *Town & Country*, and the *Elks* magazine over the next several years.

---

5. And critical acceptance, as well. It is noteworthy that critics who would never venture to remark on *Pilgrim's Progress*, for example, without acquiring some background on Bunyan's Puritan "furniture" feel no need to educate themselves about the intellectual environment of science fiction. Much sf criticism is, therefore, not so much "wrong" as it is "wrongheaded" and, therefore, beside the point.

Writers and readers of pulp science fiction were alternately amazed and scornful of the simple-minded stuff Heinlein was selling to the slicks. But the truth is, the highly conventionalized material John Campbell was publishing in *Astounding* could not be sold to the public: for many years there continued to be a perennial market for articles addressed to librarians on how to recognize and buy good science fiction, as the new market for hardcover science fiction books continued to grow. Heinlein had to figure out on his own how to sell science fiction ideas to a public that was not intellectually prepared to deal with the concepts in the same way that science fiction readers had prepared themselves. Once he defined his market, he entered a different level of commercial writing and continued to extend and expand his efforts. He branched out to films, too, writing the script for *Destination Moon* with established screenwriter Alford "Rip" van Ronkel. George Pal Productions bought the property and filmed it in 1949. *Destination Moon* is considered the first modern science fiction film.

Another commercial avenue opened up for him as early as 1947. A publisher of boys' books in Philadelphia had approached him for a book. Heinlein outlined a series of books about a team of Young Atomic Engineers, similar to the Tom Swift series and began to write the first one. But rogue Nazis on the Moon wasn't quite what the publisher was looking for. Heinlein's new agent, Lurton Blassingame, took the book to Scribner's, who liked it well enough to publish it in 1947 under the title *Rocket Ship Galileo* (from which the story for *Destination Moon* was loosely adapted). However, Scribner's, a prestige publisher, was not looking for a Tom Swift series, so the Young Atomic Engineers series was never written. Scribner's was, however, interested in more books for boys: the publishing contract contained a standard option for his next book, and this set up a wildly successful series of a dozen boy's books of enduring popularity, written throughout the decade of the 1950s. As a consequence of the popular series of books, his magazine appearances in the *Post*, and the success of *Destination Moon*, Heinlein was to become something of a minor-league celebrity during the 1950s.

In November 1948, Heinlein kept an appointment with a neighbor ten miles away in Colorado Springs to use his ham radio equipment to talk to his friend John Campbell, editor of *Astounding Science-Fiction*, who had his own ham set-up in New Jersey. The subject of the latest issue of *Astounding* came up. One of the letter-writers, Richard Hoen, had sent in a joke "review" of the next November's issue, with appearances of all the "greats." (Perhaps this is an early emergence of nostalgia for the "Golden Age" of prewar *Astoundings*.) Although Heinlein had not appeared in the pages of *Astounding* since before World War II (such an appearance would have been a significant drop in income for Heinlein during the period he was selling to the slicks), Hoen had "reviewed" a new Heinlein serial titled "Gulf."

Wouldn't it be a great "topper" for the joke, Heinlein suggested, if Campbell made the November 1949 issue come out the way Hoen had described it? If

Campbell would do the necessary leg-work to get the other authors Hoen had "reviewed" lined up, he (Heinlein) would write a story to Hoen's "Gulf" title.

Campbell jumped at the chance to have a new Heinlein story. Thus the "time travel" issue of *Astounding* came into existence.

Heinlein put the project on his professional agenda for later discussion. He didn't have a story idea on hand to fit the "Gulf" title. So in November or December, he scheduled a story session with his wife, Virginia Heinlein, who was rapidly becoming a silent partner in his writing business. He was a little limited in what he could do, for the speculative screenplay he had written with Rip Van Ronkel had been sold to George Pal, and Heinlein had been hired as Technical Assistant for *Destination Moon*. Production was scheduled to start in Hollywood in July 1949, and the Heinleins would have to be on hand for the shooting. He would only have a couple of months after finalizing *Red Planet*, the latest boys' book for Scribner's, to work on "Gulf."

Virginia Heinlein had prepared a couple of ideas for this story session. One of them, a satirical story about a man raised by aliens, Heinlein was instantly taken with—only, he thought, it would probably take more time to write than he had available. As discussion continued, the idea firmed up: it would be a Mowgli story (referencing Kipling's two Jungle Books)—with the boy raised by Martians instead of jungle animals, and he could use some of the Martian background he hadn't been able to use in *Red Planet*. He could be a Martian named Smith. He made some notes and turned to other material.

He had been thinking about writing a superman story. What, he asked his wife, Virginia, do supermen do better than us ordinaries? "They think better," she replied. This story, too, Heinlein made notes about. He could combine the *Homo superior* idea that was then fashionable in science fiction then with a three-part article that had appeared in the *Post* about Samuel Renshaw's startling work with sense discrimination the year before.

But the Martian story was very compelling. In January 1949 he wrote about the idea to Campbell, asking for input. For one reason or another, however, it was the *Homo superior* story that Heinlein wrote for "Gulf." Shortly thereafter, Heinlein went to Hollywood, only to find movie production delayed for months. He wrote a Boys' Life serial and his next boys' book for Scribner's, *Farmer in the Sky*, while waiting for production to commence in October 1949.

The "Martian named Smith" was put in the files to ferment.

Questions for Discussion

1. World War I has been called the first "technological war," and it was also followed by a period of social change culminating in The Great Depression. A period of social change also followed World War II. What factors differed in peoples' experience of the two wars? How were their experiences reflected in the social changes that took place after each? Are we still dealing with the changes of World War II?

2. There was a flood of "atomic catastrophe" books, stories, and movies in the 1950s and early 1960s. People were trying to deal with the new "atomic age" in the context of the Cold War. How is this trend related to the recent run of films set in a "post-apocalyptic" world (*Road Warrior* and *Terminator* are two prominent examples)?

3. Is it true that science fiction has become our principal source of imagery for thinking about the future?

4. Some critics assert that science fiction is no longer a living art form. Given the huge prominence of science fiction in films, why would they say that?

5. How does the science fiction that appears in film differ from the science fiction that appeared in book and magazine formats? What cultural factors contribute to this difference (if any?)

For Further Reading

Heinlein, Robert A. "Gulf." *Assignment in Eternity.* Riverdale, NY: Baen Publishing Co., 1953

Destination Moon. George Pal Productions, 1950.

– 3 –

Composition and
Publishing History

The story of *Stranger In a Strange Land* begins late in 1948, as Heinlein is finishing up *Red Planet*, his third "boys' book" for Scribner's. That story deals with a revolution of colonists on Mars against the arbitrary authority of an absentee corporate owner and introduces a unique portrait of the Martians as "elder souls"—a transformation of H.G. Wells' materialist-socialist "intellects vast, cool, and unsympathetic" from *War of the Worlds*.[6] As he wrote, Heinlein created a more thoroughly worked-out backstory for the Martians than he could fit into the confines of his boy's book. He often talked out his ideas with his wife, Virginia,[7] regretting that he would not be able to use any of the material.

---

6. In the brief summary of *War of the Worlds* that concludes the polemical introduction to his new critical edition, Leon Stover eerily converges on the general outline also of *Stranger* (if we understand the "conquest" as spiritual rather than simply military):

   "...the Martians...arrive as enemies from an older (and wiser) world to conquer a newer one (in need of wisdom). In turn...they serve as a model for earthlings in their conquest of a new world; the future created out of the destruction of a mistaken past." (*Id.*, 46)

7. The partnership of Virginia and Robert Heinlein has been somewhat explored in *Robert A. Heinlein: Popular Adult Educator and Philosopher of Education* by Phillip Homer Owenby, Ph.D., Unpublished Doctoral Dissertation available through UMI Dissertation Services, Ann Arbor, Michigan, 1996, and in Owenby's "Silent Partner: The Power Behind the Throne" in *The Power and the Potential of Collaborative Learning Partnerships*. I.M. Saltiel, A. Sgrois, and R.G. Brockett, eds. San Francisco: Jossey-Bass (1998), but as of this date there has not been a full investigation of Virginia Heinlein's many contributions to the Heinlein *corpus*.

Reading *Red Planet* and *Stranger* in parallel shows how Heinlein scavenged the underlying Martian civilization. There are the "disappearances" of various obnoxious (in Martian eyes) characters—a medical lieutenant (*Red Planet*, 32); Howe, the authoritarian Head Master (184); the Resident Agent General, Beecher (186). The Water Ceremony: "Growing Together is an imperfect translation of a Martian idiom, which names their most usual social event" (34–37). Martians not having sex in human terms (193). The idea of the Nest (109). Mike's initial reaction to a human zoo: "Jim tried to explain [a zoo], but broke off before he had finished elaborating the idea. The Martian radiated such cold, implacable anger that Jim was frightened" (118). The Martian Old Ones also have the same ghostly-spiritual qualities in both books. MacRae compares the Old One/Adult relationship to the human notion of Heaven (93).

These ideas are used as atmosphere and as the background for action. They are never brought to the fore; they are never explicated or explored. When Virginia suggested her Mowgli story as a satire, Heinlein told Campbell, she also suggested it would be a good way to incorporate all the material he had been developing.

The essential problem with the Mowgli story (tentatively titled *A Martian Named Smith* at this point) is that it didn't fit into *any* market he had previously sold to, and if he said what he had to say it wouldn't even be publishable. It had to be a satire, and you cannot pull punches in a satire, but editors—as he had special cause to know because of his increasingly unsatisfying relations with the Scribner's juvenile editor, Alice Dalgliesh[8]—were timid creatures afraid of the librarians who viewed themselves as ever-vigilant guardians of the young. Well, this wouldn't be a boy's book—but his supposed "adult" editors were starting to insist that he cut his material to the juvenile audience. If he wrote it the way it had to be written, there might not be any kind of market for it.

On several occasions over the next decade, Heinlein took out the project and worked on it.[9] Everyone he discussed it with seemed enthusiastic about it—but it just didn't come together to Heinlein's satisfaction. In 1952 he made extensive outline notes, developing up the character of Jubal Harshaw out of the Kettle Belly Baldwin character he had created for "Gulf" in 1949. He may have written the prologue to the novel at this time before putting the project away. In 1953 he made more notes, and in 1955, after returning from his first around-the-world tour, he actually wrote the first part of the book, the 54,000 words that get Valentine Michael Smith out of the hands of the Federation and into the hands of Jubal Harshaw. But he bogged down at exactly the point where the satire begins to predominate over the adventure-intrigue story and put it back in his files (*Grumbles*, 260; letter to Lurton Blassingame dated February 23, 1955).

---

8. See pages 49–100 of *Grumbles From the Grave*, and especially the letter dated April 19, 1949, starting on page 61.

9. The details of the origin and composition of Stranger are given in Patterson, "Early Chronology of Stranger."

In April of 1958 he was looking over the material again, tentatively titling it *The Heretic* in his mind, when a full page ad from the SANE Committee appeared in the local (Colorado Springs) newspaper, advocating unilateral cessation of nuclear testing. Believing this constituted an insane response to the Soviet threat, Heinlein started a counter-campaign which collapsed a few weeks later when President Eisenhower called a unilateral halt to nuclear testing. The circumstances of this event are detailed in Heinlein's 1980 collection of miscellanea, *Expanded Universe*.

Heinlein dropped *The Heretic* and instead wrote *Starship Troopers*, an anti-communist novel which was unanimously and unceremoniously rejected by the entire editorial board of Scribner's, thereby breaking their string of options. Heinlein's agent began shopping the story around. The juveniles had been such a commercial success for Scribner's that they were already legendary within the book publishing community. Walter Minton, at G.P. Putnam's Sons, heard that there was a Heinlein juvenile available and instructed his people to grab it unconditionally. *The Magazine of Fantasy and Science Fiction*, edited by Heinlein's old friend from pre-war days, "Anthony Boucher" (William A.P. White), brought out a condensed serial version, which was followed by the Putnam's publication. The book caused a storm of controversy, which still rages forty years later, and won the Hugo Award, science fiction fandom's award for the best novel of the year, at the World Science Fiction Convention in Philadelphia the following year.

Heinlein turned back to *The Heretic*, now again titled *A Martian Named Smith*. He had effectively declared his independence from the strictures of editors. From now on, he resolved, he would not write conventional books for anybody else's idea of his market. Instead, he would write "my own stuff, my own way." (*Grumbles*, 261). He wrote straight through the book and wound up with an 800 page manuscript not like anything anybody else had ever done. It wasn't a pulp serial at all; it was a kind of a fairy story—by which he meant a myth—but above all, he told his agent, it was a "Cabellesque satire on religion and sex." (*Grumbles*, 264).

Putnam's wanted it—but they wanted him to take out all the sex and all the religion. There is nothing but sex and religion in the story, Heinlein pointed out: every single event in the story is set up by Mike's miracles.

Over the eleven years during which Heinlein's Mowgli book was being written, society in the U.S. had loosened up quite a bit. The publishing industry was no longer as prudish as it had been in the years immediately before and after World War II. It had become possible to publish quite challenging material. In particular, Grove Press, a small press specializing in material regarded as literary "pornography" (e.g., Nabokov's *Lolita* and William S. Burroughs' *Naked Lunch*) fought down the last remnants of censorship left over from the Comstock laws. Olympia

Press, a French publisher of censorable "art" literature, moved to the United States. The Comstock era was over.[10]

Sex there was in Heinlein's books—but the attitude was so self-evidently reverent that eventually the Putnam's editors agreed to accept it in its own terms, though it could not be published at its current length of 220,000 words.[11]

Heinlein had always intended to cut the book to about 150,000 words. He habitually wrote large with the intention of cutting his work back to publishable size, but his boys' books were usually about 60,000 to 70,000 words. Even cut, this would be twice the size of his usual, and correspondingly more expensive to publish. He agreed to underwrite partially the cost of publication by letting it go early to a book club edition. Doubleday's Science Fiction Book Club could guarantee a minimum number of sales by virtue of their automatic selection feature. If a Book Club member did not send back a selection card marked for some other book (or for no book), the month's selection would automatically be sent and the member billed. Even though the book club edition was printed in a cheap binding and sold at a deep discount (less than half the cost of a book published in the ordinary way), the proceeds were shared among the publishers, the writer taking a much lower royalty. Consequently, publishers encourage the Science Fiction Book Club, although writers are often much less enthusiastic about it. In this case, Heinlein acknowledged that there was simply no way to tell whether the book had any market at all, so the Book Club deal made sense at the time for both writer and for publisher.

The editors did not like any of the alternate titles Heinlein gave them; nobody recalls who ultimately suggested *Stranger in a Strange Land*, but everybody agreed on it. Heinlein cut the book to 166,000 words and could not cut any more, so that was the size at which it was published. Unusually, the Book Club edition actually came out before the trade edition. Almost simultaneously with *Stranger*, Joseph Heller's *Catch-22* came out, indicating that the time was finally ripe for

---

10. "Comstock laws" refers to a series of laws regulating "objectionable" material, particularly printed material circulating through the mails. Local postmasters, usually in concert with the Society for the Suppression of Vice (the national organization of which was headed by Anthony Comstock, promulgator of the original Comstock Law of 1871), or its local equivalent, decided what was objectionable and used their official power to suppress, among many other types of material, family planning and marriage reform periodicals. (See Sears, *The Sex Radicals*).

    The Comstock organization gradually lost power. The attempted suppression of James Branch Cabell's *Jurgen: A Comedy of Justice* in 1920 was the last—and unsuccessful—major campaign of the Society for the Suppression of Vice.

11. At that time, science fiction book publishing was a relatively new business among mainstream publishers, and editorially dominated by a number of firmly held beliefs—among them that long science fiction books could not be sold. Consequently science fiction books through the 1950s and well into the 1960s were held to 60,000 to 70,000 words—just longer than a pulp serial. In fact, Ace paperbacks made a practice of combining two pulp serials of 50,000 words into a single book, popularly called a "double."

satire. Indeed, over the next several years, satires by Vonnegut, Barth, and Roth became surprisingly popular (considering that the genre had been relatively neglected for the last century). There was even speculation in the critical community that the satire might become the new model for contemporary fiction, supplanting the realistic novel. Heinlein's timing had been perfect.

Reaction within the science fiction community was immediate and enthusiastic; the book received the Best Novel Hugo Award for 1961. It sold moderately well in its trade edition, amounting to perhaps 5,000 copies in its first year. In the years before science fiction became a mass market phenomenon, that was a respectable sale.

Heinlein continued writing, each book different from the one that came before. He gave Putnam's a quasi-juvenile, *Podkayne of Mars* (1962), followed by a quasi-swords and sorcery book, *Glory Road* (1963), followed by an apocalyptic novel, *Farnham's Freehold*, in 1964 and *The Moon Is a Harsh Mistress* in 1966. Each book was very different from the one that preceded it. And each one was equally in tune with the *Zeitgeist*.

The Science Fiction Book Club began offering *Stranger* as a loss-leader, a premium given gratis to new members.

In the world outside science fiction, something was happening to the culture at large. The 1950s had been a time of great pressure to conform; now college students in the mid-1960s were deliberately and consciously rejecting the pressure to conform. They had been preceded culturally by the "Beats" in the 1950s—Kerouac, Ginsberg, Ferlinghetti and fellow-traveler William S. Burroughs—followed by the "Beatniks" later. There was a slight inheritance of influence from the Beats, but this was a phenomenon growing on its own. A handful of books circulated among college students—Walter Kaufmann's new English translations of Nietzsche, Mark Twain's just-published *The Mysterious Stranger & Other Stories,*[12] the works of Hermann Hesse (particularly *Steppenwolf* and *Siddhartha*), Thoreau's *Walden* and B.F. Skinner's utopian *Walden II*, the Ace pirated editions of J.R.R. Tolkien's 1940s fantasies, *The Lord of the Rings,* and, increasingly, *Stranger in a Strange Land*. These books together formed a kind of substructure of ideas around which the students came together. They formed a kind of culture, counter to the mainstream culture of repression and conformity. When the news media finally took cognizance of this "counterculture" in 1967, it was already fully formed. The "flower children" of the "Summer of Love" were only the most superficial aspect of a cultural efflorescence whose effects are not yet completely over.

---

12. Although Bernard de Voto had wanted to bring out Twain's masterwork, "The Mysterious Stranger," in the 1930s, Twain's only surviving daughter, Clara Gabrilowitsch (later Samossoud), suppressed publication until after her death in 1962. Twain thus had a bestseller on the *New York Times* Bestseller List 55 years after his death in 1910.

Stranger had appeared just at the moment when it could have the maximum possible impact. Terminology from *Stranger* spread rapidly around the counterculture, particularly the language of water-sharing rituals. "Grok" eventually made its way into the mainstream of the language, appearing in advertising and even in newspapers.

During this period—1968 through about 1970—demand for *Stranger in a Strange Land* far outstripped the ability or willingness of the publisher to supply it. Tattered copies of the paperback editions were passed from hand to hand in the hippie communes of San Francisco, because it was not possible to buy the book anywhere, at any price. By 1969 the paperback rights were placed with Berkeley, who brought out a multiple hundred-thousand copy edition that sold out immediately.

The counterculture mutated and evolved into other things as time went on, and the superficial jargon of water-sharing and grok have disappeared from our newspapers. But *Stranger* continues to sell briskly in new editions and even new languages. Science fiction expanded to include Heinlein's fairy tale and Cabellesque satire, but science fiction readers make up only a tiny part of *Stranger*'s audience. Heinlein himself died in 1988, but *Stranger* continues to have a lively career. In 1991, in response to persistent questions from fans and readers about the nearly 60,000 words of material Heinlein had edited out, the estate[13] allowed the as-written version to be published at 220,000 words. Astonishingly, both editions continue to sell briskly, though they are in direct competition with each other.

At the time *Stranger* was written, before he could even know if there was a market for it at all, Heinlein took heart from the advice of colleague "Murray Leinster" (Will F. Jenkins): there's always a market for a good story. *Stranger* is that, and more. The publishing history of *Stranger in a Strange Land* is an unexplainable phenomenon. It can only be that the book continues to speak to generations of readers because it is saying important things. We are going to discover some of those messages, to uncover some of the engines of the continuing success of *Stranger in a Strange Land.*

---

13. It is convenient to speak of the Heinlein "estate," but Heinlein's literary business is managed by Virginia Heinlein under an *inter vivos* trust. Mrs. Heinlein has been substantially managing the affairs of Heinlein's writing business continuously since about 1969.

Questions for Discussion

1. Why would *Stranger in a Strange Land* not have been publishable in 1948 when the idea first came up?

2. Were satires not publishable in 1948?

3. Do you think *Stranger* continues to have a commercial and intellectual life because it is a satire? What is it about satires that give them such longevity? What other satires have similar long lives?

4. Even though publishers have been selling books for a very long time, marketing practices seem to be developed by consulting the entrails of chickens. What business factors might contribute to this?

For Further Reading

Heinlein, Robert A. *Red Planet*. New York: Scribner's, 1948.

Patterson, Bill. "Early Chronology of *Stranger*." *The Heinlein Journal*. No. 6 (January 2000), p. 4–6.

Wells, H.G. *The War of the Worlds: A Critical Text of the 1898 London First Edition, with an Introduction, Illustrations and Appendices*. Ed., Leon Stover. Jefferson, North Carolina: McFarland & Company, Inc., 2001

PART TWO

"His Preposterous Heritage"

—

"But hereafter, before you read anything, ask me
or ask Jill, or somebody, whether or not it is
fiction. I don't want you to get mixed up."

– 4 –

Satire as a Literary Form

Stranger has been variously analyzed as a fictionalized theological tract (Blish), as a "subverted" novel of intrigue-*cum-bildungsroman* (novel of character-formation) (Slusser), and as a grotesquely malformed novel of manners containing a satire within an unintegrated internal structure (Panshin). These assessments are quite mistaken. *Stranger in a Strange Land* is not a malformed example of a novel; rather, it is a perfectly formed example of a satire. Mis-identification of genre renders formal analysis unnecessarily complicated—and in this case renders it impossible.

The satire is a literary form (or genre) with its own conventions of form and approach, quite different from the traditional novel. The literary prestige of the novel—and particularly the novel of manners—in the twentieth century has all but obliterated important distinctions of genre. Nathaniel Hawthorne, writing in the middle of the nineteenth century, felt his readers needed to know that *The House of the Seven Gables* was not a novel, but a romance. More than a hundred years later, romances have been relegated to sub-literary magazines and books. The term "novel" is applied indiscriminately to any long work of fiction. This designation is both informal and inadequate. Works such as *Pride and Prejudice* or *The Golden Bowl* are so dissimilar in form to *Tristam Shandy* or *Candide* or *Gulliver's Travels* that they cannot meaningfully be analyzed using the same formal standards.

Surprisingly little critical work has been done on the satire as a literary form, despite a recent resurgence of interest in the satire by writers such as Kurt Vonnegut, Philip Roth, and John Barth. For our purposes, the comments of Canadian literary critic Northrup Frye, in *Anatomy of Criticism* (1957), form a useful basis from which to analyze *Stranger*'s literary form.

Frye proposed that there are four broad genres or classifications of fiction: novel, romance, confession, and satire.[14] The satire genre appeared in the classical period, growing out of the Greek satyr plays and named for the Roman tradition of the *lanx satura* (an overflowing platter of mixed fruits). Frye proposes to reserve the name "satire" for the kind of formal verse satire exemplified by Horace, Juvenal, and Alexander Pope. The prose satires called "menippean satire," starting with imitators of Menippus—Lucian's *True History* and *The Golden Ass of Apuleius*—Frye renames the "anatomy," after a famous historical example, Richard Burton's sixteenth century *Anatomy of Melancholy*.[15] This taxonomy is particularly useful for approaching Heinlein because Frye includes some non-satirical works in the anatomy form—e.g., Izaak Walton's *The Compleat Angler* and, perhaps, Melville's *Moby-Dick*)—based on structural similarities reflecting a similar "encyclopedic" impulse. Heinlein, too, has played with the non-satirical anatomy in *Time Enough for Love* (1973). Heinlein has always exhibited an encyclopedic impulse, strewing even short stories with learned digressions (Patterson, "A Study of 'Misfit'").

Identification of genre is a crucial first step—or mis-step—in critical evaluation, for it sets the standards by which the work is to be assessed. Anatomies are typically loosely and discursively structured, with didactic and even pedantic essays and digressions interpolated into the story line. In *Gargantua and Pantagruel*, Rabelais pauses repeatedly for commentary—on monks as the world's *rejecta* or the extended digression describing the constitution and decorations of the Abbey of Thelemé. Even the story line is episodic and strung together with no particular regard for story logic. In the most extreme cases—e.g., *Gargantua and Pantaguel* and *Tristam Shandy*—it may be difficult even to *discern* a story line in the usual sense. Playfulness, *joie de vivre*, and, sometimes, a certain

---

14. Frye's reputation has been somewhat eclipsed in recent years—partly because fashion in criticism has turned away from the kind of structural and thematic analysis at which he excelled; partly also because the academic world emphasizes the kind of narrow specialization that excludes his broad inclusiveness, embracing the whole of literature in a single interpretive schema. For this reason, specialists have a hard time with Frye's schema; it cannot be viewed as a system of hard-edged categories.

     Dustin Griffin's 1994 overview of the current critical situation regarding both verse and menippean satire, *Satire: A Critical Reintroduction*, indicated no fundamental new critical categories introduced since the publication of Frye's *Anatomy of Criticism*, though there has been considerable elaboration of existing critical approaches.

15. Curiously, this is one of only two historical anatomies explicitly mentioned or referenced in *Stranger* (the other being Jonathan Swift's *Gulliver's Travels*). It is unlikely (though not impossible) that Heinlein had read *Anatomy of Criticism* in the two years between its publication in 1957 and the completion of *Stranger* in 1959–60. Virginia Heinlein has remarked that she had asked for and received a copy of *Anatomy of Melancholy* as a holiday present. The reference to *Gulliver's Travels* appears to have a special structural purpose. The references are probably coincidental—or as coincidental as they could be in the context of two writers talking knowledgeably about the same literary subject.

behind-the-back-of-the-hand malice, are the keynotes of the anatomy, and the kind of linear directness that we find in the romance or the novel of manners is neither a virtue nor a necessity for an anatomy.[16] It may even contain multiple genres within itself, appropriating other story forms for its own ends.

> "The narrative satirist tells a story in order to mock, to expose, to subvert. The story is only a vehicle; it may be interrupted at will; it may be broken into episodes; it may be extended *ad libitum* or broken off (as Butler says) 'in the middle'...Since satirists are not normally interested in narrative wholeness, in character consistency, in drawing that Jamesian circle by which a particular set of human relations appears to be bounded, they will feel no need to provide narrative closure." (Griffin, 97–98)

Heinlein's story line here is middling straightforward, for he has taken on the task of telling a gospel. But Heinlein is in tune with the best models of the form in which he is working. The loose formal structures of *Stranger*, transforming from section to section, from an apparent story of intrigue into an apparent story of *Bildung*, and thence to Myth, have been mistaken for indicators of poor plotting and interrupted writing sessions—as, indeed, they might be in a linear novel of manners. But the book's "looseness," in terms of formal structure, as well as its learned digressions on the law of property, on money as a mode of "balance and healing," on the mail a celebrity receives, on taboos, and on how to look at art, and on and on and on and on—are features of the anatomy form. In fact, what is going on is that the transforming of apparent genre from section to section of the book reveals a reality underlying appearances: the "time out" (in novelistic terms) in Jubal's menage first brings Mike to his model for his later Nest, then explores the power motivations underlying the intrigue of the first section. It is a necessary summation of what has gone before and a transition for the next, connecting, section that deals with Mike's discovery of the way the world works, which culminates in a hagiographical section that uncovers the reality underneath that working. There is a covert dynamic between appearance and disowned reality (truth) that runs through the book—a controlling unity with many and surprising dimensions. The Fosterite church is one such. But the juxtaposition of innocence (Mike) and experience (Jubal) makes the dynamic possible and is, therefore, structurally essential to the

---

16. Thus many of the classic satire-anatomies have entered perennial literature as children's stories (as at least the Lilliput and Brobdingnag sections of *Gulliver's Travels* survives and is read and enjoyed by children even today. *Alice's Adventures in Wonderland* and *Through the Looking Glass* were written for a child and can still be read with pleasure and delight by children who resonate with the juxtaposition of the large and the small and playing with relative sizes of the little girl, unaware of the sophisticated mathematical games embedded in the story structures.

book.[17] Jubal groks without learning Martian because he sees the truth underlying the appearance, and his maneuverings to free Mike from the power struggle of the merely material humans into whose power he falls at the start of the book is effective action based on an understanding of the realities involved, rather than on the mere appearances. The transformation of genres from section to section of the book is not precisely traditional for satires, but it is very much the *kind* of thing we should expect in an anatomy.

Anatomy of Criticism looks at the anatomy as a formal literary tradition. As the romance views the "human condition" through the doings of princes and heroes and the novel explores the relationship of a unique and individual mind to its society, so the anatomy, a highly intellectualized expression of the encyclopedic impulse, organizes a view of human existence by its perspective in the light of a single intellectual idea. The organizing principle need not be a weighty idea: Carlyle's *Sartor Resartus* is a cosmic or Olympian look at human existence in terms of clothing, whimsically mocking nineteenth century German academic and philosophical traditions.

Sometimes, several intellectual ideas are combined into a single anatomy. *Gulliver's Travels* uses a different shaping idea for each section. The Houyhnhnms make horses of theorizing, ivory-tower philosophers; the Lilliput section mocks the waging of sectarian religious wars—and so on. In the case of *Stranger*, Heinlein makes a synthesis of two intellectual ideas. The book, he says in a contemporaneous letter to his agent, is "a Cabellesque satire of sex and religion" (*Grumbles*, 264)—a combination that plays consciously and deliberately on the "cognitive dissonance" of ideas that do/do not "belong together" in the customary worldpicture of his readers. But satire requires a basis of agreement between the author and the reader (or a basis from which agreement can spring), and Heinlein appeals to a mutual agreement of values by attacking both satirical subjects under the aspect of hypocrisy.[18]

---

17. The terms "innocence" and "experience" are here used in the sense of William Blake's "Songs of Innocence," *w*here innocence is heavenly and experience is worldly. Mike's innocence is composed of several elements: (1) the literary convention of the Innocent Voyager, a tradition that goes back to the classical tale of the Young Man from the Provinces; (2) Blake's literary/philosophical innocence/experience dichotomy, and (3) Mike's complex ontological status: Mike is Unfallen both because of his Martian heritage and because he is an archangel (representing the theological aspects of Blake's innocence). Jubal's "experience" is the mirror complement of Mike's "innocence." Jubal is the City Sophisticate (in the Young-Man-from-the-Provinces tradition), the experienced (in Blake's terminology) and Fallen Man (in theological terms).

18. "Satire can become a vital form of literature only when there is a fairly widespread agreement about what man ought to be. The satirist needs the conviction that fixed intellectual ideas or norms can give him, and the assurance that he will receive understanding from his readers…Satire is best able to develop from a basis of general agreement on moral and intellectual standards." John Bullitt, *Jonathan Swift and the Anatomy of Satire*. Cambridge, Mass: Harvard University Press, 1954, p. 1, quoted in Griffin, 35.

Using an intellectual idea to organize the satire means that the writer is free to dispense with linearity and plot. The organization and unity is carried on a less superficial level. In the most extreme cases (e.g., *Gargantua and Pantagruel*), story unity is abandoned entirely. That cannot happen here, for some degree of unity is guaranteed by the biographical nature of the gospel—but Heinlein is not, in any case, highly invested in the conventional unities of a commercial plot structure. He has made a regular practice of relying on thematic progressions to provide story unity, rather than plots (though we often see plots, as well). There are two principal thematic unities that tie the entire book together. The first is a symbolic portrayal of several figures that resonate together at different stages of the book, on an unconscious level (for the reader at least—it is very difficult to discern how much of this structure Heinlein may have been conscious of). The two most important components of this image are Jubal's household and Mike's nest, which are complementary images of each other, one near the beginning of the book, the other near the end. The mirror-symmetry of the youth-age, innocence-experience contrasts of Mike and Jubal are thus placed in a complementary figure, dynamically changing roles at various times (e.g., after a period of eclipse, Jubal takes the ascendency again when Mike is martyred—but now he is not a parent, but a primate of the new and vigorous church).

These complementary images each have a "harmonic" image a little further removed. Jubal's household is a reflection of the "Martian set-up," as he describes it at one point, with its egg (Mike), nestling (Jill), adults (the secretaries and staff), and Old One (Jubal). On the Nest end is a complementary image of Heaven with its nestlings (human saints), adults (angels working in project management bureaus), and Old One (God/The Great Architect). Mars and Heaven are co-equal (the Martians have "their own set-up") and Jubal's household is co-equal with the Nest. It is, Jubal is assured, his "home." Thus, Mars-Jubal's Household-Mike's Nest-Heaven are all symbolically the same image, resonating together, a typological unity that gives thematic unity to the book.[19] Heinlein makes this identification explicit at the end of the book, where the location of the Nest is to become the capital of the Church of All Worlds. St. Petersburg means "The City of St. Peter," i.e., Heaven. The Nest is Heaven and in Heaven.

The fact that Mike replaces Jubal in the "Old One" position as we move from Jubal's household to Mike's Nest, and then to Heaven indicates a progression superimposed on the typological unity. On Mars, Mike is an egg; on earth he is a nestling and a human adult who functions as an Old One for his nest. When he goes to heaven, he relinquishes his earthly ministry into Jubal's hands and becomes an Adult worker for God—except that he *is* God (and all that groks is God), he is

---

19. "Typology" is technically defined as a figure of speech moving (or recurring) through time. The images are "types" of each other. Here, Mars, Jubal's household and the Nest are types leading to the comic Heaven Heinlein presents as Mike's ultimate destination.

simultaneously the Old One in Heaven. As Mike moves through the Martian life-stages, he simultaneously moves through human psychological developmental stages, from infant in the first book, nurtured by Jill, to child being parented and nurtured by Jill and Jubal, to teenager immersed in his peer group, to adult giving back nurturing and healing to the people who nurtured him. The apparent genre of the book changes as he enters each new life-stage—external action and intrigue dominating when he is entirely passive. The intrigue gives way to *Bildung* when education and discovery of boundaries dominate Mike's life; and when Mike takes over entire control of his life, he must be reported on as a journalist. Finally, he can no longer be reported on: Jubal joins the Nest and experiences Mike. Reporting is words, and we are repeatedly assured that our words are inadequate. Anything that exists can only be experienced. Mike must be experienced.

The typological unity of the four "Heavens" thus contains a thematic progression, and the second thematic unity, of development through both Martian life-stages and human developmental psychology, carries the book forward in a coordinated way, independent of the events of the story line.

The combination of innocence/experience (Mike/Jubal) must then be taken *together* as the authorial "voice." Neither stands alone. This is grossly apparent in the novel-of-intrigue and *Bildung* sections, where Jubal is to the forefront, even overshadowing Mike as a character. Heinlein even gives Jubal the "Miracle of the Loaves and the Fishes" to perform on Mike's behalf (using, true, the mundane mechanisms of a pre-prepared and frozen *smorgasbord*). Jubal is not Heinlein's voice in any simplistic sense. The character's biography and actions rise out of the demands of the fiction, and it is to the fiction that Heinlein gives his loyalty. Jubal is Fallen. His experience, albeit valid, is not capable of communication. Jubal has no disciples, founds no church. Even though he groks in fullness, the best he can do is retreat into his own bellybutton with a small coterie of support staff—the secretaries, Duke, and Larry—surrounded by an electric fence. This is the best that a purely worldly and materialist orientation can achieve. Experience, by itself, is ultimately impotent, because it knows only what has gone before. Experience must protect innocence, but it is innocence—Mike—that sees with new eyes and is therefore potent. It is innocence that can communicate the Good News. This is not a trope of *Stranger*, but biblical dicta: "[You must] be as wise as a serpent and innocent as a dove." (*Matthew* 10:16). (This is exactly what Mike says to Jubal in their "Garden of Gethsemane" talk near the end of the book: goodness is not enough; goodness is never enough—it must be allied with hard, cold wisdom [Stranger, 415/502]. This is one example among many of how strongly *Stranger* is linked to its biblical sources—and, also, of the thematic unity within the book: again and again, Heinlein seems to be moving over the edge, off the map, outside the boundaries—only to be supported by Christian orthodoxy.)

Stranger is both "correct" and "original." The ability to shape a particular literary form is a matter principally of what Frye calls "literary scholarship" (*Fables of Iden-*

tity, 42), but containing the Hero tale within the satire-anatomy is a fresh and original turn—a difficult and challenging one—still fresh a few years later when John Barth shaped *Giles Goat Boy* around the Oedipus story. Heinlein was visibly familiar with many examples of the satire-anatomy. He had referenced both Rabelais' *Gargantua and Pantagruel*[20] and Swift's *Gulliver's Travels* in a number of early stories, and his extra-textual references to *Stranger* as a "Cabellesque satire" suggests a certain degree of sophisticated literary understanding of the subject and implies a fair degree of literary "preparation" as well as sensitivity to the form.

---

20. Although there are no overt references to Rabelais in *Stranger*, there are many, many echoes of *Gargantua and Pantagruel* scattered throughout the book. Heinlein's comments about money being a mechanism of healing and balancing may be an echo of the digression of Panurge on borrowers and lenders in Book III. Gargantua's birth-cry is "drink, drink, drink!" and the first word of Martian we learn—indeed, the only one we learn formally— is "drink" (*grok*). These echoes are suggestive, rather than definite.

Questions for Discussion

1. Frye's term "anatomy" means analysis by "dissection" as a medical student learns to anatomize. Why is this an appropriate name for the satire genre?

2. We have mentioned several satire-anatomies in this chapter: *Gargantua and Pantagruel* (Rabelais), *Anatomy of Melancholy* (Burton), *Candide* (Voltaire), *Gulliver's Travels* (Swift), and *Giles Goat Boy* (Barth). Name other satires and identify the intellectual ideas that provide the focus for the anatomy.

3. Historically, anatomies have been extraordinarily influential and extraordinarily long-lived. Very little fiction prior to the nineteenth century is still read, but many anatomies are still in print, and words and expressions from the satires are still a part of the language. Identify some of these expressions.

4. Why do you think anatomies outlive the mainstream literature of their day? Can the same be fairly said of *Stranger*?

5. Literary criticism, among other things, relates a work to other works of literature. What is the relationship of literary criticism to the reader's personal experience of "good" and "bad," "like" and "dislike" in the reading?

6. It is often stated that "grok" is the only Martian word explicitly mentioned in *Stranger*. There are actually two Martian words, one used only once. Why do you think Heinlein did not invent and use more Martian words?

For Further Reading

Frye, Northrup. *Anatomy of Criticism*. Princeton, New Jersey: Princeton University Press, 1957

Griffin, Dustin. *Satire: A Critical Reintroduction*. Lexington, Kentucky: University Press of Kentucky, 1994

− 5 −
The Technique of Satire:
Ironic Inversion

Satire also denotes an attitude or approach to the materials. Satirical materials can be included within other forms. *Stranger* is satirical as well as *a* satire.

The principal technique of satire is "ironic inversion." Irony, in one form or another, is a basic technique of all literature, but satires make a particular use of irony to form a structural basis for the story, drawing story figures and literary devices by "inverting" metaphors and treating them as if they were true.

The conventional definition of irony, going back to rhetoric theory of the classical world, is to say one thing and mean another—perhaps the exact opposite of what is said—so that "…something contrary to what is said is understood…" (Quintilian, *Institutio Oratorica*, 9.22.44). One of the most famous examples of literary irony in English literature is Jonathan Swift's "A Modest Proposal." Swift's modest, ironic proposal is that Irish babies should be ranched as meat animals by the English.

Swift does not literally intend to suggest that Irish babies be raised and marketed as meat animals; by contraries, he intends to suggest that the Irish should be treated with greater respect by the British and accorded the ordinary human dignities they are not under then-current policy. Taking the metaphorical observation that English policy treats the Irish like "cattle," Swift performs an inversion by dropping the metaphorical qualifiers ("like" or "as if" or "as though"), and the Irish *become*, for his purposes, cattle (meat animals) for English tables. The bringing together of "contrary" images of babies and roast beef fuse into a baby roasted for the table and create a "cognitive dissonance" that intentionally outrages the sense of what is right and proper—and moves the reader to agree that "something is wrong."[21]

Irony is not intended to deceive, but to illuminate, to assist the reader in transcending his local and parochial values. It is intended that the reader move past the literal meaning of the overt words and perceive the underlying "true" meaning. Philosopher Gregory Vlastos, meditating on Socrates' use of irony as a mode of ethical argument, concludes that "if we choose to do it [irony] we forfeit in that very choice the option of speaking deceitfully." (Vlastos, 43) Irony is the one way of speaking truth that does not involve speaking literal truth. It is therefore highly appropriate for art, which seeks to speak truths in symbols and images at a remove from truth.

Using irony as a tool, Socrates is shown by Plato as leaving his students in a state of perplexity. He sees that they have gone astray in their argument, but would not lift a finger to help them out of their paradox. You are free to take it one way, though you are meant to take it in another, and when he [Socrates] sees you have gone wrong he lets it go.

> "Not, really, that he does not care that you should know the truth, but that he cares more for something else; that if you are to come to the truth, it must be by yourself for yourself." (44).

Here irony may deceive incidentally when it juxtaposes two conflicting moral principles—both, perhaps, perfectly valid. The case is not which is "true" but which is "truer." It is not a black-and-white dichotomy, but the endless shades of gray lumped together in the dichotomy's sides. This Socratic irony is not a game, not a method of intellectual "gotcha," but is an extremely serious attempt to uncover the basis of morality.

Heinlein in *Stranger* is playing the same Socratic game with the reader, much as Swift "teases the reader out of (or into) thought" (Griffin, 28). It is less important to him that you agree with his specific ideas than that you are moved to think about your own. So he throws out gambits and outrages to create a state in which you must confront and evaluate your beliefs. For Heinlein, not only is "the unexamined life" not worth living; it is not fit for living in human society.

Irony is uniquely suited to provoke meditation. Zen Buddhism uses ironic words, phrases, or playlets as foci for meditation in an attempt to guide the practitioner to recapitulate the enlightenment of Siddhartha Buddha. This use of irony is intended to undermine the psychological and intellectual basis of the practitioner. It is intended, through delving into the overt words, to reach the underlying, transcendental reality. A monk asked, in all seriousness, "Does a dog

---

21. The cream of Dean Swift's grisly jest is that during the Potato Famine of 1848, Irish grain continued to be exported to England while Irish children starved to death. The English literally ate the lives of Irish babies, and the metaphor inverted itself to become reality.

have Buddha nature?" Joshu answered "Mu!" "Mu" has the overt meaning of "No" or "Not," though the nuanced meaning is something like "the question is formulated in such a way that it cannot be answered 'yes' or 'no.'" The ironic meaning of "Mu" is what the student has to understand by experiencing it—grokking it. The student can derive overt meanings "till the cows come home," but until the ironic point is comprehended the koan is unresolved.

Koans, like all ironic statements, are not resolved by linear attack, but by absorption of the self into identity with the koan. When this occurs, experiential leaps not possible to linear thinking become possible.

Irony thus creates a mental state in which personal "breakthroughs" are possible. Illuminations become possible. "Paradigm shifts" become possible. By statements contrary to reality, ironically, the greater truth is apprehended and the limitations of a single mindset may be transcended.

Plato does not play the same games with irony that he portrays his teacher, Socrates, as playing with his students in his Dialogs. Socrates is credited with using irony in the "Socratic method," but it is Plato who is regarded as the founder of the intellectual tradition that profoundly influenced subsequent history. Platonism has divided into several currents—Plato's original writings have continued to be a direct inspiration to philosophical thinkers for 2,500 years; the first century C.E. school of NeoPlatonism exemplified by Plotinus became a particular influence on early Christianity (see the discussion of NeoPlatonism in Chapter 18), and several occult and underground traditions derive from from Platonism in the ancient world.

Of the Socratic-Platonic ironic tradition Jonathan Swift is the special literary master:

> "It is now something of a commonplace that Swift attacks his reader's complacency, seeks to disorient or unsettle. But Swift is often regarded as exceptional. I would argue just the opposite – that Swift is the paradigmatic satirist." (Griffin, 52)

Heinlein looks to Swift as his principal satiric model for *Stranger*, for it is his intent to "disorient and unsettle" his reader—for the excellent reason that you can't see over the walls of your mental ruts if you're in that particular groove.

Satire as a literary form uses irony as a basic structural building block for the work as a whole.

Questions for Discussion

1. Identify some of the ironic inversions used in *Stranger*.

2. Discuss the distinction between satire (anatomy) as a literary form and satire as an attitude or approach to materials. How can *Stranger be* a satire that *contains* a satire?

For Further Reading

Vlastos, Gregory. *Socrates: Ironist and Moral Philosopher.* Ithaca, NY: Cornell University Press, 1991

Swift, Jonathan. "A Modest Proposal." This short essay has been collected into numerous anthologies. It can also be obtained online from numerous sites, including Mark Zimmerman's *Encyclopedia of the Self* at:
http://authorsdirectory.com/c/rndprplo.htm
It is also available for download at:
http://www.textlibrary.com/TITLE/modest-p/

– 6 –

Ironic Dualism

Arvin Wells points out in *Jesting Moses*, his study of the comedy of James Branch Cabell, that irony can also mean *what is said* as well as what is indicated—that is, irony is or can be a technique for stating two meanings (or more!) simultaneously. This is not a new invention of Cabell's—Vlastos says Socrates created "complex irony," quoting one of Plato's characters likening Socrates to "those Sileni[22] that sit in the workshops of the statuaries, who, when opened into two, turn out to have images of Gods inside" (Vlastos, 37, quoting "Symposium", 215 A7 B-3) (just as *Stranger's* rampageous characters all have Gods inside).

Cabell dualistically values romance and the routine and uses irony to affirm conventional values at the same time he criticizes them. The lesson of *Jurgen*, he says, it that it is better for middle-aged businessmen to be faithful to their wives, and so it supports the conventional social value of marriage. Yet the story is a string of philanderings and serial bigamies as Jurgen goes ostensibly in search of his wife in the realms of myth and fantasy and romance. Cabell hides his artistic vision behind the literal truth he portrays.

Cabell was one of Heinlein's most influential "teachers" of literary technique. (Patterson, "James Branch Cabell") When Heinlein declared his independence from the Scribner's juveniles series in 1959, he turned to writing Cabellian-influenced fiction, and he referred to *Stranger*, in a contemporaneous letter to his

---

22. Silenos was a rustic demigod of the forests in Greek mythology, a kind of minor-league Pan. He was deliberately rough and ugly—and therefore extraordinarily important in the beauty-obsessed Athens of Pericles, Socrates and Plato. Socrates, with an unfashionably broad face, starting eyes, and pug nose, was said to look like Silenos.

agent, as a "Cabellesque satire." (*Grumbles*, 264) Cabell's ironic dualism is the principal justification for thinking of *Stranger* as Cabellian. It is one of the many literary techniques Heinlein learned from Cabell and applied to *Stranger in a Strange Land*, though Cabell's literary reputation had so far evaporated by 1960 that there was little point in making the reference public and explicit.[23]

Stranger's approach to ironic dualism is to take the apparatus of Christianity and invert it for the satire of sex-and-religion. But since he is writing a gospel of Valentine Michael Smith, he preserves the *functional* significance of Christian figures and devices. They remain "true" for purposes of his story and function to place the satire in the realm of myth. The ambiguity allows him to play freely between the two levels of meaning, the interplay producing elegant satiric effects. Thus the appearance of dissent and heterodoxy conceals a substance of agreement and orthodoxy—surprising and delighting in a way possible only in a satire-anatomy.

The recurring figure of Martian cannibalism, for example, is brought into the story (starting as early as page 11/22) as an ironic inversion of the Christian sacrament of the Last Supper. The implication of ritual cannibalism is clear in the biblical instructions, "Take, eat. This is my body"—but the ritual is symbolic, in that it is wheat and wine (grape juice among teetotaling low Protestants) that is being given, though the doctrine of Transubstantiation insists that the wine and wafer are mystically transformed into the actual blood and body of Christ during consecration.[24] So the Christian sacrament of the Last Supper is already inverted by substituting metaphor for reality when it presents to Heinlein's satiric gaze. Heinlein inverts the inversion (an ironic use of irony) and restores the mystical significance of the cannibalism, not by cloaking it in symbolism—the more usual satiric practice—but by stating the proposition plainly and without concealing ornamentation. Martians not only willingly eat their dead in times of famine (a practice humans also follow, but only *in extremis*), they volunteer (and it is considered an honor) to donate their bodies to the public weal.

At the end of the book, Mike cuts a finger off so that his fellow nestlings can eat the body he is about to cast aside and grok him. They make of him a soup—"Mike always did need a little seasoning" Jubal says of him. And they drink the soup, grokking and praising. "Grok," remember, means "drink." Jubal drinks

---

23. Heinlein very often tucked away references, in one form or another, to people from whom he derived ideas—but he rarely gave his literary influences the same acknowledgment, until at nearly the end of his life, he prominently featured both Cabell and Twain in a single book—*Job: A Comedy of Justice* (1984).

24. Many Protestant sects reject the doctrine of transubstantiation and treat the sacrament of the Eucharist (Last Supper) as a *symbolic* recreation of an important event in church history. Whether the wine and the wafer are regarded as actual cannibalism or symbolic cannibalism, however, both traditions fall into the anthropological classification of ritual cannibalism.

Mike and surrounds him, takes Mike into himself, in a mirror complement of what has just happened: Mike took Jubal into his Nest, into himself.[25]

The surround/surrounded by exterior/interior symmetry is used elsewhere in *Stranger*. This same ironic irony is used on the institution of baptism. Heinlein takes the Sacrament of Baptism (The Water of Life-in-the-Spirit) and has his character drink it ("'grok' means 'drink,' Mike said." [213/265]) instead of being dunked in it; he surrounds the water and the water surrounds him. When Mike is in the water and grokking, the Water of Life is both within him and around him. Grokking is all there is, everywhere. As baptism—immersion—is the symbolic joining of the candidate to the Christian church/community; so drinking/grokking is the symbolic admission of the candidate to Mike's Nest. Again, the Martian candidate surrounds the water; the Christian candidate is surrounded by water. For satiric purposes, Heinlein inverts the symbol; his method of dualistic irony, both the original and the inversion are affirmed.

The "Water of Life" symbolism of *Stranger* is clearly and obviously adapted from Christianity's rite of baptism[26], and Mike's group uses water sharing in its public and ceremonial aspects as baptism ritually reflects admission to the body of Christ and his church. But baptism itself is a late reworking of ancient-world and alchemical symbolism. For Christians, the "old man" "dies" in the baptismal font,

---

25. Following Sir James Frazer's argument of *The Golden Bough* (1912), Robert Graves in *The White Goddess* (1948) traces Christianity's particular type of ritual cannibalism to an old harvest ritual, with emasculation representing harvest reaping. Kings were chosen to reign for the agricultural year and ritually killed (usually at midsummer) and a new king chosen. In some traditions, the old king is "eucharistically eaten after castration" (*Id.*, 66). The old king then becomes immortal and is borne off to some sacred island. This rite of neolithic corn (barley) cults persists in Judaism as ritual circumcision. "God," as Jacques Derrida says, in "Ulysses' Gramophone" (in *Jacques Derrida: Acts of Literature*), "is a collector of prepuces." Jehovah reaps his followers and gathers them to Him in a harvest.

In Christianity the castration is replaced by scourging and crucifixion; in *Stranger*, the castration/emasculation is present but oddly displaced: Mike cuts off a finger for his water brothers to share his body (oddly, a fruit knife is specified for this, which has harvest implications; moreover, some fruit knives have curved blades, reminiscent of the golden sickle specified in the druidic versions of this rite); and in the lynching that follows, "Mike's right arm was struck off at the elbow" by a shotgun blast. (429/517) So Mike is emasculated twice—once for his private family and once for his public. Both Christ and Mike thereafter perform certain miracles before going to Heaven and eternal life.

Heinlein is known to have studied Frazer attentively, as *The Golden Bough* was referenced extensively in his 1940 novella "Magic, Inc." It is quite likely that he read *The White Goddess* (i.e., he was perennially interested in the subject, and the book made an international stir when it was published in 1948), but there are no specific references to it in *Stranger* or elsewhere.

26. "Baptism was not, of course, invented by the Christians. They had it from St. John, and he had it from the Hemero-baptists, a mysterious Hebrew sect usually regarded as a branch of the Pythagorean Essenes, who worshipped Jehovah in his Sun-god aspect." (Graves. *The White Goddess*, 135)

and the "new man in Christ" is born again. The original of this symbol has water
the self-consuming and self-generating of the four elements with corresponding
self-transformation of fire and earth. (See C.G. Jung on an early alchemical text,
"The Vision of Zosimos," ¶105–6) That the alchemical symbolism is meant in
Stranger is suggested by Mike's "division" through the story into the four elements:
flesh (=earth), water obviously *passim*, fire at his martyrdom and, finally as air
(=pneumatike=spirit) at the end where he "sustains Jubal."

   Interestingly, drinking—instead of bathing in—water as a religious rite was
used in *The Gospel of Thomas*. This Gospel was buried near an Egyptian monas-
tery, under obscure circumstances, and was found by two farmers digging fertil-
izer in 1947. The complete find, known as the Naq Hammadi library, comprised
thirteen codices of fifty more-or-less complete tracts. One of these tracts was enti-
tled *Peuaggelion Pkata Thomas*,[27] ("The Good News According to Thomas").
Without engaging in academic wrangling as to provenance and author (ongoing
for forty years and looks good for another forty), it is clear that this work had
some relevance to some early Christian sect, faction, group, or heresy (the characterization of the group depending on the investigator). In any event, there are several references to drinking:

Thomas 13:5	"Jesus said, I am not your teacher. Because you have drunk, you have become intoxicated from the bubbling spring that I have tended."
Thomas 28:2	"I found them all drunk, and I did not find any of them thirsty."
Thomas 47:13	"Nobody drinks aged wine and immediately wants to drink new wine."
Thomas 74	"He said, 'Lord, there are many around the drinking trough, but there is nothing in the well."
Thomas 108:1	"Jesus said, Whoever drinks from my mouth will become like me." (Funk, *The Five Gospels*)

   The publication of *The Gospel of Thomas* made international headlines when it
was published in 1959, but it is not clear whether Heinlein had read it before taking up *Stranger* for the final push. References to the timing of the different writing
sessions in *Grumbles From the Grave* (see, e.g., 208) suggest that the final 166,000
words of the book were written from January to mid-March 1960.

   Mrs. Heinlein indicates that his practice with *Stranger* had been to pick up
from where he had left off, not discarding or rewriting what was already there.
(Patterson, "Early Chronology of *Stranger*"). The Martian word *grok* is first used

---

27. If this title looks odder than usual, it may be because the title is Coptic rather than the conven-
    tional Greek it resembles. In Greek, the title would be *Euaggelion kata Thomas*.

in the verb *grokking* on page 22 of the complete version—the first time Smith is actually seen. There it is used as a referent for understanding ("Back even before the healing which had followed his first grokking of the fact that he was not as his nestling brothers…")—which would suggest the usage was planned long before *The Gospel of Thomas* was published (possibly as early as 1952 or 1953). But the neologism is not defined until page 265, by Dr. Mahmoud ("'Grok' means 'to drink'") during the discussion "in an upper room" following the conference with Secretary-General Douglas. This is probably the first passage written when Heinlein took up the manuscript again in 1959 or 1960—just at the time the newly-published *Gospel of Thomas* was topical and in the news.

Without further evidence, it is not possible to determine if *The Gospel of Thomas* was a direct influence on this crucial motif within *Stranger*. Be that as it may, there is no question that Heinlein did, in his overtly most *outré* moment, hit upon symbolism that early Christians—or at least *some* early Christians—would have considered perfectly orthodox.

The general critique of Christianity that emerges, based on its own principles, is that of hypocrisy. Martians, it is clear, believe and act on their moral principles. The implication by ironic inversion is that Christians do not, and this is what is wrong with Christianity in terms of the satire: it is not "practical." It does not deal with reality as it finds it. This is the supreme virtue of Jubal Harshaw, who groks in fullness without learning Martian, and it is the process of "conversion" of Ben Caxton to the Church of All Worlds—the only conversion presented for inspection. Jubal induces Caxton to face his jealousy squarely and disown it. Caxton confesses that it is not part of himself as he sees himself and wishes to see himself, and this removes the last impediment to seeing the Church of All Worlds clearly. Caxton joins the Nest. He thus begins to practice himself, to practice truth. It is his emotional truth that makes him free. Jealousy was not his truth—it was the screen by which he evaded his truth, just as the personal will is the screen by which people evade the divine Will within them.

While this use of irony allows Heinlein to enlist the American frontier tradition of "plain speaking" in aid of his rather sophisticated philosophy, English, the carrier of the irony, is itself ironically inverted because it is incapable of adequately describing reality. It is only when the characters are able to become fluent in Martian that they can become part of the Elect. They are forced by the Martian language to be "plain speakers," and this is the source of the Martian powers, which symbolically stand for "human potential"—the powers that are our human birthright but which we have frittered away "for a mess of pottage."

The real-world idiom "You come from Mars" means "You are not in touch with reality"; this is inverted to mean "You are more in touch with reality." Mike is a Messiah because he is able to teach others the language. He is "from Mars," but leads others into a better understanding of reality. Heinlein says, as close as he can come in the fictional form, "Look, don't take this literally. The medium with which I am saying this is not capable of saying what I am saying." This echoes an overt statement in the book: it is possible to say things in one language that cannot be expressed in another. And yet, the multiple layers of inversion of inversions undercut all the various grounds on which a reader assumes it is safe to stand. All assumptions are undercut by the irony. Whenever a plateau or cadence in the argument appears to yield a firm philosophical ground on which to stand, Heinlein cuts it away. Even the Martian Old Ones themselves are declared "as provincial as humans" (437/524). It is questions Heinlein is interested in, not conclusions. And we are back to Socrates: said to be the wisest of all men, not because he knew things—but because he knew that he was not wise, that he did not know.

Questions for Discussion

1. How can an ironic remark mean exactly what it says and still mean something else—for instance, the exact opposite of what it says?

2. Why is cannibalism a suitable subject for a religious ritual? Or, if it is not suitable, why has it been used as religious ritual? What is the relationship of taboos to religion?

3. What is the symbolism of baptism, and how does it relate to the Water-of-Life symbolism in *Stranger*?

For Further Reading

Guillamont, A.; Puech, H.C.; Quispel, G, and 'Abd al Masih, Y. *The Gospel According to Thomas*. Leiden, Netherlands: E.G. Brill/Collins/Harper, 1959

Vlastos, Gregory. *Socrates: Ironist and Moral Philosopher*. Ithaca, NY: Cornell University Press, 1991

Wells, Arvin. *Jesting Moses: A Study of Cabellian Comedy*. Gainesville, Florida: University of Florida Press, 1962.

– 7 –

Certainties Destroyed:
Ironic Use of Irony

Heinlein's discussion of the Martian language versus English is highly revealing. English is confusing to Mike-the-egg because English words have an infinite number of meanings[28], depending on context. By implication, Martian words have single, clear, and direct meanings—though, again ironically, the most important Martian word, *grok*, has hundreds of specific meanings for translation purposes.

Part of the contextual variability of human languages, the inability of human languages to fully describe reality, has to do with our expectation that the words we mean do not always mean what we seem to be saying. They express a code of assumptions as well as the objects and events they seem to denote (while Martian does describe reality because it presumably does not bring this hidden agenda to the language). Theodore Roszak addresses just this point in his 1969 *The Making of a Counter Culture*. The "technocratic" "mainstream" has a set of assumptions that automatically rejects "the images and metaphors developed to describe and discuss the 'non-intellective consciousness.'":

> "It leaves us devoid of language as soon as we enter that province of experience in which artists and mystics claim to have found the highest values of existence." (*Id.,* 52)

The real world thus presents us with an irony of language which deprives us of a means of expressing important experiences; Heinlein has inverted the real-world

---

28. "Infinite" is literally correct, not hyperbole. The number of possible referents for any given term can be extended without limit.

irony by providing just such a language. The mainstream language reflects a Positivist Materialist agenda of denying and disowning all "subjective experience"—a code to which Heinlein does not subscribe.[29]

> "The lively consciousness of men and women as they are in their vital daily reality is missing from our culture, having been displaced by…grandiose figments [of hypocritical public sloganizing]" (Roszak, 54)

This coded agenda is a part of the freight of meaning Heinlein pours into the Martian-human language dichotomy, but another part is highly reminiscent of a discussion in Korzybski's *Science and Sanity* of the infinite number of possible values a word can assume in the context of the syntactic form of a sentence. Heinlein was intensely interested in the work of Alfred Korzybski from 1933, the date of publication of *Science and Sanity*, Korzybski's masterwork and the foundation document of General Semantics. As late as a 1973 interview conducted by Neil Schulman, he attempted to discuss epistemological issues in terms of Korzybski, so his interest in General Semantics spanned the entire time in which *Stranger* was written. We are clearly intended to be thinking about Korzybski and *Science and Sanity*: the discussion of flappers in *Gulliver's Travels* is quoted as a frontispiece of *Science and Sanity*, and Swift is not referenced again in the book. The flapper discussion in *Stranger*, as Jubal Harshaw tries to remove Mike from immediate danger of being kidnaped by the Federation, is thus an extended, if indirect, reference to *Science and Sanity*. Clearly it is an in-joke for General Semantics enthusiasts, deliberately done.

What might be Korzybskian about the Martian language? Korzybski insists that each sentence describes a form that functions like a mathematical equation, into which an infinite number of constants can be dropped. The constants are words. Consider the sentences: "John ate a pear"; "Mabel glazed a donut"; "Victor polished an apple." They all have the same syntactical form, and clearly an unlimited number of nouns and verbs could be substituted into the sentences.

Moreover, the words themselves potentially represent an infinite number of concrete things. The apple Victor polishes is not the same space-time event in the evening that it was in the morning. And that is not the same apple that I had for lunch yesterday baked into a tart.

This demonstrates, says Korzybski, that language is essentially mathematical in nature, with things being constants for variables that make up Proposition Functions; Proposition Functions are subsumed into System Functions; and System

---

29. So that, for example, Heinlein's aphoristic exhortations (e.g., "The Notebooks of Lazarus Long") to look for and value "facts" does not imply rejecting one's inner experiences. Those, too, are facts that must be included in one's view of the world. Heinlein's perennial personal ideal lies in facing facts—all facts—squarely without theoretical agendas that exclude some facts. This is, in *Stranger*, Jubal Harshaw's supreme value—why he "groks in fullness" without learning Martian—and, in fact, without being 100% correct in all his esthetic judgments.

Functions are subsumed into higher level System Functions as an equation may express an infinite number of specific values and may be subsumed into larger sheafs of equations.

In the Platonic bias of *Stranger*, language being inherently mathematical assumes a special meaning. For Plato, the study of mathematics is not a merely intellectual discipline; it is the moral study that can lead certain men "upward" and "to the light":

> "…Plato's testimony to the power of mathematics to yield more than intellectual training—to induce a qualitative change in our perception of reality *which may be likened to a religious conversion.*" (Vlastos, 108; emphasis added)

The study of mathematics—and particularly geometry—is what can change a mere ruler into a philosopher-king. In the later NeoPlatonic tradition, the trained ability to visualize figures in higher dimensions is the preparation discipline for occult understanding. Mike and the Martians clearly have mastered this study of geometry, for they can turn things "ninety degrees from everything"—i.e., through an extra geometric spatial dimension.

Heinlein has adopted as a convention of *Stranger* the Platonic notion of mathematics as a key to higher wisdom. By studying the mathematical Martian language, the members of the Church of All Worlds transform themselves into philosopher-kings (and the kings of the classical world were often thought of as divine, so this ties also into the "Thou art God" trope). Just as the philosopher-kings of Plato's *Republic* are given the absolute and unconditional right to act for and upon their subjects, so do the Martian-human philosopher-god-kings assume the right to act for the un-divinely-aware, discorporating bad guys, sending them "to the back of the line."[30] Without the moral transformation produced by the study of mathematics, they would not physically have the ability to do this (i.e., to discorporate by an act of will or to destroy the planet). It is the individual will, in congruence with the divine Will, that is conditioned to use the power appropriately or not at all. The definitive statement of this proposition in *Stranger* is, again, in Mike's "Garden of Gethsemane" talk with Jubal Harshaw. Speaking of the ability to destroy the planet by mental effort:

---

30. This passage has often been misread as implying reincarnation. The terms "reincarnation," or "transmigration of souls" or "metempsychosis" refer to a spirit or soul "incarnating" in a body. Within the NeoPlatonic or hermetic framework *Stranger* uses, there is no assurance that "the back of the line" has any implication of returning to earth or to a body at all. The fact that the angel "Agnes Douglas" repeatedly incarnates as an agent is remarked upon as something unusual. Any grokking being is, after all, God and will do as it chooses after being discorporated. In this life on earth, it has chosen to be discorporated by the agency of Mike; its mysterious purposes may or may not have been satisfied and it might move on. Incarnation is an option for gods, but there are many more attractive options open to them, including letting their individuality dissolve back into the Emersonian transcendental Over-Soul. See Chapter 18 for a brief discussion of the meaning of these terms.

"'For me it would be a wrongness—I am human.'... 'Oh, I have the discipline to do it...but not the volition. Jill could do it—that is, she could contemplate the exact method. But she could never will to do it; she is human, too; this is her planet. The essence of the discipline is, first, self-awareness, and then, self-control. By the time a human is physically able to destroy this planet by this method—instead of by clumsy things like cobalt bombs—it is not possible, I grok fully, for him to entertain such a volition. He would discorporate. And that would end any threat. Our Old Ones don't hang around the way they do on Mars." (417/504–505)

Mike and Jill have been morally transformed—by study of the mathematical Martian language.[31]

But even this is inverted, as all assumptions are undercut: the supreme virtue of Jubal Harshaw is that he can "grok in fullness" without learning Martian.

Reiterating irony in this way is the rhetorical device Heinlein uses to establish the baseline of the satire. The dissonance of irony is multiplied. The ironic use of irony is the basic building block of the satire.

Heinlein, like Socrates, is in deadly earnest, but he enlists the written in place of the spoken word. Heinlein is not interested in forcing his words into someone's ears until they come out of their mouth—but he *is* interested in leading a horse to water so it can think. Irony must been seen-through by the reader; the form demands conscious action by the reader in order to pierce the veil and perceive the underlying argument. The author can not publicly point to the meaning, even outside the work, for that would destroy the ironic process. The author is trapped by the very methodology he has chosen. Embedded in ironic conversation, he must be true to the work and maintain the form. Thus, further communication must be understood to be in the same format.

Heinlein is very aware of the excesses which reiterative ironic use of irony generates—a feature of the anatomy form. In a classic self-deprecation, he later wrote "My God, what some people will do for money!" (*The Number of the Beast*, 1980). This statement should be understood as ironic and translated as: "My God, to what depths some people [meaning "I"] will go to get an idea across."

---

31. This moral transformation brought about by the study of mathematics is a trope in Korzybski as well as in Plato:

    "The definition of man as a time-binder...suggests...the possibility that one of the functions of the time-binding energy in its pure form...works automatically—machine-like, as it were, shaping *correctly* the product of its activity." (*Manhood of Humanity*, 213)

    Heinlein seems to draw the equivalence of correct language (i.e., Martian)=correct physics from Korzybski, rather than from Plato (or Whorf). Later (217) Korzybski goes on to propose a redefinition of "number" that would let mathematical operations include phenomenological rigor as well as mathematical rigor—i.e., including "truth value" within logical operations. Heinlein's Martian language is Korzybski's idealized mathematical language.

Like a Zen *koan*, these inversions and inversions of inversions, affirmations and criticisms, produce altogether a state of "cognitive dissonance" around the subject, making illumination possible.

Heinlein's stated aim in *Stranger* (and here we should take him literally, as he is not speaking publicly, but directly in the relevant "Letter to a Fan" in *Grumbles From the Grave*) is not to persuade to any particular religious dogma, but rather to cause his readers to think about their own beliefs and accept or reject them as an affirmative act of will. The koan-like dissonance serves his ends better than any degree of persuasion.

Questions for Discussion

1. Why are Plato's "philosopher-kings" different from ordinary kings—and why did Plato regard them as better?

2. *Stranger* is an exceptionally complicated book. Does understanding its wider philosophical background help in understanding it?

For Further Reading

Korzybski, Alfred. *Science and Sanity: An Introduction to Non-Aristotelian Systems and General Semantics*. Lakeville, Connecticut: The International Non-Aristotelian Library Publishing Company, 1933 (4th ed. 1958)

Plato. *The Republic and Other Works*. Trans. B. Jowett. New York: Anchor Books, 1973

– 8 –

Stranger as Myth

The anatomy typically borrows its plot-outline from another genre—as *Candide* is structured on the very traditional tale of the young man from the provinces (casually, "the hick from the sticks") and *Gulliver's Travels* and *The Sot-Weed Factor* are structured around the travel-romance of the seventeenth and eighteenth centuries. *Stranger* has borrowed its plot-outline from the myth form, specifically the Hero tale, and even more specifically, from the Biblical variant of the Hero tale, the gospel life of Christ contained in the first four books of the New Testament.[32]

This aspect of satire has not been well studied. It maybe an aspect of parody, which Russian critic Mikhail Bakhtin suggests is a very ancient way of bringing the liveliness of the contemporaneous into the solemn "official" genres.

---

32. For more than a hundred years scholars have been trying to reconstruct a "historical Jesus," with remarkably little success. Although he is supposed to have led a religious revival during the Roman occupation, and there are historical records of other Messianic prophets at about the same time, there is only one undisputed mention of Jesus to be found in ancient records. Since the resemblance of the gospel biography to the traditional form of the Hero tale is so suspiciously close, and the gospel teachings so closely resemble anthologies of "wisdom literature" that were circulating in the ancient near east at the same time, some biblical scholars have put forth the proposition that the gospels are fictionalized biography of someone who should have existed to embody the Messianic fervor of the time, but probably did not. This proposition gives a certain ironic "depth" to the notion that *Stranger* might be a literary imitation of an already purely literary creation. The perspectives of Heinlein's later "World As Myth" books (in which Jubal Harshaw participates), that all of reality might be a figment of a writer's imagination, can thus be brought, *post facto*, to the book. Thus we can observe the "text" of *Stranger* evolving over time away from the author's original intention as the work of literature takes its place in public consciousness and among other works of literature—an evolution that continues perennially and in many dimensions.

"…parodies of genres and generic styles enter the great and diverse world of verbal forms that ridicule the straightforward, serious world in all its generic guises." (Bakhtin, 52).

Parodies and burlesques can stand on their own, but the satire, with its strategic use of irony, allows the elements of burlesque, exaggeration, and travesty to be blended into the satiric treatment. Heinlein has accepted, at apparent face value, the Hero tale, but his treatment contains deliberate travesty elements, included in the very earliest planning stages of the book. Heinlein discusses, in an unpublished letter to John Campbell dated in January of 1949, a travesty-parody of the epic hero's "special birth." Valentine Michael Smith's parents "were married, but not to each other, thus making our little stinker the first interplanetary bastard of record…" (Permission of Virginia Heinlein to quote from this correspondence is gratefully acknowledged).

Thus Heinlein, in the best satiric tradition, both accepts and ridicules his generic choices. Both the acceptance and the ridicule are canonical, as Bakhtin points out of the "fourth drama" (e.g., farces and satyr-plays) of the classical traditions: it is not, after all, the hero who is being ridiculed; it is false-solemn "heroization" that is being ridiculed—literally to force the hero out of the generic canon and into the immediate emotional life of the audience. Satire, we are reminded, "…can through parody invade *any* literary form" and

"…when satire takes over another literary structure, it tends not to just borrow it…but to subvert it…and to direct its energies toward alien ends." (Griffin, 3)

In the late 1950s, literary critics complained that the realistic novel had run out of steam, and in the 1960s a series of satire-novels appeared (notably Kurt Vonnegut's *Mother Night, Cat's Cradle*, and *Slaughterhouse 5*, but also Philip Roth's *The Breast* and *The Great American Novel*) which some critics hailed (wrongly, it turns out) as the next wave of literary formula. *Stranger* appeared before this trend had clarified itself. Although critics have wished to connect *Stranger* with the other prominent satire that appeared at almost the same time, Joseph Heller's *Catch-22*, it is more closely related to John Barth's *Giles Goat Boy* (1965), which uses the Hero tale of *Oedipus Rex* as its structural axis. Curiously, although *Giles Goat Boy* was instantly recognized as a satire-anatomy, *Stranger* has not been so recognized in the critical literature.

Concomitant with the recognition of *Stranger* as a satire is the necessary recognition that *Stranger* is not science fiction in any strict sense of the term, though certainly it borrows much of its "furniture" from sf. The author wants us to understand immediately that he is dealing in terms of myth or fable. "Once upon a time, when the world was young," he begins, with the conventional opening of a fairy tale, "there was a Martian named Smith." So important does Heinlein judge this overture to the reader that, even though he needs to cut approximately 25% of the book from its as-written state, he removes only the irony-intensifying middle clause. Heinlein thus places his work immediately in the realm of myth—a story about the doings of the gods. In this case, the Thou-art-Gods.

Nevertheless, science fiction claims *Stranger* as its own. It is marketed with science fiction books, and was for decades offered as a selection by the Doubleday Science Fiction Book Club—which constitutes one of Heinlein's favored "extensional" definitions-by-pointing, if ever there was one.

Repeatedly the narrow pulp field has expanded to accommodate Heinlein's larger visions, as it was to do again for *I Will Fear No Evil* (1970), a book that makes not even a nod to the rationalistic conventions of science fiction as two and then three personalities come to inhabit the same body. Yet, Heinlein does not ignore his selected conventions; he is highly conscious of his choices and is also supremely in tune with the *Zeitgeist*. Perhaps, as Frye says, science fiction is naturally identifiable with myth and the high mimetic, in that it "tries to imagine what life would be like on a plane as far above us as we are above savagery...It is a mode of romance with a strong inherent tendency to myth." (*Anatomy*, 49)

To concentrate on the rationalist and scientific content of science fiction is to ignore the vital ritual and affirmational aspects of the mode.

Certainly *Stranger* does more than merely traffic in myth; it is myth-like in essential form. Myth tries, as Lévi-Strauss and Eliade tell us, to communicate the important information to participants in the same society. Heinlein is trying to do more; he is trying to induce his reader to pull himself out of his habitual mental ruts. Heinlein's program in *Stranger* thus lends itself to analysis in terms of the "creative hermeneutics" of influential myth-theorist Mircea Eliade. Eliade holds that all myths are stories of origins and analogically refer to the prime origin story, the cosmogony tale:

> "Origin myths continue and complete the cosmogonic myth... a myth is always related to a creation; it tells us how a pattern of behaviour an institution, a manner of working, were established." (*Myth & Reality*, 18, 21)

In its literary form, *Stranger* is an origin myth of a new era in human consciousness, the founding of what promises to be a major religion and a spiritual awakening for all of humanity.

Myth grows naturally from pointed story to cosmology, encompassing all of humanity's important concerns within itself, including all of time. There are many "techniques" for bringing everything together into a single idea-structure. Eliade discusses the placing of all the happenings of the Greek mythology in a past that never historically existed, the "timeless eternal present" of myths. Another very widespread technique for gathering everything into one structure corresponds with the many cycles of nature that repeat over and over again, as night follows day, as the Nile floods annually when Sirius rises at sunset, as winter is followed by spring. Myth assimilates nature to the human scale and establishes an analogy between its cyclical rhythms and the patterns of human personal and social life—birth, growth, death, and the succession of generations with the hope of rebirth. This type of myth, typified by the Solar myth story form explored in the nineteenth century by Max Müller, makes a grand circle (or sometimes, spiral), ending as it begins, beginning as it ends, implying that the circle is eternal and man thus abides in eternity.

> "The myth-maker establishes that line of most relevant experiences which constitutes his inner life from birth until—by anticipation—death. He takes these two ends and bends them into as near perfect a circle as possible so that the end must be ever a fresh beginning as generation follows generation." (Tarrant, 14)

Stranger is just such a circular/spiral myth-story. It begins with the death of the first Martian explorers and the birth of Valentine Michael Smith, and it ends with Smith's death and the presumed birth of a new era in human consciousness. Mike is a solar myth. This telltale circularity points also to Heinlein's debt to James Branch Cabell, for whom the circularity of the solar myth shapes the fictive conceptions of his Biography of the Life of Manuel, one after the other. His most important characters, Jurgen and Gerald Musgrave and Gray Manuel—like Christ himself—are solar myths.

The import of the circular form of myth is that the future joins with the past and becomes timeless, entering the condition Eliade calls "timeless archaic time… an *eternal present*" (*Sacred & Profane*, 88). Myth is an important social mode of time-binding—a Korzybskian expression that was the subject of Heinlein's first public address to his science fiction audience at the 1941 World Science Fiction Convention in Denver (*Requiem*). In both Malinowski and Eliade, myth presents an orientation within society and within the self.

> "Myths…fulfill human existential needs for 'cosmic' orientation. A myth speaks for the 'whole man.' Myths are generated in man's attempt to find an existential orientation." (Strenski, 75)[33]

The tight circle (or spiral) story form of *Stranger* is somewhat unusual within the satiric tradition. But the myth-form is dictated for *Stranger* by the choice of the gospel as the story-axis of the satire. There is a literary tension built into this

---

33. This important trajectory within myth analysis (both anthropological and literary) derives directly from Friedrich Wilhelm Nietzsche's writing in the period of 1870 to about 1885:

> "Nietzsche once defined myth as a concentrated image of the world…But myths are concrete in a broader sense, for they do not simply consist of significantly vivid descriptions. Instead they are figures or formulas which bring together, in a compelling embodiment or a graphic assertion, the most important values in an outlook or creed." (Foster, 137)

Nietzsche was powerfully influential at the period when Heinlein was being educated and formed intellectually. It is not, therefore, surprising that Heinlein would cast issues even as late as 1960 in terms of useful Nietzsche categories and the intellectual tradition that derived from them.

combination of choices, for myth inherently affirms established social values, while the function of satire is to critique established social values. Heinlein's use of myth here separates the inherent ambiguity of satire into two discrete levels, critiquing the superficial and hypocritical customs while affirming the values those customs are supposed to serve, but do not. With the critique and the affirmation clearly in mind, it is possible to play freely between the levels.

Myth in popular culture has been relegated to superficial stories useful for entertaining children, no doubt, but faintly silly all the same. Goblins and ogres, bowdlerized editions of "Collected Fairy Tales," and strange shenanigans of gods and goddesses are all told with a slight knowing nod. These aren't real. These don't really mean anything.

Myth arises from the basic human need to understand the world. Myth orders the cosmos and therefore man's place within it.

> "[T]eaching by myth and metaphor is the only way of educating a free person in spiritual concerns." (Frye, *The Double Vision*, 18)

Myth explains the world and therefore gives rise to a meaning of life. Any work of popular fiction, as Jungians have tirelessly shown, taps into this wellspring of meaning. Certainly any work that has been in print for forty years must have appeal beyond the mere story, the mere "mythos."[34] This fact implies that the individual work reaches into "the inexhaustible energies of the cosmos" (Campbell, 3) and is, in fact, a myth of the highest order; therefore giving rise to meaning.

> "Religions, philosophy, arts, the social forms of primitive and historic man, prime discoveries in science and technology, the very dreams that blister sleep, boil up from the basic, magic ring of myth." (Campbell, 3)

Mythos used to be contrasted with *logos*. *Mythos* is truth told as fiction while *logos* is truth told as fact.[35] Both use *dianoia* ("thought" or theme) to organize and transmit fact but they use it in very different ways.

This is best illustrated by doing. Here are two descriptions of Virginia Beach, Virginia:

1. A city called "The Virgin Strand, in the Land of the Queen, in the Land of the Virgin."

2. 36° 51' N, 75° 58' W.

---

34. In Aristotle's *Poetics*, a book which has framed our ways of thinking about fictional technique for two millennia, a fiction is made up of *mythos*, meaning story-line and *dianoia*, which translates as "thought," but is usually rendered as "theme." Myth becomes *mythos*. The story line of a story is its myth.

35. The term *logos* (Greek for "word") is taken over from theology, where its technical meaning is the thought or plan or intention of God. In literary terms (aside from the specialized use in poesy), *logos* is the "considered philosophy" component of the fiction—the rational, connected thoughts that underlie both *mythos* and *dianoia*.

To "get" the former definition, as it would be used if we are speaking *mythos*, it is necessary to know that the city is named for Queen Elizabeth I of England, who was called "the Virgin Queen" because she never married. The state is named for the same person, and the Roman Catholic Church has officially declared the Virgin Mary the Patron Saint of the United States of America.

To "get" the second, it is necessary to know that a physical location on a planet can be specified by Cartesian geometry based on offsets, called "latitude" and "longitude," from an arbitrary zero—in this case, where the longitude of Greenwich, England, intersects the Equator.

Neither of these is "correct" in any universal sense. They are two different and equally valid ways of talking about the same thing. Broadening *dianoia* to mean "what the hell you're trying to communicate" in both expressions, it becomes clear that *mythos* is the better form to use when speaking poetically (the "Virgin Strand") and *logos* when not (36° 51' N, 75° 58' W—great for navigating from Durban, but not as interesting to roll around in the mouth). "Trouble, Trouble, boil and bubble" doesn't convey the same quality of information as "The recent political disturbance can be compared to the action of water when reaching 100 degrees centigrade or 212 degrees Fahrenheit." Although both sentences *mean* exactly the same they don't *say* the same thing. The feeling used in *Stranger* that reality can be reduced to a set of mathematic constructs isn't logical, it's mythic.

The forms can't be mixed, of course, in any linear way: Allah squared plus the Holy Spirit squared divided by the square of the hypotenuse is just plain silly. And only an intellectual turnip would maintain that neither describes reality in any way at all. Both *mythos* and *logos* are *dianoia* in movement; the decision of form is a decision of rhetoric—how to get a truth across—not fiction versus fact.

What Heinlein achieves brilliantly in *Stranger* is to take the old hoary, overworked Myth of the Dying God and, while touching all bases, remold it into a perennial best seller. From the very first words we enter the world of Myth: "Once upon a time when the world was young," as the uncut version says—the words always used to start a fairy tale. And he then goes down a list of mythic elements, ticking off boxes.

The first box he ticked could be labeled Special Birth. Just as Heimdahl is said to be born on 9 different days by 9 different mothers (and Jubal Harshaw says he was born on three successive days), Michael is born of one woman but—legal as church—the son of two different fathers. Not only that, he is the "son," i.e. heir, of all of the crew of the *Envoy*. ("Envoy," indeed: "An agent, commissioner, deputy, messenger, representative." OED.) Therefore he is the "son" of four fathers and four mothers. Out of the womb, by cesarean section, he becomes molded by the sky gods (the Martians). Cast off from his human roots, he undergoes a Special Childhood (another tick here) and learns Special Wisdom (ditto). Then he is Sent Forth (tick) to Fulfill His Destiny (tick). He, like Zarathustra, "undergoes" to Earth (tick) and Reclaims His Heritage (tick) as a human being. Eventually, after suffering in the Underworld (tick) he realizes his Divine Status (tick). He gathers Disciples (tick) and Gives Unto Them the Secret of the Universe (tick). He is Slain by the Unworthy but Rises Unto Heaven and is granted Eternal Life (tick, tick, & tick). This is all pure, unadulterated Myth. Certainly this is nothing if not a "strongly-structured" story. It is even a candidate for Lévi-Strauss' Structural analysis, as it demonstrates all three of Lévi-Strauss' requirements for a myth: "logical coherence, religious orthodoxy, and collective pressure." (Lévi-Strauss, 128)

And yet...

To state *Stranger* this baldly is like describing Handel's *Messiah* as "a choral work on the birth and death of Jesus." As Jubal Harshaw remarks, "it lacks flavor." To treat it thus is to treat it as *logos*. To speak of it as *mythos* the gaze must be lifted, as it were, and focused on higher things. Heinlein folds meaning into the story of Valentine Michael Smith and he does this in several sneaky ways. First, although presented as science fiction it is, again, nothing of the kind. The trappings of science fiction—Bug-Eyed Monsters, Space Ships, Other Planets—are there, but those opening words, "Once upon a time—" inform us we are not in the genre.

The general form of the Hero tale contains all of the boxes Heinlein has just ticked off, but *Stranger* is concerned with one particular Hero tale, the one that has most influenced the development of American culture, the biography of Christ. Different critics have noted different aspects of the Christology, usually supposing that Heinlein intends a "travesty" of one or another point of the story, not seeing that the total shape of the story is identical. He performs miracles (including the specific miracle of the loaves and the fishes, though it is Jubal's Smorgasbord), gives sermons on the mount (up a bounce tube in high-rise), and gathers disciples. As his martyrdom and transfiguration approaches, he becomes increasingly Christlike. As Christ prayed in the Garden of Gethsemane, "If it be Thy Will, let this cup pass from me," but resolves finally to carry through his divine fate, so, too, does Mike confess himself to his mentor, Jubal Harshaw, and resolves to suffer his passion: "You've got me all squared away, Father [referring to Jubal]. I'm ready to show them now—I grok the fullness" (424/512).

Christ was crucified—a political disturbance to the Roman invaders. But stoning is the traditional biblical punishment for the adulterer and burning the traditional ecclesiastic treatment of heretics and witches—a treatment canonically justified as an extreme but humane remedy, cauterizing a wound in the church while simultaneously preventing the damaged soul of the unrepentant heretic from further damaging itself—i.e., the Church sends the soul of the heretic to heaven to prevent damage to the body of the soul and of the body of the church, just as Mike had sent the "evil elements" of the city "back to the beginning of the line" in the purging of the city (the Cleansing of the Temple) before his martyrdom. Mike is done to as he did, in fact and not merely in exhortation. He suffers both martyrdoms. And like Christ he appears after death to his disciples in "an upper room" of the hotel Mike's estate owns.

Mike cannot be contained within traditional dogma and so can only be viewed, from the conservative position, as a heretic because he now contains dogmatic positions within himself. Just as myth cosmically seeks to contain all of human experience within the story, Mike has contained all religious doctrine within himself.

Questions for Discussion

1. Do modern people need or use myth today? How?
2. What is the relation of archetype to myth?
3. What is the difference between a myth and a Hero tale or a legend?
4. How has anthropology influenced myth studies?
5. Northrup Frye suggests that when the dominant literature exhausts ironic naturalism, it can cycle back to myth. Is this something that you can see happening in current literature?

For Further Reading

Cabell, James Branch. *Figures of Earth: A Comedy of Appearances*. New York: Robert M. McBride & Co., 1921

Cabell, James Branch. *The High Place: A Comedy of Disenchantment*. New York: Robert M. McBride & Co., 1924

Cabell, James Branch. *Jurgen: A Comedy of Justice*. New York: Grossett & Dunlap, 1919, 1927

Cabell, James Branch. *The Rivet in Grandfather's Neck: A Comedy of Limitations*. New York: Robert M. McBride & Co., 1915, 1921

Cabell, James Branch. *Something About Eve: A Comedy of Fig-Leaves*. New York: Robert M. McBride & Co., 1927

Campbell, Joseph. *The Hero With a Thousand Faces*. 2nd ed. Princeton, New Jersey: Princeton University Press, 1968

Eliade, Mircea. *Myth and Reality*. London: Allen & Unwin, 1964

Eliade, Mircea. *The Sacred and the Profane*. New York: Harper & Row, 1961

Strenski, Ivan. *Four Theories of Myth in Twentieth-Century History: Cassirer, Eliade, Lévi-Strauss and Malinowski*. Iowa City, IA: University of Iowa Press, 1987

– 9 –

Myth, Satire, Realism

The confluence in *Stranger* and *Giles Goat Boy* of myth and satire is strangely "right"—"strangely" because the social function of myth is to present and confirm a social orthodoxy while the social function of satire is to criticize social orthodoxies. And yet, the combination is a natural possibility of literature. Literature presents, not historical fact, but "the universal in history" (Frye, *Great Code*, 46)—"to see the dimension of the possible in the actual." (49) The social function of myth is more specific than that of literature in general: the continuous re-presentation of "concerned knowledge, what is important for a society to know" (47). This quality of "concerned knowledge" has been a predominant characteristic of Heinlein's writing, an abiding concern throughout his writing career—suggesting that Heinlein was conscious of his self-presentation as a kind of public moralist. In *Stranger* he presents what is important to know about sex and religion in deliberately provocative terms, and it is the provocative intention that leads toward myth.

Heinlein's method, here as in other provocative works (see, e.g., *Starship Troopers*) is not to present doctrine, but to provoke the reader into actively evaluating his assumptions. The juxtaposition of the actual and the ideal standards of sexual morality and religious praxis suggests a conclusion or set of conclusions—but it is the testing of one's standards that is the important thing.

To lift up his satiric objects for examination (the term "examination" is used here rather than "ridicule" because Heinlein wishes us to examine his proposed solutions no less than the horrible sexual and religious practices he exposes), they must first be "made strange," seen through the eyes of an innocent voyager, the proverbial Man from Mars, who is also the messenger (αγγελος=angel=means "message" in Greek, so Mike is also implied to be the Archangel Michael) of a new

Gospel (="good news"). The necessary central myth tends to the Christian from the very inception of the satiric intent. Small wonder that *Stranger* took such a long time in gestation: Heinlein had to work out the entire literary theory, helped along, it is true, by the pioneering work of James Branch Cabell's Biography of the Life of Manuel and the long tradition of the innocent voyager.

> "The device of 'not understanding'—deliberate on the part of the author, simpleminded and naive on the part of the protagonist—always takes on great organizing potential when an exposure of vulgar conventionality is involved." (Bakhtin, 162)

The category of angels throws a schematic monkey-wrench into the conception—and yet, they are everywhere in the book and must be regarded as a device of intention. Man is created "in God's image," which means that he *chooses*; he is volitional; he has free will. He is the only creature in time able to do so (God is able to choose, but he stands outside time). An angel, however, is a special creation of God—a thought of God, as it were. Mike "is God" in a different sense, then, than the purely human characters, and the message Mike "is" is "Thou (humans) art God." This is the thought of God, the new revelation. So Mike is God, though he has become man, and Thou art God, in different senses, but equally true. Again, this is pure orthodoxy: it is a restatement of the proposition that man is created in God's image. Mike is not a man, as we are assured repeatedly by any character who happens to remark on the matter. Culturally, Mike is a quasi-Martian; biologically he is a man; and theologically he is an angel. But Mike must reject his Martian culture because he isn't Martian; he is a human. Not to do so would be to indulge in hypocrisy—the very "wrongness" it is his mission to correct.

Thus toward the end of the book, Mike achieves the fulfillment of his incarnation in the Monkey House of the zoo. A zoo is a store-house of the biological, an anatomy in real life, as the earth is the store-house of the biological and we humans swing from/occupy the *anthopoidiae* branch of the biological tree. The ironic contrast of an epiphany in the Monkey House produces a comic effect but shows that the book's view of existence is *both* comic and tragic and therefore "absurd." His incarnation is fructified, and thus he is able to bring his message to its intended recipients. He becomes man. But thereafter he begins to become distant from man. His incarnation is not a state to be rested in, but an apogee of a trajectory that returns to the Heaven from whence he came. And he takes his human family, the many who are called and who are self-chosen, with him a little distance from the Monkey House and into a nest, the home of a bird. The monkey who leaps from tree to tree has metaphorically gained wings as Mike has gained his own metaphoric wings and takes up his ministry. His followers take over his work as their particular characterizations fade. As humans become similar in misery, so, too, do they grok together in joy, and the things that distinguish and separate us seem less important than the things that unite us. The move from Monkey House to Nest expresses in image the master integration of the entire book: the hypocrisy that makes a tragedy of human existence is that we do not act on the divine will within each of us. We are apes with (metaphoric) angel wings, and we can live in either Monkey House or Nest, as we choose.

Mike's nest move toward union each with the other. They lose the tragic sense—as Mike learned to laugh by grokking the tragic sense—and they lose their laughter because they come to live in Joy. Heinlein, following Twain (see the quotation from "The Mysterious Stranger" in Chapter 5), connects laughter with the *tragic* sense of life—at exactly the point where heaven and earth meet, the epiphany of the Monkey House. But it is not an *epiphany*, an experience of the divine. Again, ironic inversion kicks in, and what Mike is awakened to—his Enlightenment—is not his *divinity* (which he knew all along), but his *humanity*. Mike groks that "Thou art God," but until the Monkey House he does not grok "Thou art Human." This "anthropophany" (a horrible term with which we will not afflict the gentle reader any further) is the final experience that allows him to complete his education and become fully Aware. This is the complete reversal of the normal Hero tale, in which the development is from humanity to divinity. It is only after Mike awakens to the tragic nature of human existence that he is capable of communicating with his fellow humans and, therefore, of fulfilling his mission.

Mike's "messagerial=angelic" trajectory takes him back into heaven, where he resumes his halo and takes up again the job(s) he left in suspension or momentarily in other hands. We are meant to realize that Mike's message—the thought of God that he "is"—is continuously at work in our reality—not a message for a particular time and place, but a continuing—indeed, subsisting—expression of all of reality, as fundamental as $F=ma$ or $E=mc^2$: Thou art God is a fundamental principle of physical existence. Heinlein explained precisely what it means in a letter to his agent, Lurton Blassingame, before the book was published:

> [After saying that the notion of a personal god is unprovable and unlikely] "That pantheistic, mystical 'Thou art God!' chorus that runs through the book is not offered as a creed but as an existentialist assumption of personal responsibility, devoid of all godding. It says, 'Don't appeal for mercy to God the Father up in the sky, little man, because he's not at home and never was at home, and couldn't care less. What you do with yourself, whether you are happy or unhappy—live or die— is strictly your business and the universe doesn't care. In fact, you may *be* the universe and the only cause of all your troubles. But, at best, the most you can hope for is comradeship with comrades no more divine (or just as divine) as you are. So quit sniveling and face up to it—'Thou art God!'" (*Grumbles*, 229)

Just as Heinlein should naturally have gravitated toward satire because of the "encyclopedic" element of his personal psychological makeup, so, too, should we expect him to gravitate toward myth for the same reason. Having settled in myth and satire, Heinlein seizes the expansive possibilities of myth to create a very advanced synthesis. Myths tend to expand into mythologies, Frye tells us, and mythology, like satire/anatomy, "has an encyclopedic quality about it: it tends to cover all the essential concerns of its society." (Frye, *The Great Code*, 51). The encyclopedic impulse of *Stranger* collects and synthesizes not self-congruent stories of ancillary characters, but parallel or variant religious traditions. It is a myth of mythologies.

Any major religion will contain within itself everything that it is possible for humans to be: if it didn't it couldn't be broadly appealing. And the major ideas get reinvented periodically in each and every major religion. For this reason, there is a strong tendency to try to trace all religions to a single source (or at any rate a small number of sources). Aldous Huxley's *The Perennial Philosophy* (1945) tries to show how the congruence of mystical ideas in Christianity and Vedanta must have come from a single source. A Hindu mystic claimed of the fourteenth century German Christian mystic, Meister Eckhart, "This man knew Vedanta"—a proposition biographically impossible.

Placing *Stranger* within the literary and religious tradition of myth allows Heinlein to access all of these perennial ideas and turn them to his satiric purposes.

Questions for Discussion

1. Myth is encyclopedic—but science is also encyclopedic in the same way: it tries to explain everything in terms of its own operating principles. Does this mean science is also a myth?

2. If myth tries to explain origins of social practices (Eliade) and satire tries to critique social practices, why does *Stranger not* appear to critique the origins of Christianity?

For Further Reading

Heinlein, Robert A. *Starship Troopers*. New York: G.P. Putnam's Sons, 1959

— 10 —

The Apollonian-Dionysian Dichotomy

Fairly early into the narrative, Heinlein introduces the Apollonian-Dionysian dichotomy as the controlling dynamic of the book. Jubal has maneuvered the Federation world state into granting Mike legitimacy; foregathered with Mike's adoptive human family in "an upper room," he discusses his observations about Mike and, through him, the Martians. He introduces the conventional classification of (Earth) cultures into Apollonian (mild, orderly, rational) and Dionysian (frenzied, disorderly, orgiastic) and remarks that Martian culture would be regarded as more purely Apollonian than any earth culture.

This observation is clearly a reference to Ruth Benedict's 1934 *Patterns of Culture*, an early and important popularization of the new anthropology of Benedict's teacher, Franz Boaz. Along with Margaret Mead's 1928 *Coming of Age in Samoa*, *Patterns of Culture* helped blast away the Victorian anthropological idea that culture is a feature of genetics or race (and that, therefore, there are such things are innately "superior" and "inferior" races). Benedict is quite emphatic about this point:

> "Not one item of his [man's] tribal social organization, of his language, of his local religion, is carried in his germ cell." (*Id.*, 26)

Boaz' principle of "cultural relativism" (also derived from Nietzsche) suggests instead that there are many possible folkways, all equally valid. Moreover, any single culture expresses only a tiny fraction of the variability that is possible to human cultures. These are propositions with which Heinlein has aligned himself repeatedly over his long career. Here, Heinlein's thinking about Valentine Michael Smith, the Man-Martian, seems to have been shaped as a direct response to Benedict.

> "The life history of the individual is first and foremost an accommodation to the patterns and standards traditionally handed down in his community. From the moment of his birth the customs into which he is born shape his experience and behavior. By the time he can talk, he is the little creature of his culture, and by the time he is grown and able to take part in its activities, its habits are his habits, his beliefs his beliefs, its impossibilities his impossibilities." (18)

And speaking of an individual adopted into an alien culture, Benedict appears to lay out the course of the Church of All Worlds after the close of *Stranger*:

> "He learns the entire set of the cultural traits of the adopted society, and the set of his real parents' group plays no part. The process happens on a grand scale when entire peoples in a couple of generations shake off their traditional culture and put on the customs of an alien group." (27)

Heinlein clearly intends us to make this association with *Patterns of Culture*, for the reference to Zuni culture, one of Benedict's specific exemplars of Apollonianism in her work with Southwestern Indian cultures, is otherwise gratuitous. (Blackmore) However, we are meant to dig deeper than that.

The Apollonian-Dionysian dichotomy was originally proposed by German philologist-philosopher Friedrich Wilhelm Nietzsche in his first major publication, *The Birth of Tragedy* (1870; wherein Nietzsche uses the German form "Apollinian" and Walter Kaufmann's excellent English translations follow this usage). Nietzsche's philosophy gained worldwide prestige, despite inadequate translation, through the remainder of the nineteenth century up until about 1930. Some of Heinlein's favorite intellectual formative influences (such as George Bernard Shaw) referenced Nietzsche repeatedly and approvingly—Nietzsche was "in the air" at the time Heinlein was educated, and Heinlein breathed in Nietzsche's ideas and made them part of himself. When he began to write, in 1939, he trod in the path Nietzsche had laid out (and Cabell had followed so well) for fusing philosophy with story-image. *The Birth of Tragedy*, in particular, is felt in *Stranger*, with its vision of human nature as not Platonically divided into higher and lower, but growing by spontaneously by self-transformation out of the earth of man's animal nature and its insistence that the only justification of human existence is "as an esthetic phenomenon" (the phrase is repeated twice in *Birth* and carried also into the much later "Self-Critique" which is often printed as a prelude or introduction to *The Birth of Tragedy*). Heinlein was to become increasingly preoccupied in his later works with this esthetic modality for seeing human existence.

Nietzsche's work—frankly difficult, though also intensely rewarding—was not served well by his admirers, particularly in English translation. H.L. Mencken reinterpreted Nietzsche as a Social Darwinist by injudicious additional commentary passed off as quotations from Nietzsche. Nietzsche could not have recognized his ideas in Mencken's explanations. Naturally, as the Victorian notion of Progress (with the capital "P") died out, Social Darwinism became discredited and Nietzsche, too, became unfashionable—except in the academic disciplines where he was galvanizing important new work in anthropology. After Nietzsche's death in 1900, control of his literary estate passed into the hands of his sister, who was married to a racist who later became a Nazi. Although Nietzsche's writings had been highly influential in the intellectual life of Europe, his aphoristic work was twisted to accommodate Nazi ideology—his violent anti-racist sentiments repackaged as racism—and he became unacceptable as an ideologue in the liberal west. It was not until long after World War II that adequate translations of Nietzsche began to appear in English—the bulk of them coincident with the rise of the counterculture in the mid-1960s. Benedict, writing just at the time Nietzsche's reputation was about to go underground (1928), acknowledges her debt to Nietzsche and points out that she has adapted certain aspects of his ideas to deal specifically with Southwestern Indian cultures. Her cultural relativism sees in Nietzsche a great force contrary to the reactionary *Rassenwissenschaft* ("race-science") then being institutionalized in Germany (Mead, *Writings of Ruth Benedict*).

Analyzing traditional Greek theater from its origins in religious festivals, Nietzsche sees a fundamental dialectic in the Greek soul between the orderly-rational and the frenzied-mystical poles of experience. A proper human life, Greek tragedy tells us, must contain both and not be limited to one or the other. In *The Bacchae*, for example, King Pentheus tries to eliminate the Dionysian rites from his city as a civil disturbance. In consequence, he is torn to pieces by the frenzied worshipers of Dionysos—which is portrayed as a restoring of proper respect for the gods. Heinlein tells us that America has much the same split personality; its prestigious public religions are formally Apollonian, while Dionysian behavior is tolerated and expected in private and is a norm for non-prestigious (particularly pentecostal) religions:

"The culture known as 'America' had a split personality throughout its history. Its laws were puritanical; its covert behavior tended to be Rabelaisian; its major religions were Apollonian; its revivals were almost Dionysian." (289/358)

Benedict uses the dichotomy as a static classification. Heinlein treats the two aspects as dynamic, complementary parts of a dialectical process, closer to Nietzsche and his view of the ancient Greeks. The stance of *Stranger* is much more Nietzsche than Benedictine. Insofar as the Church of Foster is exclusively Dionysian and insofar as Martian culture is exclusively Apollonian, they are, neither of them, suitable for fully formed, mature human beings. Mike's special message is to create a synthesis of the Apollonian and the Dionysian, a balanced *tertium quid*, neither one nor the other but a balanced blend of both, by a process of synthesizing many religions together.

Signaling the special relationship of the two made-up religions in the book, Mike sees in the orgiastic frenzy of the Fosterite service a quality "so Martian in flavor that he felt both homesick and warmly at home." (249/309) During a hymn, "Mike was so joyed that he did not try to grok words. He grokked that words were not of essence; it was a growing-closer. The dance started moving again..." (251/310) Mike sees the Martian-Apollonian flavor within the Dionysian revels. Nor is it a matter simply of being told by the author and by Jubal Harshaw that the Fosterites are Dionysian; the symbols with which Heinlein surrounds the Fosterites confirm that it is so: Dionysos is the god of wine and the god of touch, patron of all consciousness-altering, his rites communalistic and characterized by music and group dancing. At the Fosterite service, Mike's party are treated to alcoholic drinks as they observe the snake dance, the speaking in tongues. Mike recognized in the Fosterites a true devotion to Dionysos, and the reunion of sense from thought divided. It is therefore an appropriate object of his master synthesis. Fosterism becomes the "front door" to Mike's Church of All Worlds.

Apollo, on the other hand, is the god of ideas and the abstract, of deliberation and orderly dividing, night from day, rational from irrational, divine from mundane. He is the god of the abstract image, and his art is sculpture. The story of *Stranger* is defined in one dimension by the synthesis Mike will make of the Dionysian and the Apollonian, eliminating the fundamental Apollonian division of human from the divine. Its completion is signaled when the agnostic and Apollonian Jubal Harshaw—having awakened Ben Caxton to the esthetic of sculpture—rationally acknowledges the "radical union" of the divine and the human, the final synthesis of Apollonian and Dionysian.

In these terms, Ben's revulsion at the Nest is, therefore, due to his rejection of both the Dionysian/Fosterite ("He's a slimy bastard—I haven't exposed his racket in my column because the Syndicate is afraid to print it" [261/322]) and the Apollonian aspects of the Church of All Worlds (symbolized by his inability to appreciate sculpture—Apollo's art—just as Anne's acceptance of *La Belle Heaulmière* [322/396] signifies her "state of grace.") This is prefigured when Ben is kidnaped, drugged, and imprisoned and therefore not a part of the proto-nest at Jubal's house. Ben, for all that he is First Called, is an outsider because he has not had the intense personal interaction with Mike. He has two ears, but he does not hear. He has made himself theologically insane by disowning both aspects of the synthesis, both aspects of the self. This insanity is shown twice, as Heinlein often does, in his visit to the Nest, where he stares, uncomprehending, at the various Apollonian rites and then flees in terror and disgust at the Dionysian rite.[36]

Harshaw's disgust and opposition to the Fosterites has been cast as an esthetic matter: it is an act of Apollonian division. Mike's synthesis creates a church neither Apollonian *per se* nor Dionysian *per se*, but containing a balanced—and entirely human—blend of both. "Our way," Mike says, "is better" than the Mar-

---

36. The Apollonian-Dionysian dichotomy is assimilated to the sex/religion subjects of the satire. By implication, religion=Apollonian experience and sex=Dionysian. Mike is going to combine them both.

tian/Apollonian way. It blends and compounds and makes a union of male and female, yin and yang, Apollonian and Dionysian, sex and religion.

Parenthetically, this particular incident reveals the functional significance of digressions in the anatomy form. They seem to be extraneous to the story line and often irrelevant, but they serve a structural purpose, strengthening the thematic progressions of long works. Often, digressions are used to offer a commentary from a slightly divergent point of view on an important idea of the fiction, or, here, the digression pops us out of the linear flow of the story line to give a context that ties several thematic threads together into the main progression of the story. Heinlein was particularly adept at making his digressions reinforce and integrate his story line with his theme; from his earliest writing he has relied more on thematic progressions, than on the commercial-conventional plot-line of a "well made story," to carry his stories forward.

Questions for Discussion

1. What does "Apollonian" mean? What does "Dionysian" mean? Are these terms relevant to your life now?

2. Can people or cultures go to one side or the other of the Apollonian-Dionysian division? What qualities show the tendency in one direction or another.

3. Give an example of a quiet Dionysian frenzy. Give an example of a loud or noisy Apollonian activity.

4. What does George Carlin's classic standup comedy sketch contrasting baseball and football have to do with the Apollonian-Dionysian dichotomy?

For Further Reading

George Carlin. "Baseball–Football." *On the Road: An Evening with Wally Lando*. Atlantic Records, 1975

Nietzsche, Friedrich W. *The Birth of Tragedy."* Trans. Philip Kaufmann. New York: Random House, 1967

Ruth Benedict. *Patterns of Culture*. New York, New American Library (Mentor), 1934

PART THREE
"His Eccentric Education"

—

"Damn it, why can't the boy come home
and quit this obscene pulpit pounding?"

– II –

Subjects of the Satire

Heinlein proposes the way we are accustomed to "do" sex is wrong and hypo-critical—and the great majority of his readers agree. Sex is a central feature of human existence, but we have constrained it and hedged it about with the "law that kills" and irrational "thou shalt nots." Sex thus becomes the occasion of much human misery.

Similarly, the traditional approach to religion has gone terribly wrong, in *Stranger*'s view. Churches speak in the language of religion and spirit, but what they enforce is adherence to empty, irrational, and destructive forms of behavior. "Religion" is about the experience of the numenal, the divine. (Rudolph Otto). Churches—"organized religion"—have become "co-opted" in support of, or have originated, an established and orthodox social/cultural praxis. In practice, churches are authoritarian and political rather than religious in nature. The Apostle Paul refers to empty ritual and to forms observed when their meaning has died away as "dead husks," as a form of idolatry: forces of nature—or mere customs—treated as if they were divine (Frye, *The Great Code*, 164). Setting itself against the true and material world, churches make hypocrites of their adherents by forcing public lip-service to one set of ideas and practice, while another set is, privately, in place. Churches, bluntly, kill religion.

One key to the religious satire is on page 137/176 in an (a) to (f) laundry list of things Mike does not grok. The paragraph is too long, and contains too much extraneous material, to be worth quoting here (go read it!), with the exception of one point, (f):

> "It was not possible to separate in the Martian tongue the human concepts: 'reli-gion,' 'philosophy,' and 'science'—and, since Mike thought in Martian, it was not possible for him to tell them apart."

Religion, science, and philosophy all have one major component in common: they are all systematic attempts to describe the way the universe works. When Mike says "Thou art God" in English, he is translating from the Martian a prose sentence, Thou=God. In Martian, this statement is the exact equivalence of $E=mc^2$. God is as real as energy, matter, and the speed of light. The Martian language reflects the Martian experience, since "…the answers to any questions were available from the Old Ones, who were omniscience and infallible, whether on tomorrow's weather or cosmic teleology." (137/177) In human terms, this means, "got a question? Ask an angel." Because of this, *all* of the "miracles" in the book are really an illustration of Arthur C. Clarke's (third) law: "Any sufficiently advanced technology is indistinguishable from magic."[37] Here, Heinlein replaces "advanced technology" with "adequate language," possibly reflecting his lifelong interest in the General Semantics of Alfred Korzybski.[38]

The ascetic way endorsed by the Western church is right for some people, and there are other major religions based on ascetic principles. Buddhism, for example, is formally based on the idea that life is suffering and the material world nothing but a veil of illusion. The great majority of people, however, do not and cannot emotionally grasp these ascetic notions and see the material world as a place of delight, however awkward, inconvenient, or unpleasant their present circumstances have become. There is good Biblical authority for this position, as God made a gift to Adam and his descendants of the world and all that is in it and commanded him to be fruitful and multiply.

Ascetics seek to characterize the innocence orientation as simpleminded and unsophisticated, but this is a dialectical position, not a philosophical truth. Acquisition of knowledge, experience, and sophistication does not automatically make people reject the world. An affirmational orientation is as capable of sophisticated development as is the experience (demonic) orientation of the ascetics.

In the ascetic vision, sex is categorized as an attachment to materiality and therefore demonic. The delight/affirmational orientation places sex as a means of experiencing and participating in the divine or noumenal, and of celebrating our place in the created cosmos. It is therefore fundamentally a phenomenon of inno-

---

37. Clarke's Laws are widely distributed in collections of modern wisdom sayings on the Internet. They were printed originally in Clarke's 1962 *Profiles of the Future*, though only the first was labeled "Clarke's Law." A French edition labeled the second, and Clarke himself named the third in the 1973 revised edition.

38. Korzybski was a figure of considerable influence in the early part of the twentieth century— and particularly within the small field of science fiction. His *Science and Sanity* (1933) introduced the concept of General Semantics—a study of the most basic, mathematical relationships between words and their referents. Heinlein took all of Korzybski's seminars he could get to before World War II and briefly considered writing an introductory text when he retired from science fiction (also briefly) in 1941. Public interest in General Semantics faded over the years, though Heinlein maintained a lively appreciation of its possibilities.

cence (in William Blake's classification of innocence and experience) with a strong
orientation to the divine. This is the stance from which *Stranger* is written, and
the book does not fit the usual categories because it is a sophisticated defense of
knowing innocence—paradox piled upon paradox. It is carried, not by an argument, but by an image: when we first meet Mike, even before Jill, we are told,
"[h]is most marked feature was his bland, expressionless, almost babyish face—set
with eyes which would have seemed more at home in a man of ninety." (12/26)
His eyes are "oddly disturbing" to Jill. (15–16/30) They remind her of a nun,
though there is nothing feminine about him. (17/33)

Although the majority of the readers of *Stranger* find its sexual morality utopian and desirable, a significant minority of readers find it repellant, often ratio-
nalizing their emotional reaction, when challenged, by saying that the sexual
liberalism of the Nest is "unrealistic" or "socially destructive." The majority, on
the other hand, see the same behaviors and idea-sets as socially affirming. The
affirmational perspective is held by a sizeable fraction of the population—enough,
when the cultural wind was right, to support another and similar writer on sex
reform working at about the same time as *Stranger*. Robert Rimmer's *The Harrad
Experiment* (1963) made a powerful case for the liberating qualities of sexual freedom, and Rimmer followed it up with a series of popular books dealing with marriage reform and "polyamory."[39] Nevertheless, the suppressive, ascetic perspective
remains culturally dominant.

The existence, simultaneously, of these two very divergent views on the same
material—affirmational and demonic—indicates that people are looking into
Heinlein and seeing themselves, even when they believe their evaluations and
assessments are objective. A professional writer is a professional mirror, and Heinlein was among the best in this respect. He here provides us a touchstone by
which we may examine our own values—a process he said is the real purpose of
the book: to pose hard questions, not to provide answers.

The dichotomy rises as a value judgment because of the different "package
deals" of values taught to surround sex in our culture. As Heinlein says, the quality of the answers one gets from the book intimately depends on the values the
reader brings to the experience. Conventionally, Christianity dogmatically presents sex as belonging to the realm of experience, with a demonic and materialist
orientation. In this world-picture, attachment to sex is anti-spiritual by definition.
This is not, however, the only natural orientation; nor is it even the majority ori-

---

39. This new word compounded of Greek ("poly" meaning "many") and Latin ("amor" meaning
     "love") roots was devised as a neutral term for group marriages of any composition, replacing
     gender-specific words such as "polyandry" (marriage of one woman with multiple husbands—
     "andros" for man) and "polygyny" (marriage of one man with multiple women—"gunos" for
     "woman"—the same root from which "gynecology" is derived). "Polygamy" is many "mar-
     riages" simultaneously, without respect to gender.

entation, when all of humankind is considered. It is common among Eastern religions (particularly the major strains of Hinduism) and the Western hermetic[40] traditions to assign sex to the realm of innocence, with a strong tendency to the divine. In this orientation, sex is one of many ways of experiencing the divine. Thus among the Yogic disciplines is Tantra, popularly known as sex-yoga, and sex magic is a strong component of the hermetic magical traditions, paralleling the vegetative magic called condescendingly "granola magic," practiced by Wicca-revivalists and neo-pagans. *Stranger* contains the innocence orientation within the archetype of the City of God, whose literary symbol is the church—an uncommon but perfectly legitimate literary device.[41]

And, to be quite fair, there is an intellectual strand within Christianity that declares sex to be life-nourishing and spiritually innocent. See any of the fictional works of Father Andrew Greeley. Within this underground tradition (for it has never been made a major trend within Western Christianity), sex is seen as a reflection of God's divine Love (*agape*, in Greek). Just as the Trinity is united by Love, two people are united and made one. The human body is forever potentially sanctified by God becoming Man. Birth, a natural result of heterosexuality, is seen as the recapitulation of the birth of Christ, with the love of a mother for her child seen as an image or type of the Love of God for humanity.

Most English-speaking (or at any rate, American) peoples stand somewhere in the middle ground between these polarities of innocence and experience, gravitating to one pole or another, with world-outlooks that strongly limit sex as destructive to human values and world-outlooks that strongly embrace sex as affirmative of human values. Thus the disagreement rises. It is not susceptible to analysis or resolution within the framework of the story, because it rests on value judgments outside the framework of the story. The conflict is raised to be meditated upon, not to be resolved—at least, not by this book. It is a task appropriately left to the reader.

Even the most strongly innocence-oriented person in this culture is at least aware of the experience-demonic-ascetic orientation which is regarded as a norm or standard of the culture and to which behavioral accommodations must be made. Within the framework of innocence-orientation, these accommodations

---

40. "Hermetic" refers to a very long and very diverse set of alternative religious and philosophical traditions said to descend from the Egyptian religious system set up by Thoth Hermes Trismegistes. For our purposes, the most important strain of hermetic thought surviving into the modern world comes through NeoPlatonism—first by way of St. Augustine and then through a revival of NeoPlatonic thought in the nineteenth century that sparked American Transcendentalism. These terms are given a somewhat fuller treatment in Chapter 18.

41. Note that, as Robert Graves is at pains to remind us in *The White Goddess*, public and promiscuous sex—"without shame"—is a very ancient signifier of divinity and divine royalty. Heinlein's human-gods reinstate open sexuality within the context of a church—the Nest being the Ninth Circle of the Church of All Worlds.

are incomprehensible, if pragmatically necessary. Mike puts his understanding and sympathy on display in his "Garden of Gethsemane" talk with Jubal Harshaw before his martyrdom:

> "...I slowly grokked it [sex] rarely was [what it should be]. Instead it was indifference and acts mechanically performed and rape and seduction as a game no better than roulette but with poorer odds and prostitution and celibacy by choice and by no choice and fear and guilt and hatred and violence and children brought up to think that sex was 'bad' and 'shameful' and 'animal' and something to be hidden and always distrusted. This lovely perfect thing, male-femaleness, turned upside down and inside out and made horrible." (*Stranger*, 508)

Mark Twain also sees this as a permanent and irreducible feature of the human condition. He has his "Mysterious Stranger"—an angel presumably on the same level as Valentine Michael Smith—analyze the general problem of the oppression of the majority by the minorities:

> "...your race...is made up of sheep. It is governed by minorities, seldom or never by majorities. It suppresses its feelings and its beliefs and follows the handful that makes the most noise...The vast majority of the race, whether savage or civilized, are secretly kindhearted and shrink from inflicting pain, but in the presence of the aggressive, and pitiless minority they don't dare to assert themselves...
>
> "Monarchies, aristocracies, and religions are all based upon that large defect in your race—the individual's distrust of his neighbor and his desire, for safety's or comfort's sake, to stand well in his neighbor's eyes." (*The Mysterious Stranger*, 110–111)

This sense of a divergence between the values one must practice and the values one is supposed to practice inescapably engenders hypocrisy:

> "As with all hierarchies...'underneath' is a rabble of doubts telling him that his intellectual set-up is largely fraudulent. He may shout down his doubts and trample them underfoot as temptations coming from a lower world, but he is still what Hegel calls an unhappy consciousness." (Frye, *The Double Vision*, 13)

A literary analysis of the same phenomenon is given by Russian (Marxist) literary critic Mikhail Bakhtin: When "vulgar conventionality" is enforced,

> "hypocrisy and falsehood saturate all human relationships. The healthy 'natural' functions of human nature are fulfilled, so to speak, only in ways that are contraband and savage, because the reigning ideology will not sanction them. This introduces falsehood and duplicity into all human life. All ideological forms, that is, institutions, become hypocritical and false..." (Bakhtin, 162)

Bakhtin is here discussing the literary function of the figures of the rogue, the fool, and the clown (note that Jubal Harshaw refers to himself as a "professional clown") to hold up for public display the private and hidden truth, particularly in regard to sexual and vital bodily functions, decoding the symbols by which they are covered up by the official religion.[42] Jubal Harshaw knows both public and private truths. He groks in fullness.

Accommodations to vulgar conventionality usually take the form of hypocrisy, and hypocrisy is the aspect under which both sex and religion are satirically examined. Each of the perversions of human sex,[43] Heinlein goes on to say, "is a corollary of jealousy…a terrible wrongness." (420/508)

The human remedy for hypocrisy is simply to act straightforwardly on one's actual beliefs and in support of one's own emotional truth. Heinlein traces much of the ill effects of sexual hypocrisy to jealousy.

The case of sexual jealousy is more complex, and much of the second half of the book is concerned with this. Heinlein's fundamental position regarding jealousy is that it rises from personal insecurity (which suggests another reference to Nietzsche—this time, the doctrine of *ressentiment* in, especially, *On the Genealogy of Morals*). The "cure" for insecurity is the Apollonian commandment to "know thyself." Self-honesty. There are many references to this process going on in the book, but Heinlein *shows* the internal process of self-healing going on in two pivotal cases (Heinlein very frequently used a duple presentation of key ideas in his fiction).

While Mike and Jill are in Las Vegas, Jill takes a temporary job as a showgirl and discovers in herself a streak of exhibitionism.[44] At first, she denies and wants to disown this fact about herself. But she comes to realize that she cannot deny something that is a true part of herself, like it or not. The key element in the healing process is that one must "face facts" and move on—a theme Heinlein has included approvingly in his fiction from first to last. Jill contemplates her exhibitionism and incorporates it into her view of herself, instead of disowning it, as she had done before. Now she can build an empathetic understanding of the complimentary male voyeurism posed earlier in the story by Duke. Even though Duke, too, was "First-Called," his voyeurism with pornographic pictures (which had come up in the middle of a digression about the mail a celebrity receives) created a cognitive dissonance for Jill, that prevented acceptance—psychological union—with a supposed water brother. Jill acted as

---

42. Consider the words of another "professional clown": "There are two kinds of Christian morals, one private and the other public. These two are so distinct, so unrelated, that they are no more akin to each other than are archangels and politicians." (Mark Twain, "Taxes and Morals")

43. Heinlein is not speaking "sex perversions" such as homosexuality (to which he manifests in *Stranger* a relatively enlightened attitude for 1961), fetishism, or pedophilia. Rather than identify these possible kinks individually, he speaks, rather, of "wrongness" and lets the reader supply particulars, if any. Here, Heinlein means a psychologically healthy process turned to the creation of misery and dissatisfaction—sickness.

44. This is plausible in a realistic, mimetic sense because only casino jobs pay well in Las Vegas, but this development serves another structural purpose as well: Jill becomes a showgirl; Dawn is an ecdysiast (exotic dancer). By this evolution, the identity between Jill and Dawn inside the Nest is made more plausible, as well.

though Duke were a full water brother, even though she did not feel it. This, by definition, is hypocrisy. Jill's emotional dilemma is treated initially as an example of the gulf between men and woman; by this act of self-knowledge, Jill empathetically bridges that gap. Heinlein is exploring the mechanisms of community. Her grokking causes the dissonance to disappear, and the hypocrisy: she "grows closer" with Duke—self-healing as union, reflecting the major dialectical process of the book in small. Now more in tune with her self by being more in tune with her sexuality, she is able to "do" sex without the dissonances of unacknowledged personal agendas. She is in touch with her divine nature; she is God, and the divine Will works through her—which is the point of the various spiritual exhortations to suppress the self in various religions—Paul's "Christ wears Paul as a garment," the Buddhist "pouring out" of the self, the characterization of the Buddha as the one who has "gone out" like a candle, Emerson's "transparent eyeball" through which all the universe passes as light, and the Nietzsche "overman," who "over"comes himself.[45] Jill becomes the entire sequence of *magna mater* deities presented at the initiation scene when Jubal visits the Nest to see the truth of Mike's religion with his own eyes. Jill becomes God—several gods, in fact. Heinlein made great use of similarity of scale (the same structure in large and small scales—as the *Book of Job* has the same story structure as does the Bible as a whole), his artist's comprehension of this feature far in advance of the scientific understanding of fractal and chaos mathematics that would imply, twenty-five years later, that similarity of scale is a basic property of life-processes.

It is also important to note that Heinlein sees human beings as significantly in control of their own psychological dynamics. In this respect he differs from Twain, who in his late works portrayed humans as reflexively subordinate to external influences and dispositions of character, which he regards as simply "given." This is the ultimate root of the "victim complex" to which American society has given itself in the last half-century. Heinlein does not regard one's character as "given"; rather, it is something one builds oneself over a period of years, in a process Theodore Sturgeon called "slow sculpture."

The other example of sexual jealousy being healed is, of course, the most overt example in the book: Ben Caxton's self-confessed jealousy of Jill. At a piv-

---

45. "Overman" is a more exact translation of the German *übermensch* (which is usually translated into English as "superman") and allows Nietzsche's punning with *over*coming the self and *under*going or "going under" (in the sense in which the sun when it sets goes *under* the horizon), to translate from the German to the English.

"There is no English equivalent for *untergehen* (literally going under). The German verb is used for the setting of the sun, for drowning, and above all for perishing." (Walter Kaufmann, trans. *The Gay Science*, 275). Kaufmann also notes in his Translator's Notes for *Thus Spoke Zarathustra* that "...untergehen poses the greatest problem of translation..." Small wonder we have such difficulty with the term in English.

otal cadence in the book's overall structure, Caxton comes to Jubal as a parishoner comes to a priest, with an emotional problem: he has fled the Nest and is, he says, concerned for the "snake pit" Jill has gotten herself involved in. Gradually, as Ben tells the story of his own visit to the Nest, Jubal strips him of his rationalizations. Everything he saw and experienced was healthy and life-affirming. The only "problem" was the ambiguities Caxton—hypocritically—brought into the Nest. At first, Caxton is unable emotionally to experience the spiritual qualities of the Nest. Heinlein has this problem echoed on a small scale in Caxton's inability emotionally to experience the esthetic qualities of sculpture (the art belonging to Apollo, as Jubal Harshaw represents the Apollonian view of American culture in the book). Harshaw teaches him how to view sculpture—in terms of story moving one to pity and terror. Heinlein knows that sculpture cannot be grasped in terms of narrative devices. As a material object, it can only be grasped as an existential event. It can only be experienced. Human language cannot deal with the real world, though the language of art can mirror an object of art. But Harshaw wakens Caxton's spiritual potentials by teaching him how to view sculpture (the Apollonian art form). Ben weeps; his emotional response has been unblocked. The spiritual awakening then allows Caxton to see clearly that all his problems with what he has experienced are due to sexual jealousy. He then takes the important first step in self-healing and embraces the Nest. He forces himself to act on the totality of his love for Jill, and not just the erotic attraction, and thus embraces the totality of his ability to love.

There is another aspect of Ben's hypocrisy which is not discussed, but which is shown: his sexual predation of both Jill and Dawn. Every member of the Nest is a Water Brother, and Ben is accepted as a full member by virtue of being "First Called." But he treats Dawn not as a Water Brother, but as an object. Ben has no love for Dawn; he scarcely senses her as a person at all. Jill senses Ben is uncomfortable when they first meet in the Nest. When he denies it, she puts it aside for the moment. But later she tries to show Ben that she and Dawn are the same: "Jill said, with her mouth full, 'See, Ben? That's me.'" (348/429) She then leaves and Ben "cooperated with the inevitable" with Dawn. But even after "the inevitable," Ben has no love for Dawn as a Water Brother. He used her for his own gratification, objectifying Dawn as a symbol of Jill, and therefore used the healing unity Dawn had offered him to enable and perpetuate his own self-alienation.

Later, Jubal observes "He no longer trusted any 'coincidence' in this ménage; it was as organized as a computer." (408/495). This is a key observation that bears on Ben's earlier visit. Jill, having sensed that Ben was troubled—we know that she knows of his jealousy because she later tells Mike of it—manipulated her arrivals and departures so that Ben was left alone with Dawn at the proper moment. If Ben can break through to a loving experience with another Water Brother, he will be able to deal effectively with his residual jealousy; Jill knows that for her to welcome Ben into the Nest would only intensify his jealousy and sense of possessiveness. So she makes it easier for Ben, telling him she and Dawn are "the same," truthfully meaning that they are parts of the same unity, and it is the unity Ben is asked to join with, not the individual components of it. Jill attempts to cure Ben of his jealousy—or help him cure himself—by having Dawn take her place. Jill knows exactly what she is doing:

> (Jill) "'I was tempted to spend the night with you myself—I wanted to, dear! But you arrived with jealousy sticking out in lumps. I think it's gone now. Yes?'
>
> (Ben) "'I think so.'
>
> "'So? I grok a few lumps still—but we'll wash them away.' She sat up, touched his cheek, said soberly, 'Before tonight, dear. Because, of all my beloved brothers, I would not have your Sharing-Water be less than perfect.'" (357/440)

Jill knows not only what she is trying to do—she knows her attempt has failed: there are "a few lumps still."[46] Parenthetically, it should be noted that Jill has been doing art within the definition of art Heinlein has given in *Stranger* (and earlier in "Lost Legacy"), of an arrangement of emotions. In this incident, Jill, and through her the unity of the Nest, stands in relation to Caxton's psychological state as an artist to the raw materials of the artistic creation.

At the opening of the book, Jill and Ben Caxton are shown as having a relationship special but not close enough to exclude others. There is an implication Jill considered "settling" for Caxton, but there is no "anagnorisis" or "recognition" of Caxton as her true other self. Their marriage, had they proceeded to it in Mike's absence, would have been, at most a conventional marriage with "something missing." Perhaps Ben's first passage in the Nest shows us why.

When Jill and Mike make a final attempt to force-heal Ben's jealousy (for Mike has sensed, "I grok we can't hold your Sharing-Water tonight." [360]), Ben cannot. Ben only sees the reflection of his own attitude towards Dawn: sexual predation.

Heinlein was very aware that sex has two functions in human society. The first is the biological, the sharing of chromosomes by the parents in the gamete. The second is the psychological, the "growing closer," the emotional attachment of the parents. Heinlein explicitly notes the difference:

> "...Martians had it in form so different from Terran form that it would be 'sex' only to a biologist and emphatically not have been 'sex' to a human psychiatrist" (91/119).

The social function of the water sharing ceremony is to bond Martian adults socially in the same way marriage—in the highest sense of the word—bonds

---

46. This conversation shows how tightly-written *Stranger* can be. Note how, in a few lines, Heinlein has described: (1) Jill's recognition of Ben's jealousy, (2) Jill's acknowledgment of her attempt to cure it, (3) her realization that the attempt has failed, (4) her reassurance to Ben of her love for him, and (5) her resolve to take further action to cure him.

human adults. Ben is specifically told that once he joins the Nest, he will be incapable of the biological act without its psychological component of intense emotional attachment:

> (Duke) "'I could pick up a babe in a bar, share water, take her to bed—and then bring her to the Temple. But I wouldn't. That's the point; I would never want to. Ben, I'll make a flat-footed prediction. You've been in bed with some fancy babes—'
>
> (Ben) "'Uh, some.'
>
> "I know damn' well you have. But you will never again crawl in with one who is not your water brother.'" (353/435–436)

And this is underlined later, in the "Garden of Gethsemane" talk between Mike and Jubal:

> "'Jubal, I am physically unable even to attempt love with a female who has not shared water with me. And this runs all through the Nest. Psychic impotence— unless spirits blend as flesh blends." (420/508)

Heinlein's prescription for jealousy is, therefore, not only self-awareness (as necessary as that first step is), but Love. Agape. The emotional attachment that only wishes the highest and best for Other. This concern with psychological freeing of the self unfolds another dimension of Heinlein's ongoing dialog with Nietzsche (which had emerged explicitly in the introduction of Nietzsche's Apollonian-Dionysian dichotomy). Jill's exploration and acceptance of her exhibitionist impulses—and Ben's acknowledgment and letting-go of his jealousy and sexual predation (indeed, all the conversions that take place in the book)—are portrayed as working samples of Nietzsche's "overcoming" the self (Jubal must overcome his emotional scarring from living in the world—the very thing that gives him the necessary distance to let him grok in fullness without learning Martian. Jubal more than anyone else in the book must overcome himself; he must overcome his most precious faculty, his agnosticism). The progress of each individual toward recognition of his innate godhood is exactly what Nietzsche meant by two key terms of his philosophy: "over"coming and "will to power," as the power being referred to is the power of self-actualization. Hypocrisy is posed as what must be overcome in the self in order to allow the self to expand into its natural heritage.

Heinlein was startled and puzzled by the number of people who wanted to act on *Stranger* as a plan for living. His satiric purpose was to critique the hypocrisy created by the ascetic worldview in regard to sex—to force the reader to ask himself hard questions. He did not reckon with the strong reaction a new generation that celebrated the innocence-orientation might have to the affirmational aspects of the satire of sex; the world had changed since he planned his attack, and young people of the 1960s were not content to rest with the satiric-literary assumption of agreement that "something is wrong," without doing something positive about it.[47]

Questions for Discussion

1. Heinlein says that jealousy always comes down to insecurity, not having a strong sense of one's own worth. What does this mean?

2. Social commentators say that we are living in a "victim culture." What does that mean? How does Heinlein's idea that we can heal ourselves stand in opposition to the victim culture?

3. How could honest self-knowledge assist in self-healing?

4. How much would the 1960s culture of "free love" differed had not the birth control pill and *Stranger* appeared, more or less in tandem?

5. Since the natural result of sex is children, how does the wealth of the Church of All Worlds impact the lives of the female water brothers?

6. How does the concept that we are each completely responsible for our own "overcoming" fit with the realities of handicapped and disabled people?

For Further Reading

Frye, Northrup. *The Great Code: The Bible and Literature*. San Diego, Calif.: Harcourt, Brace & Co., 1981

Greeley, Andrew. *Thy Brother's Wife*. New York: Warner Books, 1982

Greeley, Andrew. *An Occasion of Sin*. New York: G.P. Putnam's Sons, 1991

Rimmer, Robert. *The Harrad Experiment*. (1965) New York: Prometheus Press, 1990

---

47. Unfortunately, far too often for comfort, what the disaffected youth of the 1960s *did* was to show up on Heinlein's remote doorstep in a redwood forest outside Santa Cruz, California, with no clear idea of what comes next. This is sudden death to a working writer's concentration. Ironically, Heinlein found it necessary to barricade himself behind chain link and barbed wire in exactly the same way that Jubal assured his privacy in the Poconos—and for much the same reasons (Gifford, 187).

– 12 –

Sex and Religion

Consideration of the satire of sex and the satire of religion separately does not complete the analysis, for Heinlein is also and simultaneously attacking both subjects together, as one integrated subject: sex-and-religion. A logically consistent treatment of the innocence orientation dictates that, if sex is a way of experiencing the divine, then sex may be treated as a religious rite or ritual. In this way of looking at the subject, an act of sex is an act of worship and can be performed as intently or as perfunctorily as a Catholic attending a daily mass. At its most intense, one can transcend the boundaries of the narrow, limited ego and achieve a transcendent union with the divine. This union is reflected in *Stranger* most clearly in Mike's "Garden of Gethsemane" talk with Jubal, when he discusses the "group sex" Jubal had unwittingly participated in with Dawn (the Fosterite complement of Jill) the night before, at the dawn of Jubal's initiation into the Nest. "Dawn told us that you were as deep into her mind as you were into her body" (420/507). Jubal has achieved union with the Thou-art-Gods through "this lovely, perfect thing, male-femaleness." (420/508).

There are hundreds of religious sects that incorporate the idea of sex as devotion, though conventional Christianity lumps them together as Satanic and treats them as demon-worship—which the practitioners of these innocence-orientated religions regard as absurd and irrational. They have a covert existence, even when very nearly out in the open, because the conventional interpretive paradigm cannot "see" them. Heinlein makes extensive use of this fact to include covert references to the main innocence-oriented sex-religions within *Stranger*—as, for example, the name of the principal character, Valentine Michael Smith combines the commonest of all surnames (i.e., "Smith" as "everyman") with the archangel who is the symbol of the Christian church-militant and the martyred saint whose name stands for erotic love.[48]

But *Stranger* is not merely concerned with the religious aspect of sex. As the book combines the cultural and political together with the religious, so, too, does it combine the cultural and political together with the sexual. The political corollary of sex as worship, is marriage reform—an issue of perennial concern to the Freethinkers, and an issue Heinlein presented consistently throughout his long writing career. That almost archetypal nineteenth century socialist John Humphrey Noyes places the context in which we find the base of Heinlein's thought:

> "But we hold that a man's deepest experiences are those of religion and love; and these are just the experiences in respect to which he is most apt to be inclined to be silent. So the nation says but little and tries to think that it thinks but little, about its Revivals and its Socialisms…" (26)

Heinlein has brought together Noyes and Twain to create his particular treatment of these subjects, suggesting, again, that Heinlein's persistent intellectual stance is that of a Freethinker, a defined political position on the radical wing of American liberalism at the turn of the century. It is somewhat surprising to think of his position in these terms, for we are accustomed to think of Heinlein as modern and even more-than-modern. But it is perhaps more useful to think of Heinlein as capturing the best, most progressive thinking of American liberalism in the nineteenth century and presenting it in opposition to "modernism," insofar as the word implies a Positivist[49] or mechanist orientation. Heinlein has criticized, *inter alia*, "Positivist Materialism" very directly in his earliest stories (see, e.g., "Elsewhen"), and the approving references to Robert Ingersoll and T.H. Huxley in his last book, *To Sail Beyond the Sunset* (1987), indicate that his Freethought agenda was persistent and perennial. It may, therefore, be fruitful to view Heinlein as an intellectual and moral "bridge" spanning a dry cultural gulch, bringing forward perennial America progressive values and affirming the sparks that yet survive but are hardly fed in the increasingly Positivist twentieth century.

Heinlein, moreover, was not merely a Freethinker—he was on the radical wing of this radical wing. He was an American socialist during a period before there was doctrinal antagonism between socialism and capitalism (a Marxist trope). In the years before the Bolshevik Revolution in Russia, Marxism was only one of

---

48. A more complete exposition of this complex combination of names is given in the Appendix.

49. "Positivism" is a philosophy invented by Auguste Comte in the middle third of the nineteenth century that relied on "positive" facts—things that can be measured—as opposed to the prevalent assumption that church and religious propositions have automatic priority. Positivism naturally tends toward materialism, and as it became the intellectual base of twentieth century philosophy, Positivism became highly reductionist, so that all spiritual or intellectual considerations were, in principle, "reduced" to physics or chemistry. Relevant aspects of Positivism are discussed in greater detail in Chapter 18.

many brands of socialism, and not necessarily the predominant one. Socialism in the nineteenth century fell into two broad classes; the Marxist version, with which we are more familiar in the twentieth century, works on the paradigm of class antagonism or conflict; the socialism of Henri Saint Simon, worked out at the time of the French Revolution (and therefore almost at the same time the U.S. was founded), works on the basis of class cooperation or collaboration. In the nineteenth century there were several "waves" of socialist experimentation in the cooperative or "associative" mode. The most widely known of these experimental communes were Brook Farm (in which Nathaniel Hawthorne briefly lived and about which he wrote), and the Oneida Colony of about 1848 to about 1890. John Humphrey Noyes, the founder of the Oneida Colony, talked about the various combinations of socialist ideals in his 1869 *History of American Socialisms* and concluded that the ideals of cooperative socialism are deeply engraved in the American character. Noyes' influence is felt in *Stranger* in the linking of Home (the Nest) with Heaven (*Id.*, 351). The truth of this position is suggested by the sudden and unlooked-for re-emergence of "communes" associated with the counterculture of the 1960s and the continuing experiments in marriage reform now going by the name of "polyamory." Heinlein, in carrying the Freethought, cooperative socialist ideas of American liberals forward into the twentieth century, helped to midwife this renascence.[50]

The Martian-human religion of the Church of All Worlds creates a synthesis of sex and religion that outrages conventional Christian sensibilities, while at the same time being contained, subliminally, as it were, within orthodox Christian doctrine. Dr. Mahmoud—a Moslem—thinks of Mike's "Thou art God" as "blackest heresy" (341/419); but note that this thought does not occur to any of the Christians in the nest—or the Jews. Perhaps this is because the proposition is part of the Christian tradition from its very earliest days. The expression "the kingdom of god is in you" (*Luke*, 17:21) is certainly familiar as a point of reference, but when St. Paul says that he is dead as an ego and only Christ lives within him (*Galatians* 2:20) he is restating, in an inverted form, the "royal metaphor" by

---

50. Noyes and the other sources on which Heinlein drew come from a period before socialism/ communism (with a small "c") became regarded as "the opposite" of capitalism. This is a Marxist trope, not an inherent or natural opposition. In fact, Noyes discussed in his book on American Socialisms the schema of Josiah Warren, an individualist anarchist and arch-capitalist, as one of the many communist experiments being undertaken in the U.S. at the time, quite closely related to the Fourier industrial management/socialist system.

Heinlein's formative years took place just after the Russian Revolution and before Marxism completely replaced other socialist ideologies in the public consciousness. His focus, from EPIC socialist ideals in the 1930s to a kind of "capitalism-consciousness" in *The Moon is a Harsh Mistress* in 1966, persisted until at least the Schulman interview of 1973 and was not a major political evolution for him; he was simply exploring two related economic aspects of master social concept, not paradoxically moving from one side to the other of an opposition.

which the individual is identified with the sovereign as a single body. The more usual way of framing the metaphor is to speak of the individual submerged in or subsumed within the sovereign, so that the individual Christian makes up the church—the "body of Christ" and thus God acts in the world. Heinlein has already multiply rejected this metaphor as story image—in *Methuselah's Children*, (1941) where he views the "group mind" of the Little People with horror, in *The Puppet Masters* (1950), where the shared consciousness of the Titan "slugs" is euphoric but debasing for humans, and in *Starship Troopers* (1959), the book that immediately preceded *Stranger*, where the "hive mentality" of the enemy "Bugs" is a metaphor for Marxist-Stalinist Communism. In *Stranger*, the metaphor is inverted, and the sovereign is submerged within the individual. St. Paul means this as an expression of being in congruence with the divine will, but it can also be read as Paul is "really" Christ—i.e., Paul is God and therefore everyone who is in congruence with the divine will is God: "Thou art God." This kind of outrageous heterodoxy contained within orthodoxy is highly characteristic of *Stranger*. It is also, in this particular formula, the key to the synthesis of sex and religion. Sex is a way of experiencing the divine; it is therefore appropriate to religious ritual: all that groks is god; thou art god; therefore: religious sex is the way of experiencing the self as divine. That selfsame Moslem, standing symbolically or analogically for all of Islam (Mahmoud is a variant form of Mohammed, the founder of Islam), comes to understand this heresy is orthodoxy in Islam, as well:

> "Submission to God's will is not to become a blind robot, incapable of free deci-
> sion and thus of sin…Submission can include—and *does* include—utter responsi-
> bility for the fashion in which I, and each of us, shape the universe. It is ours to turn
> into a heavenly garden…or rend and destroy." (*Stranger*, 396–397/482)

Christians join Moslems join Jews in the Nest—a story figure that suggests a synthesis of the religions is going on.

Questions for Discussion

1. How can there be socialism without a Marxist orientation?

2. How can Heinlein's idea of socialism be regarded as progressive?

3. The nineteenth century had more going on in terms of social and political experimentation than history textbooks tell you about. Why have the textbooks omitted these events?

4. Think about how sex might be used in religious rituals. How would a religion based on sex be different from Christianity?

5. What is paganism? What is neopaganism? How does neopaganism fit into the sex-and-religion theory?

For Further Reading

Frye, Northrup. *The Great Code: The Bible and Literature*. San Diego, Calif.: Harcourt, Brace & Co., 1981

Noyes, John Humphrey. *History of American Socialisms*. New York: Dover Publications, 1966

Sears, Hal. *The Sex Radicals: Free Love in High Victorian America*. Lawrence, Kansas: The Regents Press of Kansas, 1977.

— 13 —

Heterodoxy and Orthodoxy:
A Paradoxical Dialectic

Even within irony, and at what appears to be *Stranger*'s furthest remove from Christian orthodoxy, we find Christian orthodoxy only superficially disguised. Heinlein's dualistic irony accepts the principles of Christianity even as he critiques them as "the law that killeth." In this context, note that Mike's Martian "Water of Life" is identical to the Biblical Water of Life which, together with the Tree of Life, is taken from man in Genesis, at the beginning of the Bible, and restored to him in Revelations, at the end of the Bible. The fundamental principles of the God religions are accepted, while the tactics of its practitioners are critiqued without let or hindrance. This is metaphorically brought into the book by the figure of the Martian Old Ones, who are characterized as the true owners of Mars. Earth's dead Old Ones rule this planet, too, in terms of dead dicta which the mere adults of this world must obey.

Stranger thus is a strident call for renewal of Christian life on Christian principles—though not in the form in which it is usually presented. This is as it must be: if these principles were kept in the forefront, no renewal would be needed. But the official conventions (i.e., hypocrisy) are opposed to the truth which would set one free. The irony of orthopraxis growing out of heterodoxy requires the satirical treatment of *Stranger*.

There is an acknowledged historical dialectic within Christianity between the "Johannine" (inspired, "enthusiast," gnostic) and the "Pauline" (rule-oriented, dogmatic) traditions, between Christians who wish to live the "inspired," Christ-like life and Christians whose orientation is to dogma and ecclesiology. Traditionally, St. Paul is thought to have marked a crucial watershed in the evolution of the early church, creating an ecclesiology that included the rule-followers on an equal footing with the inspirationalists (called "enthusiasts" for much of church history). The international church evolved toward ecclesiology, though the Pauline "compromise" made it possible for enthusiasts to co-exist within the church. As Jubal Harshaw points out, Mike's Nest shares many of the characteristics of "primitive" Christianity.

Karen Armstrong in *A History of God* (1993) sees this dialectic as a feature of all the "God religions"—Judaism, Christianity, and Islam—prestige and influence flowing back and forth between the mystic and the dogmatic in each of the religions. At some periods, Cabalists predominate over Pharisees, Sufis over Moslem fundamentalists, Johannine enthusiasts over Pauline dogmatics. Within Christianity, enthusiast phases have broken out every two or three hundred years, for nearly two millennia, as "renewal" movements within the Church. In the second century C.E., it is estimated, nearly a third of Christendom was gnostic and had to be suppressed by killing off the leaders and principal congregations and castigating them as heretic. The same impulses created a series of heretical movements and suppression campaigns or crusades throughout the Middle Ages, culminating in the Protestant Reformation of the sixteenth century. The process continued in both Protestant and Catholic traditions, with periodic charismatic revivals. One such enthusiast revival played a significant role in American history: the enthusiast Anne Hutchison was thrown out of the Puritan Massachusetts Theocracy because she held that the direct inner experience of God's grace absolved her from the dogmatic requirement of Puritan ecclesiology. Hutchison and her fellow "Antinomians" then went off to found their own theocracy on Rhode Island. Heinlein has incorporated exactly this enthusiast doctrine in the "inner temple" of Fosterism, where Patty Paiwonski and her "eternally saved" brethren could not sin, no matter how they acted, because their inner light absolved them and freed them from subjection to sin. Fosterism is a parody of low Protestant Christianity, but, in keeping with the ironic dualism of the book, it is also a true representation, with elements exaggerated for comic effect. Thus, even at what appears to be *Stranger's* furthest remove from Christian orthodoxy, we find Christian orthodoxy only superficially disguised. Heinlein's ironic dualism accepts the principles of Christianity, even as he critiques the praxis as "the law that kills."

The three God religions characterize a stage in the evolution of western culture when animism was replaced by an abstract conception of God. Animism is a style of religion that places the divine within the realm of nature. The holy place—the sacred cave, the chakras (points of power) of the earth, the oak and its wood nymph—characterizes animist religions, at least in their more highly developed stage around the Bronze Age-Iron Age transition. The Hebrews' Ark of the Covenant is clearly a transitional figure in this development—a portable sacred place for a nomadic people. Upon this basis, Judaism created the abstract god, conceptualized as the One God, creator of heaven and earth, with strong resonances, probably, of Egyptian solar monotheism which had briefly become the state religion of Egypt during the reign of Akhenaton (about 1375–1358 B.C.E.)[51]

The animist impulse has by no means disappeared; it has been incorporated into the worship of the abstract god. Now it is churches that are holy places with special sanctuary privileges against the demonic forces active in the world.[52]

Christianity, in particular, came into existence at a special time in the intellectual development of western culture and owes much of its subsequent history to the hellenistic culture that was abroad in the Roman world in the first centuries of the Christian era. It could not have been otherwise, since the intellectual background of the period was Platonism—in much the same way that Positivism, though waning, is the intellectual background now.

This late-Hellenism, as a world-culture, is the result of the fusion of Roman administrative law and political theory with Greek education. But Greek education was itself a syncretic matter. In the centuries before the beginning of the Common Era, Greeks had traveled widely around the Mediterranean basin and assimilated many foreign ideas, including the prestigious Egyptian system whose distant descendants today are called "hermetic." Plato had been educated in the

---

51. This supposition is based on the idea that the Egyptian captivity of the Israelites took place during the short reign of Akhenaton. It may tend to explain why solar symbolism and mythology figures so prominently in the religion and literature of post-hellenist Western culture, after Christianity, a Jewish heretical schism, began to become culturally important in the Roman world.

52. Carl Jung points out that the process of abstraction, going from a chief god to the only god— i.e., the god of creation—brought into existence its own dialectical complement, the chief demon, or Satan, whose name means "adversary." This process was going on all over the ancient Near East at about the same time in the Classical period in distinction to the established polytheistic state religions, giving rise to Zoroastrianism—the source of the fire-and-light versus cold-and-dark, good-evil dichotomy which is still so important to us—and Mithraism, a religion based on the Perseus myth. As elements of all these religions were incorporated into Christian orthopraxis, and as Christianity gained political ascendency, the tendency to create dichotomies intellectually and assign "good" to one of the sides and "evil" to the other persists in us, the inheritors of this tradition. Of this, Heinlein was quite aware. H.G. Wells, in a book that was highly influential on Heinlein's intellectual development, made it quite explicit: "Every attempt to universalize the idea of God trails dualism and the devil after it as a moral necessity." (*A Modern Utopia* [1905]). This dualism, quite mistakenly assigned to Aristotelian logic, extends in modern thinking, even to subjects as theoretically neutral as complementary biochemicals—e.g., "good" cholesterol and "bad" cholesterol. Readers should be alert to dichotomies: even when there is something real in the distinctions, they are still and always artifacts of the thinking process (even when they seem to us like simple observations). At the very least, a dichotomy probably conceals a bunch of incompatibles lumped together on one side or the other—or both. Jill's incident of self-healing illustrates this principle: before she undertook to "know herself" and acknowledge her exhibitionism, she had been locked into the "good girl, bad girl" dichotomy. But the exhibitionism was not "bad," she discovered; it was morally neutral and (constrained by not letting it get out of hand and out of proportion in her life) psychologically healthy. A morally neutral factor had become lumped together with the "bad."

Egyptian tradition via the mediation of the Pythagoreans, and his philosophical system owes a great deal to Egyptian religious thinking. Originally secret doctrines of the Egyptian priesthood, through the teaching of the Greeks, hermetic ideas became the basis of secular education in the classical world. Western Christianity formally adopted NeoPlatonism through the influence of St. Augustine, among others, and so developed an underground hermetic tradition within the church, that resonated with the gnostic heritage and flavored the periodic Johannine renewal movements within the church. *Stranger*, more than any other of Heinlein's work, appeals to this hermetic trajectory within the church.

The satire of *Stranger* could not be made to work unless it appealed to a fundamental agreement of values between the writer (or, at any rate, the terms of the fiction) and the reader. And yet, the satire cannot be effective in its criticism unless it is a real flaw being ridiculed. This is a dilemma Heinlein surmounts most elegantly by appealing to "marginalized" elements of the shaping worldview of western culture.

Questions for Discussion

1. Is the "inner light" versus "rules of behavior" dichotomy still alive in religious practice today? Does it have secular overtones, as well?

2. Why is the "inner light" experience of God linked to mystical traditions? How do mystical traditions differ from the mainstream traditions of the various churches?

3. Do you find this "historical" examination of Christianity disquieting?

For Further Reading:

Armstrong, Karen. *A History of God: The 4,000-Year Quest of Judaism, Christianity and Islam*. New York: Alfred A. Knopf, Inc., 1993

– 14 –

Synthesis of Religions

It is initially tempting to agree with the gambit, slyly advanced in the book itself, that the Church of All Worlds, *Stranger's* principal made-up religion, is "syncretic"—that is, assembled from bits and pieces of other religions and not supposed to make sense in terms of the organization of its ideas. The incautious reader who takes this gambit stumbles into an intellectual and dogmatic cul-de-sac, unable thus to recognize important relationships in the book.

With respect to the different religions mentioned (and not mentioned by name) in the book, the methodology is significantly *synthetic*—that is, subsuming other religions into itself by a centripetal and progressive process of absorption. There is an overt progression in the story line of absorption of the three "God religions" (in Karen Anderson's terminology). Mike starts his ministry by earning a Divinity Degree within the mainstream of Protestant Christianity—a "poor but respectable" Protestant denomination—and foments a schism—a process, Jubal notes in disgust, as traditional as church on Sunday and just as nauseating as last week's garbage. (322/394) This is a formal acknowledgment of the relatively undifferentiated mainstream Protestant background of the majority of the characters in the story gathered into the Church of All Worlds as the First Called, Mike's human "family of origin."

There are significant minorities, however, even among the First Called: "Stinky" Mahmoud, the first human to learn the Martian language, is a Moslem. In fact, he is *very* Moslem: his name is a slight orthographic variation of Mohammed, the founder of Islam. He takes to wife a woman—also First-Called—with the name of Miriam—a very *Jewish* name, in keeping with the close relationship of Islam and Judaism—but also a name which, in a slight orthographic variation, is very Christian: Mary. Mary is Miriam; Mahmoud is Mohammed.

This implied synthesis of Judaism and Islam with Christianity is confirmed late in the book when Jubal finally is induced to visit the Nest. There he speaks with twelve of Mike's apostles (echoing by writerly sleight-of-hand the Last Supper of Christ with his disciples in "the upper room"), among whom are Saul and Ruth, practicing Jews, as well as Mahmoud, who now assures him all the religious practices are compatible.

The progressive synthesis of the god religions into Mike's "Godism," as Jubal at one point calls the Church of All Worlds, is strengthened by the "conversion" of Ben Caxton. Caxton, we are given to understand, is a disaffected adherent of one of the major Protestant sects, but, just as he is not moved by the esthetic experience of Jubal's statuary, he is no longer moved by his professed "faith." Not quite a skeptic, he is not a practicing believer, either. He has become indifferent to the noumenal. But the direct experience of the Nest makes him into a practicing Godist. So, too, is Patty Paiwonski, the Eternally Saved Fosterite who shows that the Church of the New Revelation, with its secret, inner-temple "Happiness services," contains within the church a temporary prototype of the Nest.

The fourth "god religion" synthesized into the Martian nest is represented by Jubal Harshaw, the agnostic.[53] Agnosticism (from the Greek *a*=not and *gnosis*=knowledge) makes sense only within the context of a dogmatic assertion of the existence of God as a distinct and specific entity (for example, agnosticism would make no sense in Spinoza's pantheistic system: to deny knowledge of the existence of God would be to deny knowledge of the existence of nature); the collapse of the assertion into "Thou art God" removes the "knowledge" of which the agnostic claims no possession. Jubal is the protagonist of the book,[54] and his conversion—a matter of evidence and experience, as befits an agnostic—is the signal that the story is complete. All of the God religions, and their dialectical antitheses, have disappeared beyond the event horizon of Mike's Martian synthesis. Just as he has synthesized the Apollonian and the Dionysian, so, too, has he synthesized the God religions.

---

53. There is some reason to believe (based on Heinlein's working notes) that the character of Ben Caxton was originally given the agnostic-observer role Jubal Harshaw occupies in the finished book, but Caxton's necessary conversion was recast as symmetrical to Jill's—which elegantly supports the book's hermetic-initiatic subtext—so that Jubal became the prime observer and the principal agnostic whose final conversion signals the functional end of the preparatory phase of Mike's new religion.

54. Heinlein frequently made a practice of having the focal or viewpoint character of his books able to observe the hero; in his initial notes, the journalist Ben Caxton was to be the viewpoint character, but as the character of Jubal Harshaw was developed, it took over the position and Ben was relegated to the demanding role of being kidnapped and drugged for most of the book. We are not often given the opportunity to see the seams and selvages of Heinlein's word-joinery, but this late decision clearly has resulted in a stronger book overall: now there are two protagonists in the story: Jubal is the protagonist for the *mythos*, though Mike is the protagonist of the myth or divine dimension of the story.

The centripetal synthesis of the God religions, capped by the conversion of the agnostic Jubal, forms an overt subplot of the book, but the overt subplot is shadowed by a parallel synthesis of *unnamed* religions into Mike's Godism, so that synthesis is taking place both visibly and invisibly. The "theology" of the Church of All Worlds contains elements from many different sources, gathered from a miscellany of research during his "seeking" phase. Rather than discuss them individually, it will be convenient to list some of the points in the form of a table (Table 1):

Proposition	CAW doctrine	Religious Source
"truth cannot be expressed in our language"	Members must learn Martian	Early Christianity (2nd century)— Clement of Alexandria
"The sage occupies himself with inaction…Tao is eternally inactive and yet leaves nothing undone… Practice inaction. Occupy yourself with doing nothing"	"waiting is"	Lao Tzu—taoism
"Animals often give the mystical sensation of nature to men."	Mike groks with the cat	Hindu mysticism
"The yogi…who has…overcome the obscurations of his lower nature sufficiently, enters into the condition termed *samadhi*, 'and he comes fact to face with facts which no instinct or reason can ever know.'…	Reason for learning Martian—the core transformation or illumination of the CAW	Hinduism—yogic practices
The Buddhists use the word *Samadhi* as well as the Hindus, but *dhyana* is their special word for the higher states of contemplation.	Meditation, contemplation	Buddhism correspondence with yoga
"*Tat tvam asi*"—thou art that [Brahman]	Thou art God	Hinduism—Indian philosophy in general

Table 1: Theological Comparisons

Proposition	CAW doctrine	Religious Source
"…it would be self-contradictory to admit that there could be anything besides the Infinite or Brahman, which is All in All, and that therefore the soul also cannot be anything different from it, can never claim a separate an independent existence."	"All that groks is God."	Vedanta; Meister Eckhart; Eleatic philosophers
"The Sufi holds that there is nothing in human language that can express the love between the soul and God so well as the love between man and woman, and that if he is to speak of the union between the two at all, he can only do so in the symbolic language of earthly love."	"The great gift of male-femaleness" and "Our way is better."	Max Müller on Sufism
"I felt myself one with the grass, the trees, birds, insects, everything in Nature."	"All that groks is God"	William James, Varieties of Religious Experience

Table 1: Theological Comparisons (Continued)

And we must now confess to playing a trick on the reader: this entire table of multiple religious propositions, which seems almost a direct commentary on the made-up religion of *Stranger*, comes from a single source Heinlein was undoubtedly familiar with, which, itself, denotes a religion synthesized into the Church of All Worlds. The "theology" of the Church of All Worlds encompasses Hinduism, Taoism, Islam, and Christianity. It is, in fact, "borrowed" from one of Heinlein's oldest philosophical "sources," the *Tertium Organum* (1912, rev. 1932) of Petr Demianovich Ouspensky.[55] They all come from a chapter near the end discussing the nature of mysticism. This allows us to add a final few items to the table (Table 2):

---

55. Heinlein probably appreciated Ouspensky's attempt to synthesize science, philosophy, and religion. Certainly Ouspenskyan material is very broadly reflected in Heinlein's writing. For a more comprehensive discussion of Ouspensky's influence in Heinlein, see Thornton, "Mythos and Logos: The Influence of P.D. Ouspensky in the Fiction of Robert A. Heinlein," published in three parts in issues 1, 2, and 3 of *The Heinlein Journal*; particularly Part 2: "Ouspenskyan Ideas in *Stranger in a Strange Land*." *The Heinlein Journal*, No. 2 (January 1998), pp. 8–16.

Proposition	CAW doctrine	Religious Source
"…probably only a small part of humanity is capable of growth… and the fate of that greater part of humanity which will prove incapable of growth, depends not upon itself, but upon that minority which will progress… In men capable of development, new faculties are stirring into life, though not as yet manifest, because for their manifestation they require a special culture, a special education. The new conception of humanity disposes of the idea of equality" [279–280]	What Mike learns from Jubal in his "Garden of Gethesemane" talk: the role of his select elite in human evolution.	Occultism
Christianity and Buddhism are complementary views that complete each other	Fosterism (Christianity) belongs within the Church of All Worlds	Ouspensky
"The future belongs, not to man but to superman [a continuously self-aware being], who is already born and lives among us. A 'higher race' is rapidly emerging among humanity, and it is emerging by reason of its quite remarkable understanding of the world and life." [295]	Q: What do supermen do better than us ordinaries? A: They think better.	Nietzsche; Occultism

Table 2: Additional Theological Comparisons

And so Nietzsche, brought into the book through the Apollonian-Dionysian discussion, can be seen as having an impact on the shaping of the myth, of the Hero tale. Ouspensky extends his discussion of the Nietzsche Superman, or "Overman" in *A New Model of the Universe* (1932), wherein we discover that the Superman is at the basis of all religious ideas, in the sense that the major religions seek to model themselves around illuminated individuals; that he is a being continuously in contact with the noumenal (i.e., he is God) so that his thoughts and his emotions are the same thing and his language—the famous aphoristic language of *Also Sprach Zarathustra*—is incomprehensible because he is not split within himself, he has learned to speak directly truth which is beyond the comprehension of the "all too human" (i.e., he speaks "Martian"); that he must "overcome" himself, the human sentimentality that prevents him from being in touch with his divine self (Archangel Foster cannot forestall Mike's martyrdom: "Mercy was not possible for an angel; angelic compassion left no room for it" [373/456]); that there is in the Overman something lawless, as Mike demonstrates the futility of weapons against a self-aware being and lands himself in the stockade—and then cleanses the jails before his own martyrdom; and, finally, that once an Overman becomes fully self-aware, he disappears from human sight.[56] Thus in *Stranger*, Mike does not hang around Earth, but returns to Heaven and the concerns of an adult.[57] The specific development of story line in *Stranger* owes a great deal to the synthesis and summary of Nietzsche in *Tertium Organum* and *A New Model of the Universe*.[58] Although there is no record of when Heinlein encountered Ouspensky, the most likely timeframe is sometime between 1932 and 1938—i.e., at the time *A New Model of the Universe* and the second English edition of *Tertium Organum* were published. It is quite possible that Heinlein was initially drawn to the books not by their mystical content, but by the translators. One of the English language translators was Claude Bragdon, a mathematician and popularizer of mathematical ideas whose writings Heinlein had followed since his own youth. *Tertium Organum* begins with a mathematical-geometric treatment of Kant's critical idealism (similar to the tantalizing mentions in Heinlein's 1940 *"By His Bootstraps"*), discusses Relativity theory knowledgeably (which was quite esoteric for 1912 and still not popularly understood as late as 1932), and draws heavily on another of Heinlein's

---

56. An additional, not fully developed, dimension of Nietzsche reference may be the pairing of Jill and Ben at the beginning of the novel. The pairing is never developed; Ben wants marriage but Jill is not reconciled to the idea—though she might "settle" for it. The discomfort with the prospect of union suggests that Jill and Ben may represent the complex involvement of sexual and marital relations with the "master-slave" psychology Nietzsche poses (principally in *On the Genealogy of Morals*) as the bipolar fate of natural man—the "human condition." D.H. Lawrence wrestled with this subject in *Women in Love*. Nietzsche, however, raises the possibility of transcending the master-slave psychology and becoming a "sovereign individual." This is the nature of the moral transformation worked on humans by the Martian language.

57. This religious tradition continues to be active in Western arts. The 1999 film *The Matrix* showed us a Nietzsche Overman wakening from his slumbers in the matrix of consensus reality, and at the end, when he has his transcendent experience of himself and sees all the material world as a dance of binary digits, he delivers his message to humankind and removes himself.

58. Heinlein specifically mentioned Ouspensky by name only once, in the 1939 short story "Elsewhen." But there are literally hundreds of more or less indirect references to Ouspensky—particularly *Tertium Organum* and *A New Model of the Universe*—throughout his writing, of which the table of the religious dogmas of the Church of All Worlds given above is a prime example.

Ouspensky is principally remembered since his death in 1947 as a popularizer of the mystical doctrines of George I. Gurdjieff, but *Tertium Organum*, the first edition of which was written three years before Ouspensky met Gurdjieff in Russia, in the waning days of the Romanoff dynasty, show that Ouspensky had spent years sifting through the religious and mystical traditions of the world. *Tertium Organum* is thus particularly suited for use in *Stranger*, as it shows Ouspensky doing essentially the same "seeking" that Mike does.

youthful enthusiasms, the mathematician C.C. Hinton, from whom Heinlein probably learned the n-dimensional visualization exercises that play so prominent a role in his 1941 short story, "—And He Built a Crooked House—."

The Superman/Overman concept, in its religious mode, suggests that societies form themselves around individuals and that, therefore, at least certain individuals contain societies, or the germs of societies, within themselves. They begin surrounded by societies, which they must overcome to bring forth the new society that is within them. Judaism had institutionalized this social role in its pre-Temple Prophets, and Christianity inherits a sensitivity to the beneficent possibilities of lawlessness within the prophet in his role in "grounding" the divine and bringing it among men, which is expressed by Christ's paradox: "I come not to destroy the law, but that the law through me might be fulfilled." (*Matthew* 5:17)

Questions for Discussion

1. What do you think of the idea that all religions might come from a single source?

2. Critique the idea that the Superman is at the root of all public religions.

3. What do you think of metaphysical or "new age" ideas?

4. Compare and contrast the Nest "superman" concept with Hitler's Aryan superiority theories.

5. What place do the non-elect play in *Stranger's* society?

For Further Reading

Nietzsche, Friedrich W. *Thus Spoke Zarathustra*. Trans. Walter Kaufmann. New York: Penguin Books, 1966

Ouspensky, P.D. *Tertium Organum* (1912, 1932). Trans. Claude Bragdon and Nicholas Bessaraboff. London: Manas Press, 1922

Twain, Mark. *The Mysterious Stranger & Other Stories*. New York: New American Library, 1984

— 15 —

Fosterism as Foil for CAW

The Church of the New Revelation (Fosterism), the other created religion in the story, is not part of the synthetic progressions. It has a different role in the structure of the book. It is, first of all, a symbol for American low Protestant religions and is in this aspect absorbed into the synthesis of the other religions; but it has other functions and so remains separate and special even within the Church of All Worlds.

We are encouraged, by another tricky gambit, to adopt Jubal's esthetic revulsion to the Fosterites as the book's "position" on Fosterism. After all, Jubal is the only one who groks in fullness without first learning Martian. His function in the book is to be the speaker of "plain truths," and he despises Fosterism. This gambit is, again, an intellectual cul-de-sac from which the actual position of the argument cannot be seen.

Jubal's rejection of the Fosterites is clearly placed on the level of social and personal politics: "I don't enjoy snake dances, I despise crowds, and I do not let slobs tell me where to go on Sundays." (259/321)

Jubal himself acknowledges that his preferences in this matter are conventional for his culture (and therefore esthetic rather than natural law), typically by teaching Jill, whose own revulsion is based on the orgiastic qualities of the Fosterite service they observe:

(Jill) "That's not a church—it's a madhouse!... You can't tell *me* that *that* is worship."

(Jubal)"...Their brand of snake oil is utterly orthodox in all respects." (255–259/316–321

Again, Heinlein ironically cuts the ground out from under a possible firm foot-ing in the satire, requiring his readers, not to agree, but to question: once Jubal has been subsumed into the Nest, his esthetic objections disappear, and he unites with Fosterism and the Nest simultaneously in an act of sex with Dawn Ardent, the Fosterite complement of Jill Boardman. Heinlein craftily has Jubal pose the Church of the New Revelation in opposition to the Church of All Worlds using the Dionysian-Apollonian dichotomy introduced earlier in the book, but he also cues us that the dichotomy is false by the humorous incident in which Jill first meets Dawn and recognizes/does not recognize herself:

> "Jill thought that Miss Ardent looked as if she had just wiggled out of bed and was anxious to crawl back in. With Mike. Quit squirming your carcass at him, you cheap hussy!" (248/307)

While Mike's church is the epitome of the Apollonian, the Church of the New Revelation is posed as the epitome of the Dionysian: "…as the secret [Fosterite] church was that Dionysian cult that America had lacked and for which there was enormous potential market." (290/360) Note, though, that while our ground-work of assumptions links sex with the Dionysian, there is no sex associated with the outer services of the supposedly Dionysian Church of the New Revelation, whereas there is abundant sex associated with the supposedly Apollonian (and therefore supposedly intellectual or spiritual) Church of All Worlds. Something is screwy here.

In terms of the "argument" of the book, this opposition is a dialectical straw man: Fosterism is created as a foil for the Church of All Worlds, and it is similarly synthesizing. As Heinlein finds that America treats its religions as culture and even politics, it is necessary to include a cultural and political synthesis in parallel with the religious synthesis going on. This is a rather forceful example of what Mikhail Bakhtin called "heteroglossia."[59]

The Church of the New Revelation is a synthesis of various elements in American cultural life as much as in America's religious life. There is certainly a good bit of the kind of slick holy-rollerism that brought pentecostalism into the twentieth century with Billy Sunday and Dwight Moody and Aimee Semple MacPherson. Heinlein imagines a masterful synthesis of holy-rollerism with Las Vegas—"sin city" become the City of God by a process of irony exposing cul-ture and politics masquerading as religion. St. Petersburg, Florida (St. Peter's city=heaven, by implication), will become the capital of Mike's new religion. Surely this is only a little beyond the revulsion contemporary Protestant conser-

---

59. Bakhtin defines "languages" in terms of rhetorical unity of i.e., a character or a genre, so that a novel—and in Bakhtin's analysis, the satire is explicitly considered as a novel—contains many languages ("hetero" means "other," and "glossia" means "languages") in dialog with each other. See *The Dialogic Imagination*.

vatives voice about the blatant hucksterism of the television ministries typified by Jim and Tammy Fae Bakker.

Reacting to this obvious hucksterism, some critics have assumed that Fosterism is "materialistic" and the Church of All Worlds is "non-materialistic" or "anti-materialistic," but this assumption is not well grounded in the text. The Church of the New Revelation and the Church of All Worlds are each equally materialistic in orientation and not anti-materialistic at all. It is only their "styles" that differ. Both CAW and the Fosterites are firmly committed to living "in the world," so both may be said to reject the Christian and Buddhist rejection of the world. They are identical in an extremely important aspect: neither is hypocritical. Each is exactly what it is, without pretense otherwise. We see their divergent styles in high contrast because we only see the most public, "outer temple" of the Fosterites, with its apparatus of exhortation to keep the financial affairs of church members within the church community—and we see the private life of the Nest (the public-to-private contrast is used for many purposes in the book). But we are equally told that there is a public side to the Nest: the boundary is marked by the bowl of money. If the Nesters were "anti-materialistic," they would have no need of a bowl of money—they would take the traditional Buddhist monk's begging bowl, instead. Equally, there is a private side to the Fosterites: if we had witnessed a private "happiness meeting of the eternally saved," the contrast would probably not occur to us.[60]

Jill and Jubal tell us that the Church of the New Revelation is a "real" church, though it does not appear, from the outside, to have anything Jill can understand as "real" religion about it. About this Jubal cannot, as a strict agnostic, testify. But Patty shows us that there is a kernel of "true religion" in the huckstering and very political Fosterite Church. Symmetrically, the Church of All Worlds, we are told by Ben Caxton, is not a real church, though it is absolutely permeated by "true religion." This is another of those mirror image dialogs Heinlein uses throughout the book, for there is the seed of a new culture, with its attendant commerce and politics, inside the Nest; we see it "in bud" in conversations when Jubal finally visits the Nest. The Church of the New Revelation and the Church of All Worlds are mirror-complements, not polar opposites.

---

60. The proposition that the Fosterites are "materialistic" and the Nesters "anti-materialist" cannot be read or inferred from the literal text; it comes, rather, from the set of assumptions in the intellectual "package deals" the reader brings to his reading. However, this is not to say the author has not produced this effect intentionally and deliberately; he has chosen his portrayals of the two groups for just this contrast and knows that his highly-controlled rhetoric invites the reader to "complete" the images with their private understanding of what they mean. Heinlein does not make the contrary explicit because his *purpose* is to elicit these package deals and allow the reader to examine his assumptions. There is ample contrary evidence in the book, and the open mind will weigh its assumptions against the evidence, rather than assert its assumptions over the text.

There is also a bit of Mormonism in the Church of the New Revelation. The Church of the Latter Day Saints had its own New Revelation circa 1830 and its centripetal emphasis on the community of the saints may serve as a basic model for the communitarian emphasis of the Nest. Smith's name may be an evocation of Joseph Smith, the founder of Mormonism, and the group marriage is often talked about in terms of polygyny, though its actual form is a group marriage—a "group theogamy," as Jubal calls it (362/445).

The largest single component of the Fosterite synthesis, however, is probably Scientology—another cultural movement deliberately in the form of a religion.[61] Close to the end of World War II while both Heinlein and L. Ron Hubbard were in Philadelphia (and years before Dianetics came into being), they are said to have had a conversation in which Heinlein is said to have pointed out to Hubbard that a church could engage in a wide variety of activities free from regulatory interference because of the protection given in the U.S. to churches and religions. Years later (1950), Hubbard introduced his "new science of mental health" under the name of Dianetics. Initially Hubbard's work had been welcomed by orthodox psychiatric practitioners (there are contemporary records in which he mentions being delighted by the cooperation he is receiving), but by the time Dianetics began to become a popular "movement" (1952–1954), Hubbard was under attack for practicing medicine without a license.

Hubbard had originally expected to publish Dianetics in the medical journals, but after his initial article was rejected by the *JAMA* and other peer-reviewed medical journals, he placed it in *Astounding Science Fiction*. John Campbell was one his earliest and most enthusiastic converts. Dianetics spread rapidly through *Astounding's* readership, Dianetics auditing becoming something of a parlor game, and a Dianetics book, *They'd Rather Be Right*, won the Best Novel Hugo Award for 1954—the science fiction community's equivalent of film's People's Choice Award.

In 1955 Hubbard set up the Founding Church of Scientology in Washington, D.C. and in New York, and gradually withdrew from Dianetics.[62] Scientology, unlike Dianetics, has a religious cosmology—though decidedly not a Christian one. By the time *Stranger* was published in 1961, Hubbard's principal antagonists were no longer the medical establishment, but now the IRS, bent on proving that Scientology was a fake religion—a battle the IRS eventually lost in the courts. Heinlein's "take" on the question, thirty years earlier, had been directly on point, and he puts the same understanding into *Stranger:*

> "Look, Ben, a skating rink is a church—as long as some sect claims that skating is essential to worship—or even that skating served a desirable function. If you can sing to the glory of God, you can skate to the same end." (331/407)

---

61. Scientology is not being singled out here: in terms of the discourse of the satire, any church, insofar as it is an organization, is political and social.

62. Dianetics persists as a secular parallel to the Church of Scientology.

Heinlein appears to have digested and transformed story elements of *They'd Rather Be Right* and incorporated them into *Stranger*. The character of Patty Paiwonski, for example, is probably adapted, by a process of transformation, from the character of the landlady in *They'd Rather Be Right*, who is portrayed as a former hooker, now aged and obese, her face painted with "varicolored enamels." It is not hard to see how she has become Patty—fleshy but no longer obese, and comprehensively tatooed. The landlady was the first superman "cleared" by the therapy of the book's supercomputer, and Patty Paiwonski was among the first to receive "Foster's Kiss" and the first of the Eternally Saved Fosterites to be incorporated into the Church of All Worlds.

However interesting it is to contemplate a topical reference, the Church of the New Revelation Heinlein synthesized is not an allegorical representation of the Church of Scientology. At most, Scientology is a contributing element in the mix. *Stranger* is not highly topical in any of its references, and it is unusual even to be able to identify one element in the mix. Pointing too directly to Scientology would obscure Heinlein's actual target, which is an abstraction—the long American tradition of hysterical revivalism now identified with Midwestern (Bible Belt) low Protestant fundamentalism. Avoiding topical references actually strengths the satire (whereas it might weaken a novel).

> "Even when satire is referential...we should remember that historical particulars in satire always have a curious in-between status, neither wholly fact nor wholly fiction. Once inserted into a satire, the particulars become the satirist's thrall, to use as he wishes." (Griffin, 123)

Fosterism appears to function in the book to synthesize important cultural elements in the same way that Mike's Church of All Worlds synthesizes important religious elements—necessary in view of the way the book "sees" sex and religion. We are, very early on, given a strong clue that Jubal's Apollonian-Dionysian theory is not so much "true" as it is a useful descriptive device for some purposes.[63] Viewing the orgiastic and superficially Dionysian Fosterite service, Mike is filled with homesickness for the supposedly Apollonian Martian water-sharing. Mike sees the underlying unity of the Apollonian and the Dionysian in the Church of the New Revelation that makes it a suitable connection to the Church of All Worlds. At the end of the story, the New Revelation has become a kind of "front door" to the Church of All Worlds, an "outer temple" with its own inner temple of the eternally

---

63. It is possible also that Heinlein sometimes uses the dichotomy as *misdirection*, much in the way D.H. Lawrence characteristically misdirected the reader at particularly fraught, symbolic moments that might come too close to a direct statement of his theme (as, for example, in *Women in Love*, Gerald's remarks to Birken about "wrestling with his good angel" lead the reader away from the deliberate homoerotic content of the wrestling scene). The dualistic irony of the book makes it possible to use a truth to misdirect—always the very best way of propagating a believable lie.

saved. Patty Paiwonski, the Fosterite inner templar, is the bridge to the Church of All Worlds—"the most advanced of any of us" (346/427). The symbolism is made more explicit; as the (Christian) church is the bride of Christ, so is Patty analogically the bride of Mike: ("If anybody is Mike's wife, it's Patty..." [402/489]). This is the "position" of the book on Fosterism, and Heinlein hammers in the point at the end: when Mike gets back to Heaven, he picks up his heavenly work—not where he left it, but from the ministering hands of *Archangel* Digby, who has been continuing Michael's work. The angelic work of the Archangel Michael is to sustain the heavenly hosts and in particular the church militant, so the implication is clear that Digby, and Foster before him, was engaged in some sense in preparing the way for Mike's earthly ministry: the New Revelation refers to the Church of All Worlds in the same way that John the Baptist prefigured Christ.

Just as America is both Apollonian (publicly) and Dionysian (privately, albeit hypocritically), so, too, will the Church of All Worlds synthesize these dialectical opposites into one. First the God religions and then everything else, and finally the American culture-religion disappear into Mike's Godism. The two made-up religions of the book model America's cultural split between the Dionysian and Apollonian impulses—and the synthesis Mike brings about is emblematic of the healing that is possible when one faces reality squarely, acquires self-knowledge and self-control.

Questions for Discussion

1. What does Jubal's opinion about Fosterism imply about the way readers should look at Jubal's opinions in general? Why does Mike respect Jubal anyway?

2. Why would Heinlein put these "gambits" into *Stranger*?

3. What elements of Mormonism are found in the Fosterites?

4. What elements of Scientology are found in the Fosterites?

For Further Reading

Allen, James B. and Glen M. Leonard. *The Story of the Latter-Day Saints*, 2nd ed. Salt Lake City, Utah: Deseret Book Co., 1992

– 16 –

Anagogy in *Stranger*

The making and setting aside of divisions—particularly between man and the divine, but also between man and his proper society—is one of the most fundamental of literary impulses and may be viewed as the emotional "engines" of the basic forms of fiction. Tragedy is concerned with the isolation (division) of the tragic hero from his proper society, while comedy is concerned with the overcoming of obstacles to the creation of a union within a proper society (hence marriage as the natural end of a comedy).

Stranger in a Strange Land is formally a "divine comedy," containing both comic and tragic catharsis, its "group theogamy" ("theo"=god(s) plus "gamy"=marriage) a figure of the union of the human and the divine. It is myth in its overall structure. The tragic separation of its mythic hero (martyrdom) creates a divine union with man—the paradox of a self-sacrifice that makes possible the fulfillment of the work of the self. "The tragic symbol of the fully realized self is…to borrow from Jung—the crucified Christ." (Wells, *Jesting Moses*, 107). *Stranger* places the tragic symbol within a comic setting, as Mike assembles his proper community as a type of the proper humanity, set about with comic gods and angels.

The point on which Mike's synthesis of the Apollonian and the Dionysian pivots is the element that must be shared by both Apollonian and Dionysian worldviews—sex. There is Apollonian sex and there is Dionysian sex. Sexual hypocrisy rises from the denial of one or the other of the two. It is a religious idea under examination, and in *Stranger* sex is treated as an aspect of religion, an expression of the divine in man.

As an ironic gospel, *Stranger* may be approached by any of the methods developed for biblical literary criticism. In medieval (Scholastic) critical theory, scripture—and, indeed, any prose work—must be examined on each of four levels:

1. The "literal," in which the mythos or story line is viewed as an analogy of history;

2. The "allegorical" or "metaphorical," in which the actors and events are viewed as symbols or representations rather than as "simply" historical narrative;

3. The "archetypal," in which both story line and symbol sets are viewed as representations of common or universal human experiences; and

4. The "anagogical," by which the merely human is identified to the divine.

Thus, to take one scriptural story at random, the forty-year wandering of the Israelites in the Sinai desert is viewed, on the literal level, as a national (or racial) epic of suffering, endurance, and, ultimately, emergence into heritage. On the allegorical level, the story can be read as a family tale of disobedience, estrangement, and finally reconciliation of child with father. Viewed archetypally, it can be seen as a type-specimen for all the experiences of confusion, weakness, loss of personal focus or direction identified in myth-criticism terminology as the "Long Dark Night of the Soul." Anagogically, the story can be seen as a fragment or "beat" of a larger story, of separation from and reconciliation with the divine—though the divine is always present and always sustaining in the pillar of fire and the pillar of cloud and in the manna from heaven—reconciliation when it comes will dissolve the partitioning of heaven from earth and unify the nation of Israel with the will of their God.

Even individual figures or devices that make up the story can be read in this multi-leveled, "polysemous" manner: any partitioning or separation or division can be read in the literal mode as an *act* or *circumstance* that sets a story in motion (and which implies the union or reunion which will resolve the dramatic tension created by the division or partitioning)—as the wall of *Pyramus and Thisbe* separates the lovers; in the allegorical mode the wall itself may disappear, as Shakespeare mutates it into the family feud of the Montagues and the Capulets. In an anagogic reading, the wall or division or partition echoes the basic division between God and man, as the Bible itself begins with the act of creation which is also an act of partition and separation. God sets the ocean apart from the dry land and divides earth from sky and light. God is partitioning himself in the act of creation; the remainder of the book will be about other divisions—but it will also be about the dissolving of partitions and reunions of God and man, centering (in a

Christian reading) on the specially-significant union of God and man in the person of Christ incarnate.

Taking this anagogic device back down a level to the archetypal, we see that division is the province of (human) wisdom—as Adam participates in the division-work of creation by naming all the creatures—but that unification is the province of divine wisdom. Thus the creation of the world may be seen as the type-specimen for all tragedy, as it is the first and most fundamental partition or division: separation from God. Thus, our universe begins in tragedy, and thus the image of the creator or the creative artist lends itself to tragic treatment. Creation itself, in its fundamental aspect of separation of the created from the person of God, presents the artist with his primary dramatic tool: a dialectical tension between division and unification.

The polysemous method of interpreting fictional figures, thus, has built into it "similarity of scale," a feature of which Heinlein made persistent and deliberate use throughout his career.[64] *Stranger* presents in the form of a scripture (particularly in the form of a gospel) and so lends itself very neatly to this "polysemous" approach. All of the four levels of interpretation are not only present in *Stranger*, but they are deliberately used to give form and unity to the book. We have, in fact, been exploring some of these various levels. The symbolic level of interpretation is dominated by the typology of Heavens: The "Martian set-up"[65] of egg-nestling-adult-Old One is a type of Jubal's household, where Mike is the egg and

---

64. See, for example, the discussion in Korzybskian terms of the structure of "Misfit," his second story (Patterson, "Study of 'Misfit'").

    George Edgar Slusser, in *Classic Years of Robert A. Heinlein*, has identified a characteristic Heinleinian narrative device which may be related to the author's use of the progressive possibilities inherent in polysemy to drive his stories. Heinlein makes little use of the conventional linear plot structures of commercial fiction, but Slusser sees him expanding upon and developing a narrative center, then abruptly contracting to a point, so that the succeeding narrative moves from center to periphery and back upon the point. The plot point development is thus relatively static within the parts of the story, while the thematic progression carries the story through its parts. The "expansion" phase is complete when all the levels of reading have been incorporated into the narrative, and the writer can move up and down the levels to initiate the collapse of the narrative "upon the point" and move to the next point or center of narrative.

65. The "Martian set-up" may be partially referred to Alfred Korzybski's first book, *Manhood of Humanity: The Science and Art of Human Engineering* (1921), in which Korzybski reconceptualizes wealth as the summed product of the efforts of our forbears, now dead. *Passim*, but see especially 115: "...*nearly all the wealth of the world at any given time is the accumulated fruit of the toil of past generations*—the living work of the dead." In Heinlein's Mars, the dead—i.e., the "Old Ones"—own everything. More: note the passage on p. 119: "...humans do not die—their bodies die [i.e., "discorporate"] but their achievements live forever—a permanent source of power." It has long been known that Korzybski was an important influence on Heinlein, though little critical work has been done on this subject. Here, Heinlein has allegorized Korzybski's first book to create his Mars—no wonder the Martian language is mathematical in nature: that is the subject of Korzybski's second book, *Science and Sanity* (1933).

Jill the nestling. The staff are the adult hewers of wood and drawers of water, and Jubal is symbolically the Old Ones. Jubal's household is itself a type of the Nest, with its apparatus of offstage children and busy adults and Mike corresponding to Jubal in his household. Finally, the Nest itself is a type of Heaven, in which we see Michael in his Adult role managing the cosmos. The various heavens have their complements of earth—the carnival for Jubal's household and the monkey house for Mike's Nest.

The allegorical level of *Stranger* is dominated by a developmental progression in which Mike's story is an allegory of growth and maturation of an individual human being. There is no evidence that Heinlein was familiar with the formal work being done in developmental psychology over the middle decades of the century, but he does repeatedly show a writer's sensitivity to the "beats" of the process. The five "books" of *Stranger* correspond to five developmental stages.

At first, Mike is allegorically an infant; everything must be done for him, and he must learn even to walk. His identification in this phase is with Jill, who functions as his "mother," his primary caregiver. Then he is a toddler/small child in the household of Jubal Harshaw, learning to speak human language and to hold his own in social conventions. His identification during this phase is with Jubal, who functions as his father in the sense of parenting function.

For a time, Mike is psychologically a teenager immersed in the peer group of the household, and his identification with Jubal weakens. The process of individuation begins: he leaves the nest of Jubal's household and as a young adult seeks out his life's work. The epiphany in the monkey house marks the end of the individuation process.

Finally, as a self-determining adult, he begins his life's work. Although the story is told in third-person omniscient, the material under consideration in each section is formed by the perspective of a significant other on Mike. The first section, for example, is focused on the care and protection he receives from Jill secondary to Ben Caxton's professional interest. The longer middle section is concerned with the care, protection, and teaching he receives from Jubal Harshaw as a parent.

At the moment he becomes an adult, caregivers are no longer relevant. In place of caregivers, Mike relates to peers, and Ben Caxton—who had entered his life as a journalist, in a professional capacity—returns to father Jubal to make a journalistic report and comment on Mike's adult activities. Mike teaches Ben through the mediation of Jubal. Then Jubal himself is taught. Shortly thereafter, Jubal himself comes to the Nest as a peer—though a highly valued and respected peer—and receives learning and healing from Mike.

The implication is that an adult *gives back* to the individuals and to the community at large a reflection of the care and nurturing he received as a child. Or, since one cannot truly pay back the love and care of a parent, one must pay it forward, to the human community as a whole.

In *Stranger* the extended digression about the interpretation of art, particularly sculpture, also reinforces a point of orthodoxy that is relevant to the godism: Jubal's objection to Fosterism is deeply esthetic, and esthetic judgments penetrate the book. St. Thomas Aquinas tells us that the four levels of interpretation are built into the cosmos in God's act of creation and man is most like God in the creation and apprehension of a work of art. This idea is multiply echoed in succeeding generations of literary criticism, down to our own age, when critic John Burt Foster, discussing Nietzsche's decision to pursue his highly theological philosophy in terms of art, and its effect on future generations of writers, noted:

> "But the climactic moments of direct contact occur when writers are pushing their capacities for expression to the limit. By and large these moments come in imaginative writings..." (Foster, 10)

The connection here of Nietzsche in the nineteenth century with Aquinas' thirteenth century theological approach (then Thomas Mann's twentieth century writing, in a succeeding passage) is particularly appropriate for *Stranger*'s use. In overcoming the self, the Nietzsche becomes as God and participates in the ongoing creation of the universe. This notion has been extended to another of Heinlein's particular influences, contemporary with Mann, James Branch Cabell:

> "Thus the imagination is regarded as participating, by imitation and within the limits of the human mind, in the forces of creation at work throughout the whole universe." (Tarrant, 4)

Jubal is, therefore, teaching Ben Caxton how to be God.

In the twentieth century, Northrup Frye's *Anatomy of Criticism* (1957) created a critical apparatus for polysemy, much as myth critics had earlier created a critical apparatus for archetypal criticism based on Carl Jung's notions of myth figures or archetypes rising out of the "collective unconscious."[66] Frye's critical approach relates each interpretive level to the body of literature as a whole and to other literary works so that, for example, the archetypal mode or phase relates a work's formal structure of symbols, not to the signifying taking place in the narrative, but to the literary forms on which it draws.

> "Within this perspective, we see that the term archetype designates the genesis of a conventional and generic bond, stemming from a poem's *external relations with every other poem*." (Ricoeur, 9. [Emphasis added])

---

66. In his earliest writings on the subject—dating from 1916 through 1918—Jung may have posited some sort of actual "shared mind" underlying the collective unconscious, but by the 1940s he was characterizing the collective unconscious in passing remarks as a purely formal and descriptive device, and in this later interpretation it retains validity, even though the notion of the collective unconscious as a biological-neurological phenomenon has been rejected definitively by both scientific and literary-critical communities. It remains and retains validity as part of the iconography of the Jungian-Transpersonal approach to literary values.

In Frye's terms, the "anagogic phase of criticism" deals with "radical union(s)" which dissolve conventional distinctions, demarcations, partitions, boundaries in ways that outrage reason and propriety. The distinctions between subject and object, between God and man, between the noumenal and the phenomenal dissolve and melt into a "monad" (Frye's terminology), which Paul Ricoeur discusses as "…imaginative experience's capacity to attain to totality in terms of some centre." (10) Thus the "encyclopedic" literary forms of myth and satire naturally tend toward anagogy on one level or another: Candide spends the book searching for Cunegonde and when he finds her, outraged and writ upon by outrageous fortune, concludes that cultivating their garden—the garden is the literary symbol of the natural world—is the best place for the two of them (and, of course, this is just where we find Jubal Harshaw at the start of *Stranger*, having spent his life cultivating his earthly garden).

Heinlein presents just such a radical union, outraging reason and propriety, as the core of the novel and, paradoxically, stated on the surface of *Stranger in a Strange Land*. Center and periphery identify. In "Thou art God," the boundaries between God and man are forcibly and outrageously violated. Frye's literary typology may have fallen out of fashion with critics, but this presentation cries for analysis by Frye's categories.[67]

Structuralism has since been succeeded in ascendency by Deconstructionism, a critical modality centered in rhetoric and even more hostile to the notion of literature as a tool for confronting the noumenous. Despite some pregnant remarks by scholar Paul Ricoeur relating Deconstructionist methodology to Frye's approach, neither Structuralism nor Deconstructionism provides analytic tools for confronting the obvious anagogy of *Stranger*.

---

67. Frye introduced his literary typology just at the time Structuralism was gaining ascendency. Structuralism, a descriptive modality with a positivist and reductionist set of assumptions, centers its approach in formal and narrative elements and may be regarded as fundamentally hostile to anagogy. Lévi-Strauss created a Structuralist approach to myth criticism which ignores as irrelevant the noumenal component of myth. With such a set of assumptions, anagogic treatment can see unions but it cannot see union with the divine.

Anthropology in the twentieth century has wavered between noumenal-"irrationalist" (Müller, Otto, Eliade) and structural-rationalist (Lévi-Strauss, Malinowski) approaches to the role of myth in society. While the defined structure of the myth-element of *Stranger*, as well as its apparent emphasis on cultural relativism, would seem to lend itself to a Structuralist approach, the serious integration of religious and spiritual elements into *Stranger* leads away from the Structuralist approach. Structuralism begins in anthropology and looks at myth as a psychological and social phenomenon, not a religious one. The translation of Structuralism out of anthropology and into a method of literary criticism yields a comparative study of forms. "Lévi-Strauss holds that myth shows order or form, the manipulations of which constitute the stuff of imagination…" (Strenski, 183) Consequently, a Structuralist analysis of *Stranger* would yield little unique commentary: Heinlein has adopted the Christ-gospel as his structural axis, and the well-worked territory of commentary on the Hero tale and solar myth are all applicable, without particularly bearing repetition.

Stranger presents its radical unions in the form of a satire, and in it we find even the creation of unions ironically inverted. Heinlein leaves the reader with no illusion of a firm ground on which to stand: the conventional partitions between God and man are dissolved, but in their place Heinlein has playfully erected a comic—and equally outrageous—multiplication of new partitions—of heaven now, rather than of earth. Heinlein inverts *Stranger's* orthodoxy-hidden-within-heterodoxy to show us not "heaven," but "the heavens." There is one for conventional Christians, to be sure, which bears a passing resemblance to "the heaven of Jurgen's grandmother" and also to Captain Stormfield's heaven. But there is more than a touch of the greater cosmos of the Mysterious Stranger. Islam has its own conventional heaven, with houris (from which the English word "whore" descends), and "the Martians have their own set-up." (268/330). Even the "reality" of the fiction is made to shimmer like the veils of Maya: Mike is, ultimately, not human at all, but an archangel—the archangel Michael of the church militant, playing for a time at multi-person solipsism. When the reader apprehends the essential meaning of the book, he (the reader) is joined into the synthesis by exercise of his own god-like esthetic and intellective functions.

Questions for Discussion

1. How can a work of art be interpreted on four levels simultaneously? Is this a common practice among writers?

2. Does the mythic nature of *Stranger* make this view of the text reasonable? Does it let Heinlein use biblical themes and symbols in a particularly useful way?

3. Explain the difference between "analogy" and "anagogy."

For Further Reading

Frye, Northrup. *Anatomy of Criticism*. Princeton, New Jersey: Princeton University Press, 1957

Parker, Patricia. "Anagogic Metaphor: Breaking Down the Wall of Partition." *Centre and Labyrinth: Essays in Honour of Northrup Frye*. Toronto: University of Toronto Press, 1983

Ricoeur, Paul. "'Anatomy of Criticism' or the Order of Paradigms." *Centre and Labyrinth: Essays in Honour of Northrup Frye*. Toronto: University of Toronto Press, 1983, p. 9. Emphasis added.

Twain, Mark. "Captain Stormfield's Visit to Heaven." *The Bible According to Mark Twain: Irreverent Writings on Eden, Heaven, and the Flood by America's Master Satirist*. Howard G. Baetzhold and Joseph B. McCullough, eds. New York: Simon & Schuster, 1995

Voltaire, *Candide*. Trans. Tobias Smollett. Franklin Center, Penn.: Franklin Library, 1979

– 17 –

Carnival and Monkey House

Mike achieves radical union with man (as incarnation is an anagogic "radical union") in the Monkey House of the zoo. A zoo is a metaphor for earth; it is, in human terms, a storehouse of the biological, as the earth itself in cosmic terms, is the storehouse of the biological and we humans occupy/swing from a branch of the "biological tree." Mike's incarnation is completed when he groks the tragic sense, and thus he is able to bring his message to its intended recipients. This could only happen at one of the two places in the book where heaven and earth meet in one place: the Monkey House and the Carnival.

During his days of "seeking," Mike is a magician and mentalist for a carnival, echoing the experience of a friend of Jubal who worked as a doctor in a carnival. In the carnival, Mike is "Dr. Apollo," his Martian-Apollonian aspect in dominance, without the necessary balance of the Dionysian epiphany of the Monkey House. The Carnival is metaphorically Heaven, the storehouse of wonders, magic and miracles—in just the way that the zoo is the storehouse of the biological.

The carnival experience ties together a number of the characters and motivating forces in the story and is a particularly fraught device.[68] The unconventional

---

68. Note that Heinlein used a carnival setting only twice previously. The 1939 short story "Requiem" opens with Delos D. Harriman visiting a county fair in Butler, Missouri (Heinlein's birthplace), and the carnival is exactly the place where Heaven (in the form of a rattletrap rocket) touches the earth. Harriman, who has been earthbound by the creative act of establishing space travel, can only come to Heaven where Heaven and Earth touch—in this case, a county fair. The other significant use of the carnival figure is in the short story "The Man Who Traveled in Elephants"—which he told Spider Robinson was his favorite among all his stories. There, the carnival was literally, as we find out, Heaven as afterlife.

behavioral standards of carny folk represents freedom from conventional ideas and conventional behavioral standards. The carnival represents freedom, release from at least some earthly constraints.

This gives us a clue to the nature of the carnival but also insight into the Patty Paiwonski character. Patty works in the carnival, as well: she is the tattooed lady for the blow-off and therefore a well-paid worker in the Carnival, a kind of "star." She also uses her "artwork" in the Happiness Meetings in the Circle of the Elect in the Fosterite Church. "She's a very holy temporal herself," (298) an angel says of her. Also, in the Nest, "She's the most advanced of any of us…" (346/427). And immediately after Patty is "saved" by Mike (279–297/346–347 or all of Chapter XXVII) we cut to "Heaven," where Foster, as an archangel, tells off Angel Digby, who resents and is outraged by Patricia's "blasphemy." However, the union of the Nest and the church of Foster is typologically prefigured by the coming together of Mike and Jill with Patty Paiwonski: the union of the churches is figuratively "born in heaven," the heaven-earth of the Carnival.

The Carnival is a "little bit of heaven" but it is a *tragic* heaven (for those who do not *know*, like Mike)—until you go through the epiphany of the Monkey House, awakening to humanity: Until you know that life can be tragic, you can't laugh; unless you can laugh, you can't see what has to be done. Heinlein, like Twain, connects laughter with the tragic sense of life—at exactly the point where heaven and earth meet, the epiphany of the Monkey House. On epiphany, Mike awakens to the tragic sense and learns to laugh:

> "The ten thousand high-grade comicalities which exist in the world are secreted from their dull vision. Will a day come when the race will detect the funniness of these juvenilities and laugh at them—and by laughing at them destroy them? For your race, in its poverty, has unquestionably one really effective weapon—laughter." (Mark Twain, "The Mysterious Stranger," 117)

Out of the partitions erected, partitions dissolve. Mike fails in the Carnival (bringing heaven to earth). He has mastered the technical and materialistic—the Apollonian—aspects of his grift; it is the personal, "spiritual," and "human" aspects he fails at. But Patty succeeds because she has transcended the tragic Carnival (where Mike is) and found the "little bit of heaven." She makes the marks happy—a slaunchwise reference to the Happiness Meetings of the Fosterite church. After Mike's tragic epiphany in the Monkey House, when he finally groks people, carny argot is incorporated into the Church of All Worlds in an echo of the task to learn Martian. We humans are all "marks," credulous and food for spiritual grifters—the more so as we are the more sincere. Learning carny argot is a step in the process of inheriting the carny's power of freedom from convention. Learning Martian is a step in the process of inheriting the power of Martian freedom from certain physical limitations.

The Carnival also includes the Apollonian-Dionysian motif, but since it is the tragic heaven, it is the tragic, or Fallen, version of the synthesis. Outwardly Dionysian in its use of "sex and blood and money" (274/339), inwardly the carnies despise the attendees: "...marks weren't people; they were blobs whose sole function was to cough up cash." "The Carnival was a nest where troubles of the outside world did not reach." (276/341) But it is a nest available to insiders only. The "marks" long for initiation into mystery, but the carnies' cynicism is matched by their own inability to see it in front of their eyes. During the magic show, a mark makes a running commentary, pooh-poohing the—real—magic as fake. Like the Church of All Worlds, the Carnival has its outer and its inner circles, but, unlike the CAW, the outer circle of the Carnival (the marks) are never allowed in; they forever attend Seeker Services. In the Carnival, the wonders are not to be touched or participated in—only viewed from a distance. Touching the illusion spoils it.

The Carnival and the Church of All Worlds are directly linked in other ways. The "girls" who work in the Carnival, in one town, are arrested by the sheriff for public lewdness; the Inner Nest is later attacked, and "[t]he sheriff announced that he's going to run us whores out of town." (385–386/469). While the marks pay to attend the "outer services" of the Carnival, in the CAW baskets of money are handed around and the marks are given the option to "help themselves." The point is underlined by Jubal observing, in carny lingo, "That pitch, properly given, should result in people giving *more*..." (340/419) The words of the announcer just before Mike's martyrdom are "This is it! This is it! This is the blow-off!" (428/515) And afterwards:

> "'Golly!' Patty said reverently. 'That's the best blow-off ever used.'
>
> "'Yes,' agreed Becky, judicially. 'the Professor himself never dreamed up a better one.'" (430/518)

The Church of All Worlds is the Carnival divine. The terminology of the carnies is used to underline the fact that the Carnival, along with the Church of Foster (linked by possessing Patty at the start) is part of the synthesis and cannot be disowned.

In essence, the Carnival, in its Fallen aspect, is the "Seeker Service" that Mike (and Jill) have to go through in order to reach the Monkey House. It is the period of study and preparation that precedes illumination. Without the failure of the Carnival, Mike is not able to join the Elect and fulfill his mission. The very first thing Mike says, after they get back to their room, is that he can now make the marks laugh—a reference to the Carnival. At this point the Carnival becomes a *comic* heaven. So the dual nature of the Carnival tells us that it is a "cusp," a point of "The Kingdom of God" or where heaven touches earth. It is a place where you can step from earth (Tragic) to heaven (Comic). It is a sacred space touching, surrounded by earth but also its own enclosed space, untouched in its essence. Thus *Stranger* again shows its structure as a divine comedy containing both tragic and comic catharsis.

This is not "private symbolism" of Heinlein; similar evocations of the circus or carnival as the resolving point of contact between tragedy and comedy show up even in television programs such as *The Prisoner* and *Twin Peaks* and is a well-spring for much of the "silly" imagery of *Help!* and the calliope/carnival evocations of *Sgt. Pepper*. So, too, does Ray Bradbury use the carnival as a point at which the world beyond the world, of mystery and magic, touches the everyday lives of people, as did Charles G. Finney, almost explicitly in *The Circus of Dr. Lao*. Canadian dramatist-scholar-author Robertson Davies made the significantly named World of Wonders carnival the focal figure of an important trilogy of novels.

In this use of the carnival as archetypal device, the circus is seen as a vehicle for the Pan-mystery, or all those mysteries not authorized by the low Protestant faith of Our Fathers. Heinlein is dipping into the springs of mythic imagery in his inclusion of the carnival.

The Monkey House is the mirror image of the carnival, since it is an enclosed space primarily located "on Earth," mythically speaking. Zoos reflect a human act of will, containing the living part of earth and thus image man as God. It does, of course, touch Heaven (and is therefore a space wherein an epiphany can occur), but it looks to Earth as the Carnival looks to Heaven: it contains the wonders of biological earth, as the Carnival contains the wonders of magic. It is where the Hero has to "undergo" as Zarathustra has to "undergo" in darkness in order for the soul to be tested and break forth into the light. Without the Monkey House the true nature of the Carnival is unappreciated. The Monkey House is protected by bars where the animals, or source of epiphany, are separated from the marks—people. In both Monkey House and Carnival, the biological cosmos is enclosed and protected from the people who view it. The Monkey House, the house of us hairless apes, is thus the ironic complement of the Carnival.

The Carnival and Monkey House is only one of the many important mirror-complements used as a structural element of *Stranger*. In a sense, Heinlein has chosen to represent the basic anagogic movement of the book as a series of polar opposites that are revealed, as the book goes on, as complements rather than as opposites: Mike and Jubal appear with contrasting characteristics of youth and innocence, age and experience, but at the end they integrate: Jubal joins the Nest and then Mike comes within Jubal to sustain him after his martyrdom. Jubal's household in the Poconos is a type of Mike's Nest. There is an undiscussed dualism of water outside (baptism) and water inside (grokking) that is a contrast-feature of the satire, integrated by having the grokkers bathing in the water of life. And as we come closer to the Nest, we find a complementary pair in Jill and Dawn. We are initially given the Church of The New Revelation as an opposite of the Church of All Worlds, but by the end of the book they have become integrated as outer and inner temples through Patty Paiwonski. Jill and Dawn are mirror complements—the same body from the Fosterite side and from the Goddist side. The basic anagogic progression of the book is expressed in these mirror divisions and complementary unions.

Mike's epiphany in the Monkey House brings about the necessary union. Mike incarnates and fully becomes man. But he immediately begins to become distant from man-as-he-is, for he is what humanity should be and could be—and will be—fully awake and fully potent. Mike's nest was prefigured by Jubal's household, where the three secretaries seemed also almost interchangeable—but curiously they gain characterization within Mike's nest. Mike's nest moves toward radical union each with the other. They lose the tragic sense—as Mike learned to laugh by grokking the tragic sense—and they lose their laughter as they come to live in joy.

Questions for Discussion

1. What is the difference between "comedy" and "humor"? Can humor be a tool of comedy, as irony is a tool of satire?

2. What is "divine comedy"? How might *Stranger* be related to Dante's Divine Comedy? Can you think of other divine comedies?

For Further Reading

Nietzsche, Friedrich W. *Thus Spoke Zarathustra*. Trans. Walter Kaufmann. New York: Penguin Books, 1966

Tarrant, Desmond. *James Branch Cabell: The Dream and the Reality.* Norman, OK: University of Oklahoma Press, 1967

– 18 –

Philosophy and Logos

Heinlein made a regular practice of dropping references to his sources into his stories, and *Stranger* is no exception—but here his references are almost all multi-dimensional. For example, and recapitulating material already covered in passing, two historical satires are mentioned explicitly—Burton's *Anatomy of Melancholy* by name, and Swift's *Gulliver's Travels* by recounting the "flapper" anecdote, when Jubal is trying to reach someone in authority at the Federation's Secretary General office. However, the flapper story is also a reference to Korzybski, inasmuch as this anecdote is quoted as a frontispiece to *Science and Sanity* (1933), a book which profoundly influenced Heinlein.

Another indirect reference to Korzybski is found bound together with several other direct and indirect source references. After the meeting with the Secretary General, Jubal and several of Michael's water brothers from the vessel that brought him to Earth are waiting for Secretary-General Douglas' response in a sealed and tiled[69] hotel suite. Their talk turns to the Martian language and the nonce-word "grok." Heinlein asserts as a given that the structure of the language one uses determines the world-outlook possible to one. This is a restatement of the Whorf-Sapir Hypothesis, a position in linguistic theory which emerged in about 1940. But it more probably derives from statements in *Science and Sanity*, seven years before Benjamin Whorf began to publish his papers in linguistics.

---

69. Or "tyled," closed to and guarded against outsiders.

Korzybski is now widely regarded as a crank,[70] so he is not referenced directly—but neither is Whorf referenced by name.

In the same conversation, Dr. Mahmoud asks if Jubal is familiar with the distinction between Apollonian and Dionysian cultures and remarks that Martian culture is Apollonian to a degree unknown on earth, even in comparison to the Zuni culture. This is another "twofer." The Apollonian-Dionysian dichotomy was first proposed by Friedrich Wilhelm Nietzsche in his first publication, *The Birth of Tragedy* (1870) (a book about esthetics and therefore quite an appropriate reference for *Stranger,* which is a book full of esthetic judgments), and since the reference occurs in the context of a philological discussion, we may infer that the reference is intended to evoke Nietzsche, an academic philologist by profession; however, the specific reference to the Zunis also marks this as a reference to Ruth Benedict's *Patterns of Culture* (1934).

The direct reference to Benedict adds to the intellectual "richness" of *Stranger,* but the indirect reference to Nietzsche is structural; for Heinlein's "spin" on the Hero tale owes something to Nietzsche's depiction of the religious figure of the superman, starting with *Thus Spoke Zarathustra* (*Also Sprach Zarathustra*) and the various succeeding books intended to gloss *Zarathustra* (e.g., *Beyond Good and Evil; Genealogy of Morals, Ecce Homo,* etc.)[71]

During the middle years of the twentieth century, Nietzsche's name and reputation had been tainted by an unwarranted and manufactured association of his philosophy with Nazism, and he would not have been considered suitable in 1961 to reference directly. As a successful commercial writer, Heinlein was always aware of his market and the intellectual freight it would bear, and he seldom taxed the reader with names or associations likely to provoke a "kneejerk" rejection. Instead, he allowed the ideas to speak for themselves.

This particular set of ideas, by 1961, was particularly prone to provoke reflex rejection: Heinlein's treatment of the superman material does not seem to derive directly from *Also Sprach Zarathustra*—which is, after all, an extraordinarily difficult book (equally so in English or in German)—but rather from P.D. Ouspen-

---

70. This does not mean that Korzybski was mistaken or that his notions were not valuable; it means only that the academic discipline of semantics has, over time, mutated away from the logico-mathematical concerns about language Korzybski was addressing. In fact, semantics as a discipline hardly exists any more; its place is taken by semiotics.

71. *The Will to Power* is not a fully-fledged part of the Nietzsche canon; after his death, Nietzsche's sister compiled this book out of fragments from his notebooks and imposed a racist, anti-semitic agenda on the selection and interpretation of the fragments. Nietzsche's deliberately "aphoristic" method was turned against him and obscured his intended meanings. For example, the "blond beast" that crops up in *Zarathustra* and elsewhere occasionally is supposed to refer to the lion of mythology, not the blond "aryan" race; and the Will to Power is intended to refer to the drive to be self-actualizing, not to a program of political hegemony. It is an irony of history that, by turning Nietzsche's "internality" to externality, the Nazi philosophers made it impossible for their "Aryan superman" to achieve the Nietzsche *Übermensch.*

sky's summation and synthesis of Nietzsche's treatment with the occult tradition of the superman in *Tertium Organum* (1920) and *A New Model of the Universe* (1934). Heinlein had referenced Ouspensky once before, by name, in "Elsewhen" (1939), but hundreds of times indirectly and by making use of Ouspensky's notions to shape his own fictions. (Thornton, Part 2) The various doctrines of Smith's Church of All Worlds, from "waiting is" to "all that groks is God," are found in a single, 25-page section of *Tertium Organum.*

Thus, a single conversation unfolds to an astonishing richness of references that shape the whole of the book—Benedict, Korzybski, Whorf, Nietzsche, Ouspensky. *Stranger* is rich and diverse, its sources and arguments are familiar but not quite familiar. *Stranger in a Strange Land* is more explicitly NeoPlatonist than any other of Heinlein's books. Its analysis is thus placed within a prestigious tradition—which renders the attack on the received wisdom of the status quo more tolerable to a wide range of readers.

NeoPlatonism is the label attached to group of Late Hellenic philosophers *cum* teachers *cum* theologians (the distinctions we now make between these specializations were not possible, or conceivable, during their time), who all claimed inspiration and intellectual descent from the Greek philosopher Plato. As usual with intellectual labels this one is applied to a diverse range of thinkers who in all probability hated and despised each other while they were alive but who did have a commonality in their thought and, hence, the label.

Of the many connecting ideas that form the commonality of NeoPlatonism four are immediately relevant to *Stranger*:

1. There are many spheres of being, arranged in a hierarchical order, with one of these being the "Reality" we see.

2. Degree of being (which sphere one lives "in") determines the degree of unity.

3. The higher up in the hierarchy you "live," the more unity, truth, and reality you grasp and use.

4. There is continual up and down motion within the hierarchy of Divinities, Aeons, Angels, etc., giving illumination of the higher to the lower beings.

It is easy to see how these ideas are used in *Stranger*. Mike is not merely a human raised by Martians but is the Archangel Michael sent on a divine mission. He is an archetype, a being from a higher sphere of existence, whose reflection is humanity, come to spread Good News, an anagogic message. The Martians have "a different set-up" (268/330) operationally since their Old Ones—beings existing on higher spheres (which are identified with higher dimensions in modern versions of the NeoPlatonic theory)—directly interact with their reflections. In "our" set-up the archetypes are a step removed and are not seen directly, although they also interact constantly. Thus, Archangel Foster is able to comment on (267–268/330–331, 297–299/368–370, 373/455–456) and even manipulate the action, as when Foster arranges for Mike's "minor martyrdom." (373/456) Because the higher subsume lower spheres, Digby, as an angel, is sent as a "Guardian-in-Training in a new sector." (299/370)

If the lower spheres are always being showered with Truth then is possible for beings on these spheres to receive it and, thus, Jubal Harshaw can "grok in fullness" without learning Martian.

The foremost transmitter of these NeoPlatonist ideas to us was (Saint) Augustine of Hippo (396–430 C.E.). Augustine has had major influence on the intellectual and cultural history of Western Civilization. Before his conversion to Christianity he was a follower of Manichaeanism, a late-Roman religion that proclaimed the universe we see was the battleground of light and darkness with the soul of man being an element of light trapped in darkness. Manichaeanism also partook of the NeoPlatonist climate of opinion. The higher circles of Manichaeanism were ascetic and celibate, since procreation only served to entrap more particles of light. The lower, and distinctly inferior, circles were allowed to marry and have sex as a concession to human weakness.

If this is beginning to sound familiar, that may be because it *is* familiar. It is the world-as-demonic paradigm. Look again at number 4 above: If all those "good guys" can come down the hierarchies disseminating knowledge and virtue, then the "bad guys" (devils, demons, etc.) can move *up*, spreading ignorance and depravity. If "up there" are heavens then "down there" are hells, and in the middle is this rather awful place, a battleground between the two.

> "Augustine was particularly attracted to Manichaeanism by the easy solution which it offered of the problem of evil, to which in later life he devoted much attention, and he was very deeply affected by Manichaean materialism." (A.H. Armstrong, 207).

Augustine never surmounted his emotional attachment to Manichaeanism, even as he rejected it intellectually, for he did reject it intellectually. At some point he read Plotinus and became an ardent NeoPlatonist.

> "[The] transmutation of Plotinus's [sic] theology is particularly clear in St. Augustine, because his thought is at once so authentically Christian and so very close in some ways to Plotinus [the foremost NeoPlatonist philosopher]." (211)

But Augustine never rejected Manicheanism emotionally, and in his doctrine of Original Sin, abhorrence of sex, and rejection of the world, transmitted Manichaeanism along with NeoPlatonism, down through western religion and culture. He was named a Doctor of the Church, and when Martin Luther, a member of the Augustinian Religious Order a thousand years later, wanted to reform the Medieval Church, he wanted to return it to its Augustinian roots (though Augustine would probably not have recognized anything Luther thought as deriving from his ideas—and Plotinus would certainly have been startled to be accused of starting this particular tradition). Calvin, heavily influenced by Luther, grafted Augustinian ideas—predestination, *et al.*—and they thus became incorporated, eventually, into low-church Protestantism.[72]

Here again Heinlein comes around full circle. He uses the very foundation of what he is satirizing as the basis of the satire.

Through the medium of St. Augustine, NeoPlatonism became a part of the background of Western Christianity. There were also secular strains of NeoPlatonic thought in the background, carried along with the learning of the hellenistic world that was preserved in the middle ages. One of these secular strains re-emerged into overground culture in the mid-nineteenth century, with the invention of American Transcendentalism and the writings of Ralph Waldo Emerson. Emerson was greatly influential in forming the groundwork of liberal thought in the nineteenth century. His essays were widely read in the U.S., and also by Nietzsche, who admired him greatly. Heinlein appears to have picked up Emerson's Transcendentalist/NeoPlatonic idea of the "Over-Soul" for his own purposes. Emerson's idea was that there is only one fundamental reality, the Over-Soul, and that the appearance of individual human beings is an illusion. We are all tendrils of the Over-Soul intruded into time. Thus we are all connected to—we are all—the one fundamental reality. In *Stranger* this proposition is voiced as "All that groks is God" and "Thou art God" and in a chestnut Mike tells during his bally:

> "…one of his parables was the oldy about the earthworm burrowing along through the soil who encounters another earthworm and at once says, 'Oh, you're beautiful! You're lovely! Will you marry me?' and is answered, 'Don't be silly! I'm your other end.'" (339/417)

This particular notion appears over and over again in Heinlein's writing, in many different forms, from his very first stories. In some iterations, the universe is "a game we whipped up among ourselves and agreed to forget the rules." The presence of these NeoPlatonic ideas in a very modern writer suggests that Heinlein is philosophically interested in "perennial truths" and forms a living link to our philosophical history.

---

72. This is a very simplified sketch of a complex series of events and interactions. In short, NeoPlatonism is on all sides of Christianity and on both sides of the satire of *Stranger*.

Questions for Discussion

1. Plato's central idea is the distinction between the world of things (phenomena) and the ideal world. How does this relate to Christianity?

2. Nietzsche's central idea is the superman, who contains within him the seed of new worlds. How does this relate to Christianity?

3. How did Heinlein combine Nietzsche, Plato and Christianity?

For Further Reading

Emerson, R.W. "The Over-Soul." *Essays* (1841). New York: The Modern Library, 1941

Nietzsche, Friederich W. *The Birth of Tragedy*. Trans. Walter Kaufmann. New York: Random House, 1967

Nietzsche, Friederich W. *Thus Spoke Zarathustra*. Trans. Walter Kaufmann. New York: Penguin Books, 1966

Thornton, Andrew. "Mythos and Logos: The Influence of P.D. Ouspensky in the Fiction of Robert A. Heinlein," Part 1: "Foundations Laid in 'Elsewhen.' *The Heinlein Journal*, No. 1 (July 1997), pp. 9–14; Part 2: "Ouspenskyan Ideas in *Stranger in a Strange Land*." *The Heinlein Journal*, No. 2 (January 1998), pp. 8–16; and Part 3: "*Glory Road* and the World As Myth Books." *The Heinlein Journal*, No. 3 (July 1998), pp. 13–18.

− 19 −

Esthetic Theory

One of the more interesting of Heinlein's satiric digressions is on esthetic theory.[73] *Stranger* shows a minor preoccupation with esthetics; comments that bear on esthetics are scattered throughout, showing that Heinlein intends to include it within the subject matter of his satire. The core discussion of esthetic theory, however, takes place in one particular spot: Ben Caxton has come back from a visit to the now fully-functioning Nest in a state of what he characterizes as moral perplexity. In a series of casual comments, Caxton unintentionally indicates that he is emotionally "blind" to the statuary Jubal has been collecting, with help from Mike. Harshaw interrupts dealing with Caxton's moral perplexity to show him "how to look at sculpture," by converting his own esthetic experience of Rodin's *La Belle Heaulmière* (The Helmet-maker's Wife) and *The Fallen Caryatid*[74]—and the statue of *The Little Mermaid* that sits in København (Copenhagen, Denmark) Harbor—into linear exposition. Caxton can be moved by the linear exposition (he, like Harshaw, is a writer) and so learns how to be moved by sculpture. The digression is purposive: it contains preparatory material for the resolution. There are four basic ways of relating to the world—that of science, of philosophy, of religion, and of art, and they can all be converted into the terms of the other, in just this way, though they can only be experienced in their own terms—i.e., you can talk about the experience of art, but the talk is not the experience. Auguste Rodin

---

73. Esthetic theory is the philosophy of art.

74. Also known as *The Caryatid Fallen Under Her Stone;* it appears on the jacket of the earliest hardcover editions of *Stranger.*

(1840–1917), one of the greatest sculptors of all time, was particularly adept at capturing pregnant images and embodying them in sculptural terms. As Harshaw remarks, his kind of esthetic work was labeled "literary" or "narrative" by later generations of, mostly nonrepresentational, art critics.

Harshaw remarks that the world went nuts about the time Rodin was working and that the ability to create works so moving has disappeared, so it is not surprising that a youngster like Caxton (Jubal was born, according to *The Cat Who Walks Through Walls*, in either—or possibly both—1903 or 1904) had not been taught this basic esthetic skill.

Heinlein touches briefly on technical issues in Rodin's sculptures, but then invokes *The Little Mermaid*, contemporaneous with Rodin, but sculpted in 1913 by Edvard Eriksen based on the tale of the same name by Hans Christian Andersen. This switch of sculptural subjects is an obvious pedagogical device, as *The Little Mermaid* is a simpler sculpture, esthetically pleasing, and does not challenge Caxton's—and presumably the readers'—undeveloped faculties for technical appreciation. Jubal Harshaw then draws a parallel of Mike's situation to hers, which brings the literary/narrative values implicit in the story the statue illustrates into the thematic ambit of *Stranger*.[75]

The figure of the half-human/half-fish (or serpent) is a very ancient archetype. Equally adapted to different worlds, she is a source of wise counsel during "sudden collapse of a form or style of life." (Jung, 177) This now-buried meaning is what Jubal is pointing to; Mike, unlike the Little Mermaid, does not look longingly back to Mars; he has embraced his humanity and has become adapted to two worlds. As Valentine Michael Smith is engaged in creating a "sudden collapse" of our customary "form or style of life," The Little Mermaid is needed by humans.[76] But, equally significantly, she "must return to the watery realm if the work is to reach its goal." Humans can make their watery return, the possibility of which the Little Mermaid has forever given up, by their baptism (a second—i.e., return—for Christians who are already "born again") in the Martian Water of Life. The "work" referred to above, Jung goes on to explain, is to unite conscious-

---

75. The story of the Little Mermaid was used as the basis for a recent series of animated films by Disney, but in their trademark fashion, they eliminated anything from the story that could challenge its viewers or form the basis for personal growth. Like many of the fairy tales collected by Hans Christian Andersen and the Grimm brothers, the well-known version of the story is somewhat "sanitized" from its source materials. Andersen reworked the story's dramatic arc to play down the older elements that would not appeal to his sentimental Victorian readers.

76. Interestingly, the fish-woman/serpent-woman archetype is also the source of the Melusina imagery—a feminine image alluring from across a void—on which James Branch Cabell built his "witch woman" stories in the Biography of the Life of Manuel, one of Heinlein's principal sources and models for writing technique. Cabell attaches yearning for the ideals of romance to Melusina imagery and makes another Melusina-figure, Etarre, the centerpiece of the *Biography*, whose name is reflected in Star and Star-Light names in Heinlein.

ness and the unconscious, male and female: the whole of which fragmented individuals are but latent parts. This is what the CAW conspicuously does.[77]

Critic and science fiction writer James Blish has taken Heinlein to task for a "naïve," "engineer's" esthetic theory, but it is quite clear that Blish does not understand much of what Heinlein is saying. Heinlein's esthetics are rather well developed in their own terms—though they are quite definitely not "modern."[78] The key to interpreting the context of Heinlein's esthetic theory is given by Jubal Harshaw in the same passage:

> "Because the world has gone nutty and art always paints the spirit of the times. Rodin died about the time the world started flipping its lid. His successors noted the amazing things he had done with light and shadow and mass and composition and they copied that part. What they failed to see was that the master told stories that laid bare the human heart. They became contemptuous of painting or sculpture that told stories—they dubbed such work 'literary.'" (325/399)

Rigidity and inability to see what Heinlein is talking about are qualities of the way the world has gone "nutty" in the twentieth century. Heinlein appears to be talking specifically about painting and sculpture—the plastic arts—and it appears superficially that Heinlein—or, at any rate, Jubal Harshaw—simply does not like non-representational art. But Heinlein is casting a much wider net than that; he is here giving us another facet of a general critique of modernism, in which he has been engaged since he began writing in 1939.

What does Heinlein mean by "the world went nutty"? He is not talking about "the Crazy Years," for that is a specific cultural phase of his Future History, and *Stranger in a Strange Land* takes place in our (Heinlein's and the readers') consensus world, rather than in the Future History (Heinlein makes this clear in his later,

---

77. Jung's discussion of the Melusina imagery was given in October 1941, on the 400th anniversary of the birth of Paracelsus, but it is not likely RAH read this address—though he may have been familiar with some collateral source material.

78. Blish's esthetics are, apparently, even more limited than Heinlein's: Blish expresses doubt at Heinlein's passing reference to a nine-"movement" symphony somewhat parallel to Holst's tone-poem, "The Planets." Blish seems to think the term "symphony" *means* a four-movement musical form (i.e., the Rococo symphony form of Mozart and, for the most part, Hayden). But the term "symphony" has been applied to a wide variety of forms, from single-movement "tone poems" to multi-movement forms. Insofar as there is anything like a "rule" for the application of the term "symphony" to a long work, it is only that of "symphonic" development applied to the material. A working composer might prefer to call a long, multi-movement program piece a "Nine Planets Symphony" rather than the "Nine Planets Orchestral Suite" or "Tone Poem," if he weakens the traditional connections between the three parts of a traditional sonata movement form within a conventional three-movement symphony. Heinlein's passing reference is thus more in line with the actual practice of working composers than Blish's naïve theoretical objection.

This is not the first of Blish's outrageous dogmatic assertions, but it is in some ways the most offensive. Heinlein seems to bring this out of Blish.

World as Myth books).[79] Heinlein is talking about something that is taking place in "our" mutual history.

The changeover from the predominance of representational art to the predominance of non-representational art, which historically took place starting in about 1910, was an esthetic manifestation of a general change in Western—and particularly American—culture at about the same time and is profoundly connected with the differences we feel between ourselves and our Victorian forebears. Initially, the general cultural trend was called "modernism," and, although the term has become connected with the 1920s and the Jazz Age in historical circles, so that we now feel compelled to think of ourselves as "post-modern" in some sense, it is still a good enough term for a general descriptor. We feel ourselves to be "modern," in contradistinction to the "quaintness" of Victorianism.

True, the Victorians believed themselves to be "modern," also—but modernism meant to them something quite different. That difference is attributable partly to the Victorian idea of unlimited progress, but more to the fact that we live in a Positivist Materialist age and the Victorians did not.

What does "Positivist Materialism" mean? It is a theory so pervasive in the twentieth century that we are no longer aware of it as a conscious choice, but it shapes our worldview quite considerably. Positivism tries to base all knowledge on sense data alone. It is the notion that only the physical world is important, and of the physical world, only things that can be positively measured—weighed, numbered, tasted, etc.—are important enough to be taken into consideration in making decisions. The more nebulous qualities of "spirit," for instance, or "soul"—in fact, all internal or subjective experiences—must be left out of decision-making. Strictly speaking, they cannot even be talked about in any coherent way. Even "mind" cannot be quantified or reduced and so must be left out of the evaluative process. So studies that rely on the concept of mind have been radically reformulated over the last century. All philosophical problems that cannot be reduced to matters of language and rhetoric are discarded. In many universities, Philosophy Departments merged into Languages Departments. Skinnerian Behaviorist psychology is regarded as a branch of biology—though biologists have been less willing to accept Behaviorism. In literature, focus has narrowed from formal structures in fiction (Structuralism) to rhetoric (Deconstruction); abstract paint-

---

79. The Future History is a projected historical development of the next several hundred years which Heinlein used for a great many of his earliest stories, abandoned for a time in the middle of his career, and finished off with *Time Enough for Love* (1973). His books written after about 1980 *(The Number of the Beast,* followed by *Friday* [1982], *Job: A Comedy of Justice* [1984], *The Cat Who Walks Through Walls* [1985], and *To Sail Beyond the Sunset* [1987]) belong to a series called by one of the central characters "World as Myth." Jubal Harshaw shows up in certain of these books, again in his role as a speaker of essential truths. The internal structure of these books is quite interesting, but beyond the scope of this work.

ing and sculpture (particularly in the school or style of "Abstract Expressionism")
Heinlein sees as the plastic embodiment of Positivism.

Speaking specifically of the rise of the counterculture of the 1960s—an event
of some importance in consideration of *Stranger*'s place in literature—Theodore
Roszak considers an important effect of Positivist Materialism which *Stranger* specifically addresses:

> "It is quite impossible any longer to ignore the fact that our conception of intel-
> lect has been narrowed disastrously by the prevailing assumption, especially in the
> academies, that the life of the spirit is (1) a lunatic fringe best left to artists and mar-
> ginal visionaries; (2) an historical boneyard for antiquarian scholarship; (3) a highly
> specialized adjunct of professional anthropology; (4) an antiquated vocabulary still
> used by the clergy, but intelligently soft-pedaled by its more enlightened members.
> Along none of these approaches can the living power of myth, ritual, and rite be
> expected to penetrate the intellectual establishment and have any existential (as
> opposed to merely academic) significance." (Roszak, 146)

Since about 1980, the iron grip of Positivism has finally began to disintegrate.
Philosophers are again discussing the meaning of subjective experience, and Cognitive Psychology is replacing Skinnerian Behaviorism as the preferred model for
psychology. Statistical mechanics, though still the most prestigious "method of
science," is giving way to chaos mathematics and nonlinear dynamics. Gradually,
we are able to see the utility of Heinlein's very long-standing criticism of Positivism as a transient style of world-outlook, not as a fundamental truth about reality
having a special claim to intellectual allegiance.

Positivist materialism was "invented" early in the nineteenth century by Augus-
tus Comte (1798–1857), under the philosophical name of "Logical Positivism."
It is thus roughly contemporaneous with Hegel. Comte's ideas were enthusiastically adopted as a *progressive* reaction against the same religious "package deals" of
ideas against which Nietzsche was, a little later, still inveighing. In this sense, Positivism can be seen as a late offshoot of Enlightenment-Era rationalism.

The Victorian Era was intellectually diseased with sentimentalism, and progressive thinkers of the late nineteenth century looked to Positivism, and its ancillary philosophies of Pragmatism, Operationalism, Reductionism (developed later
in the century), as counterbalances or cures for excessive sentimentality. Gradually, Positivism was taught widely enough to become self-sustaining and self-per-
petuating as the preferred worldview, first of scientists, then of the "social
sciences," and, finally, even of artists. It did "cure" sentimentality, by setting up a
rigid and arid orthodoxy for the arts. From about 1910, fine art and popular art
began a process of radical diverging that has not yet ceased. Popular art and popular culture remained "accessible," with varying degrees of tolerated sentimentalism, while fine arts tended to develop highly specialized idioms and become the
province of sophisticated specialists, ignored by the public. As Positivism gained

ascendency as the philosophy of the twentieth century, fine art has died as a mass medium.

There is something missing from official, Positivist materialist culture—something that feeds the emotional needs of people. They feel trapped in a machine. Lacking any way of satisfying the emotional need within the official orthodoxy, they turn to irrationalism—the philosophy of will and blood or religious revivalism or newspaper horoscopes or new age mysticism. Even popular art forms polarize, dropping the nuances that used to be possible and becoming crudely insistent. Romance forms that used to be published in prestige magazines are relegated to the low-prestige pulps, and finally, to comic book formulas.

People do tend to carry an idea to its logical perversion, no matter how much it hurts. The overly intellectualized "academic art" of the twentieth century is an exact, inverted counterpart of the overly-emotional claptrap of the Victorians. The point here is that the necessary reaction against Victorian kitsch by the Moderns has thrown out baby, bathwater, and bathtub—which seems a tad excessive. Heinlein seeks to find art's native ground and stand with its natural power, regarding both Victorian sentimentality and Modernist abstract aridity as excrescences.

In Heinlein's critique of Positivist Materialism, materialists ignore blatant facts and are thus equally as unrealistic and unpragmatic as are the most vaporous mystics. "Elsewhen," among the first stories Heinlein wrote in 1939, contains a specific critique of Positivism; he counterposes two engineers: one, who faces and accepts the observed fact of trans-dimensional travel, is able to engage with the reality he finds in a useful and productive manner; the other, a positivist materialist so identified in the story, is crippled by his reality-denying beliefs and cannot even transport himself but must be carried by the teacher.

Heinlein's solution is simply to ignore modern esthetic theory—to ignore modernism, in fact. Instead, he takes up where the philosophical development of the nineteenth century left off and extends it. Art, he proposes, is an arranged "sequence of emotions." It is Martian art that is specifically being described, but the same description applies to human art (Heinlein has, in fact, applied just this description to human art, in the short story, "Lost Legacy," also written in 1939. The consistency of Heinlein's positions on these matters over a very long period of time is remarkable).[80]

This formulation requires us to view *Stranger's* comments about Martian art as in some sense relating to human art. In this light, we can recognize a wonderful in-joke: Heinlein tells the story of a Martian artist who discorporated while in the

---

80. In the sense that life itself is an artful arrangement of emotions, Heinlein's esthetic theory can be regarded as teleological. This aspect of the theory is dealt with explicitly in Heinlein's later, World As Myth books—and particularly in *Job: A Comedy of Justice* (1984). Heinlein has thus been saying exactly the same thing from the beginning to the end of his long career. This fact suggests further critical examination of the commonplace assertion that Heinlein changed his political philosophy over the years.

middle of composing a work of art, so it was composed partly by an adult and partly by an Old One. This event put the critical community of Martians in a dither as to how the work was to be evaluated, and it is this debate that delays the Martians tapping their "spy," Valentine Michael Smith, and which may give the human race a grace period of several hundred years before the Martians act on their grokkings.

The artist is a reference to Heinlein himself, and the work of art being composed was *Stranger*: the book was started in 1949, when Heinlein was 42 years old—an adult of vigorous middle age—but finished and published in 1961, when Heinlein was in his mid-fifties—that is, on the verge of elderliness (i.e., an Old One). Heinlein humorously acknowledges foreknowledge that the readership of *Stranger* will not know how to evaluate it—as, indeed, he himself did not.

Questions for Discussion

1. This chapter has presented a rather strong position on development of art forms in this century. Do you agree?

For Further Reading

Blish, James (writing as "William Atheling, Jr."). *The Issue At Hand*. Chicago: Avent: Publishers, 1964

Heinlein, Robert A. "Elsewhen." *Assignment in Eternity* (1953). New York: Baen Books, 2000

Auguste Rodin WebMuseum: http://sunsite.unc.edu/wm/paint/auth/rodin. There are several pictures of *The Caryatid Who Has Fallen Under Her Stone*, but none of *La Belle Heaulmière*. The Los Angeles County Museum of Art has a copy of this piece, among many others.

— 20 —

Minor Digressions

The major digression of the book is on esthetic theory. And, as we have seen, the digressions of the anatomy form are actually part of the thematic development of the satire. Heinlein included a number of other digressions, each with its own structural purpose(s).

Money

Mike's flash of insight about the nature of money is the first of his many important illuminations about how we humans go about being human. Heinlein had been particularly interested in fiscal theory since his political days. When he was retired from the Navy in 1934, he briefly attended the University of California, Los Angeles, but went to work for the EPIC campaign, an attempt by social-ist writer-social activist Upton Sinclair, working through the Democratic Party, to reform the economy of California along cooperative lines and provide Depression relief. In the course of working for EPIC, Heinlein read widely among coopera-tive and socialist reform schemes and seems to have been particularly drawn to the Social Credit theory.[81] Contemplating an early retirement from fiction writing in

---

81. The basic notions of Social Credit are that currency can be regarded as an accounting book entry rather than a representation of redeemable value and that the state can use a combination of monetary techniques to raise and then control the amount of consumer spending—i.e., the economy as a whole. The initial proposals of the founder (Douglas) proposed to deal with the Great Depression by inflationary "pump priming" grants of unsecured new money to individu-als, a price-freeze setting prices at lower-than-production-cost levels, which would be made up for by subsidies, guarantees or other forms of "credits" to manufacturers. Social Credit never made much headway in the United States, but it figured in Canadian politics until about 1971.

1941, Heinlein speaks of writing a book on fiscal and monetary theory. Regrettably, no formal exposition of Heinlein's system was ever committed to paper, but certainly the next book he wrote—*Beyond This Horizon* (1942, 1948)—incorporates many Social Credit ideas.

Mike's insight seems to encapsulate the "meta-theory" of Social Credit. Money is not simply a medium of exchange; in the largest sense, it is a way of integrating and achieving union of interest: "Money was a great structured symbol for balancing and healing and growing closer" on a very large scale. (*Stranger*, 236/292) Symbolically, a bowl of money stands as the interface between the private home of the Nest and the outside world. As the nest grows into political ascendancy, it will extend its internal socialism to the whole world, fulfilling John Humphrey Noyes' idea that socialism brings the idea of the home into the industrial setting (as opposed to the twentieth century fear that Marxist socialism will bring the regimentation of the industrial setting into the home). Noyes presages Heinlein's sentiments almost exactly:

> "Every family is a little example of Communism; and every working partnership is an example of joint-stockism. Communism creates homes: joint-stockism manages businesses." (Noyes, 194)

It is tempting to view Mike's money insight as a reference to *Atlas Shrugged*, by Ayn Rand, with its famous "money speech," which starts dramatically: "'So you think that money is the root of all evil,' Francisco d'Anconia said. 'And what, do you think, is the root of money?'" But this attribution is unlikely. *Atlas Shrugged* was published in 1957—probably, in fact, *after* the corresponding passage in *Stranger* was written.

As with many another important idea, Heinlein may here be continuing his ongoing dialog with H.G. Wells—and in particular with *A Modern Utopia* (1905):

> "Money…is a good thing in life, a necessary thing in a civilized life, as complicated, indeed, for its purposes, but as natural a growth as the bones in a man's wrist, and I do not see how one can imagine anything at all worthy of being called a civilization without it. It is the water of the body social, it distributes and receives, and renders growth and assimilation and movement and recovery possible. It is the reconciliation of human interdependence with liberty." (73)

Note the water symbolism.

The confluence of Wells, Rand, and Heinlein on this one point helps to define the nuances of Heinlein's overall stance. Commentators have tried to pigeonhole Heinlein as a political conservative—even though *Stranger* is manifestly not the product of a right-wing mind, any more than is *Time Enough For Love* (1973) or *To Sail Beyond the Sunset* (1987).

There is no resolution to this paradox possible within the interpretive framework of the left wing/right wing dichotomy. Heinlein simply does not fall within that scale.

It has conventionally been assumed that Heinlein was a left-wing socialist as a young man (Jerry Pournelle's assertion that he was a "moderate democrat" is without factual basis), but that he changed into a conservative as he got older. Isaac Asimov believes that the Heinlein he knew in Philadelphia during World War II was politically "ultraliberal" but that he became a conservative when he married Virginia Heinlein in 1948. (*In Memory Yet Green*, 488). Heinlein's later participation in the anti-disarmament movement in the late 1950s and in the Goldwater presidential campaign in 1964 are seen as evidence of a change of heart.

Thus Heinlein's political evolution is seen as fitting into a known paradigm: if a young person is not a liberal, it is said, he/she has no heart; if he/she does not become a conservative in middle age, he/she has no brain.

However, Heinlein's correspondence with this paradigm is something of an illusion. The late Heinlein, even up to the end of his life, is actively concerned with sexual liberalism, portraying contract marriages and stable societies based on "polymorphous perverse" sexual practices; this is a radical liberal position, which would be anathema to a true conservative mentality.

Libertarians are inclined to adopt Heinlein as one of their own, because libertarianism sees itself as holding liberal social issues at the same time as conservative economic issues. The symbol of the Libertarian Party is a horizontal line representing the liberal-conservative continuum, with an arrow pointing upward and to the right, representing this view. Not only did Heinlein write what is widely regarded as the exemplary libertarian novel, *The Moon Is a Harsh Mistress* (1966), his polemical writings from about 1980 onward, and particularly in *Expanded Universe*, show a clear concern for economic matters in terms acceptable to both libertarians and fiscal conservatives.

However, Heinlein never characterized himself as a libertarian,[82] and it is unlikely that any current political label will ever be found with a clear "fit," though all the likely candidates fall within the sphere of "individualism." His writing contains a great many apparently contradictory positions, adopted, in *all* cases, for the purposes of the fiction. That is, he put in his fiction ideas that suited the story he was working with, but the story always governed the ideological content. Perhaps the final answer is that the Heinlein we see through his public utterances—of polemical prose as well as of fiction—was an artist first and a linear political writer a distant second.[83]

---

82. Indeed, Heinlein appears never to have characterized himself as subscribing to any creed or sect. This curious fact may be related to the Korzybskian injunctions against "identification." The phrase "I am 'x'" may simply not have been in Heinlein's vocabulary, as a deliberate act of will on his part.

83. One political label that does seem to fit is "Freethinker," but it is not a label with any currency.

Headlines

At various places in *Stranger*, Heinlein stops the action for a comic "snapshot" of the world in which the story is taking place. Cynthia Duchess, we learn at various times, is going to have a baby by artificial insemination; then she joins a nunnery with great fanfare and leaves a few days later, with no fanfare at all. A baby wins a lottery. A cult prepares for the end of the world. These headlines, shocking and outrageously comic at the time, have since gained an eerie feel of familiarity.

Heinlein has made extensive use of the newspaper headline quotation throughout his entire career, for similar purposes. Other writers were experimenting with similar devices at the same time: Steinbeck used a similar technique an early chapter of *The Grapes of Wrath*, and it has since become familiar to us because of the film montage. Heinlein probably (though not assuredly) inherited this montage device from James Branch Cabell. In *The Rivet in Grandfather's Neck* (1915), Cabell had used headline quotations and recitations of "newsworthy" items of the period in which the novel was set (approximately ten years before it was written) for comic effect, linearly for setting the stage and ironically to show the contemporary reader how ephemeral these concerns, now forgotten, really are—and by implication how important are the readers' own contemporary concerns.

> "Though these references to current topics and events indicate that the world is larger than the characters of the comedy assume, yet the way in which Cabell jumbles together fads, gossip, and history serves to point up the ultimate lack of distinctive importance even in these once supposedly vital subjects." (Wells, *Jesting Moses*, 83.)

In *Rivet*, Cabell thus focuses the reader on the enduring human situations of the private lives of the individuals, in contradistinction to the supposedly objective importance of events happening outside the bounds of Litchfield. It is a device which at once describes and breaks the novelistic circle defining a social grouping. Heinlein uses the device for even more comic effect, making the external world a silly place, deeply irrational—and thus deeply in need of the balance and healing that Mike's "Martian wisdom" can bring suffering humanity. The comedy reaches a high pitch when the interruptive headlines are translated into commercials that interrupt Mike's televised martyrdom. Now we get not only the news flashes and "content" items—we get the ephemera of soap ads and the like that go along with the commercial media, as well. Just before Mike comes out of the hotel for his martyrdom, the humor of the satire reaches a peak of howling irony: the last commercial break is for a housing development built on Florida swamp land, called The Elysian Fields—the place of the blessed dead in Classical mythology (i.e., just where Mike is going to be). Irony piles upon irony. Nothing is too extravagant for this blow-off.

Many of the events detailed in these headlines appear less shocking or funny to us now than they were when first published. We have come a long way toward the very strange and absurd land in which *Stranger* takes place.

The Fair Witness

The conception of the "Fair Witness" is one of the most strange and fraught of all Heinlein's creations.

> "As the critics of the god Thoth, the inventor of writing, remark in Plato's *Phaedrus*, the ability to record has a lot more to do with forgetting than with remembering: with keeping the past in the past, instead of continuously recreating it in the present." (Frye, *The Great Code*, 22)

The difference between a human memory—however shaped by "renshawing"—and a mechanical document is that human memory does "continuously recreate" the past, and this suggests a connection with, or reference to, the social function of myth around which the book is shaped. The culture portrayed in *Stranger* is bourgeois-secular to an extreme degree and gadget-oriented to such an extent that is has lost the ability to think rationally or critically about spiritual issues—hence the Dionysian abandon of the Fosterite services and the inability of human languages to think about the mode of spirituality contained within the vessel of the Martian language. The Fair Witness as a highly respected social institution functions to impose the human dimension on bourgeois-secular culture and by "continuous recreation" of important commercial facts—wills and contracts are specifically mentioned—brings what Mircea Eliade calls "a timeless present"—the timelessness of the spiritual eternal—back into human affairs. This important social function is included deliberately within Jubal Harshaw's household and then transferred to the Nest. Jubal's household prefigures the Nest, and both are types of Heaven.

Duple presentation of important figures and ideas was a favorite writerly device of Heinlein's, and the Fair Witness also appears in two persons in *Stranger*—James Cavendish, the public practitioner called upon to Witness the public fake Man-from-Mars, and Anne, the private practitioner who witnesses the real Man-from-Mars in his development. The figure of the Fair Witness is thus used to imply a dual concern with public versus private, in which the public is not-true and the private is true. This figure is mirrored in large and small throughout *Stranger*—as the orthopraxis of the Church of All Worlds is private and personal and protected from the outside world by the walls of the Nest, while the destructive practices of the outside world continue in the glare of publicity, culminating in the televised martyrdom of Valentine Michael Smith by stoning—the traditional Jewish punishment for fornicators—and by burning—the traditional Christian punishment for heretics. Similarly, the public services of the Fosterite church are Dionysian revels, but the private services—the "Happiness Meetings" of the Eternally Saved—

are Apollonian sharings that bridge from Fosterism to Mike's "Godism." Truths are held in private. The public religion of Fosterism stones and burns Mike.

The figure of the Fair Witness is doubtless not intended to be "believed" in the linear, naturalistic and rationalistic sense; it, rather, suggests connections in a non-linear and mythic sense.

Questions for Discussion

1. Why do you think Heinlein has been labeled a conservative?
2. What do you think of money as a medium of "balancing and healing"?
3. Are the headlines and advertising excerpts Heinlein uses to punctuate the book more funny than realistic or more realistic than funny?
4. Is the Fair Witness idea believable? Why do you think Heinlein included it?

For Further Reading

Cabell, James Branch. *The Rivet in Grandfather's Neck: A Comedy of Limitations*. New York: Robert M. McBride & Co., 1915, 1921

Rand, Ayn. *Atlas Shrugged*. New York: Random House, 1957

Wells, H.G. *A Modern Utopia* (1905). Lincoln, Nebraska: University of Nebraska Press, 1967

Wittels, David G. "You're Not as Smart as You Could Be" *The Saturday Evening Post*, 220: 42, 43, 44 (April 17, 24 and May 1, 1948)

PART FOUR

"His Scandalous Career"

Narrator: "You understand, friends, that this wonderful community is in an unique condition today. Something strange has been going on and these people are in no mood to trifle. Their laws have been flouted, their security forces treated with contempt, they are angry, righteously so."

— 21 —

Martyrdom...

Remarkably little critical work has been done on *Stranger*, and even the commentary has been sparse, considering how widely read and discussed the book had become by 1970, and how influential in a social sense. Furthermore, the sociology of the public's response to the book presents interesting features which have not been investigated. The major commentary is explored in this chapter; a list of other, less-available essays is included at the end of the chapter.

The first wave of comment took the form of reviews at the time of original publication. The book was widely reviewed in both professional and fan press in 1961 and immediately acknowledged as breaking new ground. At 166,000 words, it was the largest science fiction book published—more than twice the size of Heinlein's juveniles or the magazine novels. Its daring sexuality was a matter of comment also, though reviewers were divided on the subject. There was also uniform skittishness on the subject of the book's religion.

એ

Science fiction writer James Blish (*Cities in Flight*; *A Case of Conscience*) reviewed *Stranger* for a fanzine, writing under the pseudonym of "William Atheling, Jr." Blish's reviews were later collected as *The Issue at Hand* (1964) and *More Issues at Hand* (1967), and published by the fan press Advent. Both books have important critical essays on Heinlein.

Blish's review of *Stranger* appeared under the title "And Another" (dated October 1961 and, therefore, during the book's initial release) in *The Issue At Hand*.

Blish struggles with the religious content of *Stranger* and comes to the conclusion that the book is, in essence, a fictionalized religious tract,[84] laying out the ecclesiology of a seriously proposed new religion. (This is probably the origin of the somewhat incoherent assertion that sometimes rises in the fan press that the book is a "put on").

Blish tries to read *Stranger* as a polemic and comes to the (unsurprising) conclusion that Heinlein's argument fails because the Martian "miracles" do not exist. He raises a host of metaphysical questions at the end, apparently not recognizing that the cosmogony of the book rests on a historically well-explicated hermetic framework, in which an infinite number of intelligent beings on multiple levels inhabit the cosmos.

Astonishingly, Blish never seems to recognize the relationship of the made-up religion of the Church of All Worlds to orthodox Christianity.[85]

> "Heinlein-Smith's eclectic religion is a fascinating potpourri, amazingly complicated to have come from a single brain rather than from centuries of accumulated haggling and hagiography." (*Id.*, 64)

While one has no wish to detract from Heinlein's ingenuity, it *did* come from "centuries of accumulated haggling and hagiography."

Blish also prefigures a number of later critics and commentators by raising the puzzling and rather absurd objection that Heinlein did not develop his material in just the way he would have.

Bracketed between attacks on the religious content of the book, Blish develops a second argument about Heinlein's esthetics, some of which we have already encountered. Blish sets up, in a footnote, a Procrustean bed of illusory theory: he likens Heinlein to "other engineers-turned-writers." Then all the subtleties of Heinlein's esthetics must be fitted into the "engineer-turned-writer" paradigm. Heinlein likes reincarnation because "it would naturally appeal to a writer trained in the sciences because it is conservative of souls." (65)[86] Again, setting the stage for much later criticism, Blish elaborates the contradictions, logical tangles, and plain inadequacies of his critical stance and attributes the resulting mess to Heinlein and to *Stranger*. "On this showing," he says, after supposing that Heinlein's

---

84. At first he says only that the *subject matter* of the book is religious (65), but within a page he has moved the discussion to the theoretical real-life orthopraxy of such a religion—and he ends the review-essay with a series of questions about the metaphysics of the system.

85. This is not the most astonishing lapse of critical faculties in the criticism of *Stranger*, however: another contemporaneous review that came to Heinlein's attention, fortunately never published, failed to notice that there was any sex in the book.

86. Apparently Blish does not realize that there is no reincarnation in the book. There is one passing reference to a baddie Mike has discorporated "being sent to the back of the line," but within the hermetic schema of the book, this does not imply that this god-unaware will be returned to the earth at all. For a fuller exposition of this point, see note 30.

esthetics are only an engineer's unsophisticated defense of "representational or story-telling art," "if the Martians ever do turn out to be a menace, we can ship them the score of Liszt's *'Mazeppa'* or a Post cover and immobilize them to the end of time." (68) This manifest nonsense Blish rationalizes as Heinlein having not thought out the esthetics he has so carefully delineated. How he rationalizes "Heinlein is also a thorough-going Freudian" is not apparent.

Nor does Blish seem to recognize the historical context of the sexual liberalism Heinlein portrays as the ideal of Mike's Nest (the nineteenth century American socialist/freethought tradition). Blish's blindness and failure to comprehend the context of the material he is reading sometimes leads him to appreciate elements that are not there. Of the moral transformation Jill undergoes when she realizes the appropriateness of her exhibitionism to her total personal makeup, he says,

> "There is an extended defense of the joys of strip-teasing and feelthy [*sic*] pictures which is both extremely funny (Heinlein's wit is surer here than it is almost anywhere else in the book) and rather touching..." (69)

Blish's program for the Atheling essays that make up his two books of critical essays was to build a critical apparatus for "technical criticism" of science fiction. Blish was a relatively sophisticated practitioner of the science fiction art, relatively well educated—and yet he could not "see" much of Heinlein's technique or, indeed, much of the material in the book that is directly on the surface. The attitude in Blish that the critical universe must and can only consist of what the critic understands (rather than what is in the work) was to become a keynote of his immediate successor in Heinlein criticism, Alexei Panshin.

⟢

Alexei Panshin's *Heinlein in Dimension* appeared in 1967, the first full-length work about Heinlein. In its survey of all Heinlein's work to date, it set the terms of discourse for the next thirty years—a very unfortunate fact, because many of Panshin's judgments, though superficially attractive, are fatally incomplete. To give just one example, Panshin proposes a "three stage Heinlein individual," with the adolescent characters of his juveniles (Stage One) growing into the "competent men" of vigorous middle age (Stage Two) and then becoming the older guide figures (Stage Three). This schema is superficially attractive, in that it proposes to define a relationship among the character types which the reader can sense—but it fails in important respects to agree with the texts. The older wisdom figure, for example, is of a different physical type than the other two, and, although there are many examples that could be regarded as a Stage One individual transformed into a Stage Two individual, there is no example anywhere in the canon of a Stage Two individual transformed into a Stage Three individual. Even granting that Stage

Two is a progressed version of Stage One, the wisdom figure is simply not a progressed example of Stage Two.[87]

Panshin appears to have assumed that the minim he understood of what was in Heinlein was all there was. His analysis has not proceeded to a full synthesis, but he presents his incoherent analysis as though it were complete and judges Heinlein to be incoherent.

Panshin does not like anything Heinlein wrote after *Citizen of the Galaxy* (1956). The next book, *Have Space Suit—Will Travel* (1958), commences what he calls the "Period of Alienation." Panshin particularly does not like *Stranger in a Strange Land* and says so right at the beginning of his comments. He sees *Stranger* as a badly written novel of manners containing three stories that do not mesh together—an adventure story, a story of the founding of a religion, and a satire (it is clear from subsequent comments that the only model of "a" satire Panshin considers is the innocent voyager tradition of, e.g., *Candide*). He resisted reviewing the book during its initial release because his distaste made him reluctant to cope with the book's difficulties in a public statement. It is a "thoroughly annoying" book (*Id.*, 98), though "worthy of respect" (108) "It is almost impossible to read *Stranger in a Strange Land* without bleeding a little, which is, of course, a very good reason for reading it." (102–103)

Following Blish's lead, Panshin interprets the made-up religion as an attempt at polemical ecclesiology on Heinlein's part and extends the critique of the book's primary religion to absurd lengths. It is "a romantic ideal, unworkable in practice." (151) Heinlein fails as a writer because the religion is self-justified by fiat. "This sort of built-in self-protection for the author is no more than a way of writing around a subject without ever coming to grips with it." (151)

The flaw with this analysis is, of course, that Mike's religion is a fictional conception, created for the satire, and does not require justification outside the work. Panshin is not extending to *Stranger* the status of fiction. The characters in the book react to the events in the book, not to events in our external reality, and the assumptions used in the book need only meet standards of internal self-consistency; they do not have to be "true" in the real world. Panshin seems to be criticizing Heinlein for writing a work of fiction.

---

87. The relationship of Stage Two to Stage Three seems to be complementary rather than successive, and the so-frequent incidence of a female figure forming a triad with these two suggests that the triad is the intended story figure. (Patterson, "The Hermetic Heinlein") Panshin simply leaves the female element out of his considerations.

It may well be that Panshin simply never noticed Heinlein's creative dialog with Nietzsche, particularly pronounced in *Stranger*. Panshin's notion of the "competent man" as a character type seems somewhat alien to Heinlein, not so much "untrue" as "overstated." Heinlein's leading characters have the leading characteristic of what Nietzsche calls simply, and more accurately, "adequacy." Both Nietzsche and Heinlein regard the ressentimental sense of personal inadequacy as pathological.

Heinlein was never confused on this point. He points out in a letter to his agent that he cannot remove the "miracles" from the book—they are the "convincers" for all the subsequent events. (*Grumbles*, 265) Heinlein is defending the conception as a work of fiction, with internal self-consistency, not as a religious tract.

Panshin's failure to treat *Stranger* as a work of fiction renders his criticism of the book incoherent. He stands so much in his own light that he cannot see the book. *Heinlein in Dimension* gives us a much fuller portrait of the mind of Alexei Panshin in the early 1960s, when the various essays that make up the book were published in fanzines, than it gives us a penetration of the intellect or writing of Robert Heinlein. It gives us a historical snapshot of the views of a certain type of mind at a certain age and is more useful for purposes of historical criticism than of formal criticism.[88]

ↄ

Of all the critics and commentators to date, George Edgar Slusser has brought by far the most sophisticated critical apparatus to bear on Heinlein in two monographs published by the now-defunct Borgo Press in the mid-1970s. On the down-side, he also has one of the most rigid and ill-adapted interpretive schemas in the literature, forcing Heinlein into the procrustean bed of a Calvinist reading in ways that are inappropriate and often bizarre.

Slusser sets forth his aim in the 1977 introduction to the second edition of his 1976 *Robert A. Heinlein: Stranger in His Own Land*:

> "[The focus of this study] holds at that point where certain broader patterns (be they American, Romantic, or mythic) interact with various literary conventions Heinlein the writer chose to use…my essay seeks to bring to light patterns in Heinlein's fiction below the level of themes, conventions, doctrines, and see how these central dynamics (which belong, if anything, to the realm of cultural myth) generate formal structure." (*Id.*, 8)

Slusser sees Heinlein using and "subverting" the conventions of the adventure novel by a process of ellipsis: "Increasingly in the later novels, the traditional center of the adventure story—reasoned and willed deeds—is emptied and elided." (4) He sees this process starting as early as *Time for the Stars* and *Double Star* in

---

88. In 1974, Alexei and Cory Panshin published an extended book of critical essays, *SF in Dimension*, which enunciated a "subjective" reading of Heinlein—that is, an attempt to see Heinlein's total work as dealing with individuation crises. A fascinating interpretive schema gone dreadfully and infuriatingly awry, Panshin's subjective reading ignores the context of the various stories as commercial fiction addressed to an audience of young people concerned with their own individuation crises, and imputes these characteristics to Heinlein. Panshin writes from the assumption that that Heinlein was psychologically an alienated and arrested teenager who had never progressed from adolescent crises into adulthood. The germ of this "subjective" reading is in *Heinlein in Dimension*. The Panshins' comments on *Stranger* in *SF in Dimension* are more descriptive than analytical and so will not be dealt with here.

1956, as the heroes find their place in destiny rather than shape themselves by their deeds and decisions, which have been elided. The "destiny" is provided by Calvinist predestination.

Slusser's Calvinist scheme of interpretation firmly shapes all of his comments and so requires examination. The theory is enunciated in *Classic Years of Robert A. Heinlein* (10). Noting Heinlein's frequent use of a superior man who gives shape to the history he inhabits, Slusser sees this figure as a type of the Elect of Calvinism, with a corresponding Predestination that shapes his ends.

John Calvin (1509–1564 C.E.) was one of the great Christian theologians. He sees all of creation as having been done in one act of God's will, with the implication that every human act—everything that takes place in time—was ordained or "predestined" from the moment of creation. Certain individuals God has elected to fulfill his purposes in human history. These are the Elect. Calvin wrote his theories in the multi-volumed *Institutes of the Christian Religion*, and Calvinism as a Protestant sect based on the *Institutes* was codified in the Synod of Dort (1618–1619) as based on five principles:

1. Total depravity of man

2. Unconditional grace of God

3. Limited atonement

4. Irresistable grace

5. Perseverence of the Saints

Calvinist doctrine spread all over Europe as the predominant theoretical model of Protestantism. English Protestants who wished to "purify" the Church of England adopted Calvinist theory and adapted it to their particular concern with ecclesiology—the organization of the church. For the English Puritans, membership in a rectified church was an essential precondition of salvation, which they read as election (a proposition not in—and in fact contrary to—Calvinist theory), and over their long history, the Puritans developed a "covenant" theory that God would bestow grace on an individual based on the individual's contract with God to belong to an approved church. This is quite contrary to Calvin's notions, explicitly addressed in the *Institutes* (Book 4) that only God knows who is Elect and there are no signs of Election that a mere human can read. There are unrecognized Elect in the secular world and unrecognized Reprobate within the body of the church. Slusser enunciates the covenant theory in *Classic Years*, so he is clearly talking about Puritanism more than Calvinism, though Puritanism does inherit a certain body of belief from Calvinism.

Puritanism came to the New World principally in the Massachusetts Theocracy, where it developed a third "sign" of Election—the public profession of a transforming spiritual experience. Slusser nowhere claims that Heinlein uses this

American tradition, but he does read predestination, fate, destiny, everywhere in Heinlein, vigorously suppressing counter-examples. Slusser, therefore, appears to make the anomalous proposal that Heinlein somehow inherited European Puritanism rather than American Puritanism—not impossible, as Heinlein's family emigrated to North America in about 1750, at the very end of the living American Puritan tradition, but highly unlikely nonetheless.

Before turning to Slusser's critique of *Stranger*, the reader should be cautioned: it is nearly impossible to discuss Slusser's ideas in any detail without acknowledging, and finding some way to cope with, a very serious personal failing in his dealing with textual matters: between carelessness with generalizations and the dogmatic requirements of his Calvinist reading, it is often not possible to recognize what Heinlein wrote in what Slusser says about it—or even to guess what Slusser might have been thinking. Statements like:

> "Mike eschews 'possession' and ownership in all forms. Yet his disciples, inspired by more than mere earthly appetites, dream of clandestine control of the world and in the process become a band of super capitalists" (Slusser, *Stranger in His Own Land*, 33)

bear only the most glancing relationship to anything in the book and cannot be squared with statements that *are* in the book—e.g., money is "as abstract as an Old One's thoughts" and a mode of "structured balancing and healing" (both, 236/292) One is often left in a state of confusion, as if Slusser might be talking about some *other* Robert Heinlein, perhaps in some alternate universe.

Slusser's monographs were promptly and loudly rejected in the fan community when they were first published—a circumstance of which Slusser loses no opportunity to complain, supposing that the fans would not countenance criticism of their icon (in view of the amount of iconoclasm in science fiction fandom about the subject of Robert Heinlein, this view is somewhat ludicrous). The truth is, it is extraordinarily difficult to sort the wheat from the chaff in Slusser; for all that, there is good sustaining wheat there.

Slusser sees *Stranger in a Strange Land* as fitting into Heinlein's scheme of subverting the adventure novel by eliding the choices by which an individual grows:

> "Heinlein's first overtly philosophical novel *Stranger in a Strange Land* (1961), goes farther yet. Heinlein goes through an elaborate ritual of formation, produces his 'representative' man, only to drop the mask suddenly—Smith is a superman." (5)[89]

---

89. Let us cope: Although Smith has an "everyman" family name, there is no evidence that Heinlein presents him as "a representative man," though he may represent mankind, symbolically; nor is there any "mask" dropped suddenly. Mike exhibits his Martian powers even before he is brought into Jubal Harshaw's menage; the analogy of the snake conveys that it is a mistake to think of him as harmless; and his powers are relatively fully developed long before Mike begins to collect his church. It is, therefore, difficult to understand what "ritual of formation" subverted by dropping a mask Slusser might be referring to.

Slusser sees the adventure novel (of which he seems to have an excessively rigid notion) as subverted by Jubal Harshaw's legal and diplomatic maneuverings.

"Once sanctuary is reached, things bog down and the action slows to a crawl. What is more, there is a subtle change of focus...In [the ensuing] welter of protocol and legal subtlety, the initial intrigue is hopelessly lost.

"Onto this trunk Heinlein grafts several sections [including] *digressions* on the Fosterite church where satire is mixed with an obvious fascination for the workings of this organization." (30 [emphasis added])

Slusser speculates that the different genres correspond to breaks in the writing of the book, much as *Huckleberry Finn* transforms at the point where Twain abandoned the manuscript for thirteen years. Subsequent research has shown, however, that the main body of *Stranger* was written in only two sessions; the first session does roughly correspond to the adventure-intrigue story, but the second session includes *both* the remaining genres Slusser detects. (Patterson, "Early Chronology," 5). Slusser's notion of the genres is excessively rigid. The transformation of genres is a device of intention, characteristic of the anatomy form, and probably functions to reveal new truths hidden by the apparatus of the abandoned genre, based on the book's dynamic of public hypocrisy and private truth.

Slusser's need to validate the Calvinist reading leads him to do violence to the stated propositions in the text. Mike is clear, for instance, that anyone can learn the Martian language and the attendant powers. All it takes is the will and the work: "A person must start with a willingness to learn and follow it with long, hard study." (403/490) To Slusser, however, the Martian language is a sign of grace reserved for the Elect of Calvinism:

"The Martian tongue is not at all universally accessible; in fact it poses an insurmountable barrier to all but the fortunate few who possess some mysterious insight into its workings." (33)

The statements cannot be reconciled; Slusser simply ignores the direct statements of the text. He multiply repeats the falsity and builds his interpretation of the book around it.

An even more insidious imposition of theory takes place with regard to Calvinist predestination. The notion of destiny appears to be weakly present in Heinlein's body of work because of a mistaken reading of Heinlein's Darwinian evolutionary bias. "Misfit" embodies this bias in story terms: Heinlein supposes that the change of environment (the "punctuation" of Eldridge and Gould's punctuated equilibrium view of evolution) causes characteristics suppressed or not expressed in the old environment to become valuable and blossom in the new. This is biologically orthodox. The exemplary story of those blossoming aspects of human variability in humanity's new cosmic environment may look to the casual observer like a character fulfilling his destiny and therefore be read to imply predestination in the Calvinist sense, but that is a mistaken reading, and Heinlein insisted in response to a direct question that he was not a Calvinist.

Slusser insists on the Calvinist reading by falsifying the contents of the text; the members of the Church of All Worlds are an Elect of Calvinism, he insists, because the new dispensation is not for everyone (contrary to direct statements in the book). The bald assertion "Many struggle and master the letter [i.e., the Martian language], only to be ultimately denied the spirit" is utterly without foundation; there is not an example in the book of someone who went through the effort of learning Martian without also acquiring Martian powers and a place in the Nest. Without these falsifications, the Calvinist reading of *Stranger* falls apart. The natural interpretation of a Jubal Harshaw that groks in fullness without learning Martian is to suppose that he is one of the "hidden elect" of Calvin's *Institutes of the Christian Religion*, Book IV, but this view Slusser cannot take, for he has cast Harshaw as a polar opposite—center to Mike's circumferential philosophy. By the nature of things, in the telepathic Nest there can be no such thing as hidden reprobate. Slusser is forced into positions increasingly absurd: "Heinlein's new religion is archly Puritanical." (36) In the next sentence, Slusser entirely loses contact with the text, discussing "sexual license, body painting, and togetherness orgies" as "strange garbs for fundamentalist religion."[90] He must blind himself, with high art, to what Heinlein states plainly and with high technique, in order to make his predestination argument.

In point of fact, the Calvinist interpretation, with its cumbersome and inapposite apparatus of predestination, is fundamentally wrong for Heinlein. There is one element of Slusser's schema which manifestly does correspond to something in Heinlein, and that is the figure of the Elect, but it is not a figure of the Calvinist Elect. In discussing another of Heinlein's characters, Slusser enumerates the total figure, without realizing the inherent coherence of the "beats" he lays out and that they point to an entirely different religious tradition:

> "He was picked, provided sanctuary, aided by teachers and all the marvels of science, and led by the hand to his final moment of 'recognition.'" (19)

Slusser is describing the process of initiation of a candidate into an esoteric brotherhood. The Initiatic pattern used by secret societies is a persistent feature of the hermetic and NeoPlatonic traditions, and it is a persistent feature in Heinlein's corpus in terms of a secret society of illuminated individuals working for the betterment or protection of humankind (i.e., a White Brotherhood). The Nest of *Stranger in a Strange Land* is just such a white brotherhood—very far, indeed, from a Christian fundamentalist religion, "archly Puritanical"!

---

90. Body painting was a fad that appeared and disappeared late in the 1960s—five years or more after the book was published. There is no body painting in *Stranger*. Slusser has read his extra-textual experience back into the book.

The Calvinist schema is Slusser's great critical failure; but his successes are quite remarkable: the identification of what Slusser calls an "undulatory pattern" in Heinlein's writing is a considerable intellectual achievement.

The basic pattern is to expand upon a center and then contract to a point. The narrative thus gains its impetus, not from the linear demands of a conventional plot, but from the expansion of the kernel. The clearest example in Heinlein is *Have Space Suit—Will Travel*, which begins on earth—and, in fact, in a family, the psychological center of the teenaged hero's experience of himself. Progressively the action expands from the Moon to Vega to a rogue planet in the Lesser Magellanic Cloud. The distance from the center brings with it an expansion of perspective, and finally Kip becomes a representative of all humankind in the cosmic judgment. Thus a thematic progression is carried along with the physical expansion and the narrative develops. At the end, it contracts back to the point, but the contraction carries with it the expansion of perspective: The center of Kip's self has successfully grown out of his family and an adolescent desire to please father and peers.

This center-to-circumference pattern is very persistent in Heinlein until at least *Time Enough for Love* (1973), which contains the master contraction of the Future History: Lazarus Long returns to the Earth of his childhood, to his family of origin, even to his mother.

In *Stranger*, Slusser's application of the undulatory pattern is somewhat less successful. He sees Valentine Michael Smith and Jubal Harshaw as the polar opposites of innocence and experience (the innocent self being the center and experience existing on the periphery of the self) between which the narrative oscillates or undulates, in a dance of acquisition: Mike acquires Jubal's experience, and Jubal acquires Mike's religion—and then *is acquired by* Mike's religion as all collapses into Mike as the center. However interesting such a pattern is to contemplate, it does not put us much forward in understanding the text. Perhaps the gospel/Hero tale pattern superimposed on Heinlein's habitual undulatory pattern restricts his usual play with the pattern.

Slusser's most intriguing intellectual feat, however, lies in the preliminary to his theory: he draws the basic undulatory pattern out of Ralph Waldo Emerson's essays, where we also find the basic pattern of "Thou art God" in his conception of the "Over-Soul," a perennial trope of NeoPlatonist thought. It is quite unfortunate that Slusser does not go on to explore in greater detail the link of Heinlein's literary corpus to the tradition of Transcendentalism, of which Emerson was the leading figure in the U.S.[91] Norman Spinrad, in an article that appeared in French in *Magazine Litteraire* and in English, briefly, on his website (www.nor-

---

91. Although Transcendentalism has been called America's only native philosophy, it was, in fact, an international movement in the middle third of the nineteenth century, with links particularly to Scotland and England.

manspinrad.com), links both Heinlein and the Beats to the Transcendental movement and speculates that the Transcendentalist worldview persisted in the U.S., erupting again in the counterculture of the 1960s—which *Stranger in a Strange Land* specifically influenced.

☙

In 1978, Joseph Olander and Martin Harry Greenberg collected nine substantial academic essays about Heinlein that had appeared in various magazines for Taplinger's *Writers of the 21st Century* series. The editors' introduction to *Robert A. Heinlein* sets forth in relatively cool terms what might be regarded as the "academic" view of Heinlein as thought-provoking but not essentially literary. Again, the viewpoints the editors bring to the work color their description of Heinlein; though the restricted scope of the Introduction makes extended analysis impossible, it is nevertheless possible to identify two clear ideas of "intellectual package dealing" in which alien attitudes are blended in with Heinleinian propositions, apparently unconsciously: "He assumes that man has an evil, aggressive nature" (*Id.,* 8) is a value judgment that would be foreign to Heinlein, who views the basic facts of human nature as morally neutral—a substrate for moral evaluations rather than morally positive in themselves. In the next paragraph the editors characterize Heinlein as portraying a "drive to survive and dominate" (10) that, again, folds a foreign perspective into Heinlein's writing. Survive, the Heinlein character does (most of the time)—but domination is not a significant part of his emotional needs. His will to power is played out in terms of self-actualization and self-determination, often within the context of a group effort at liberation—classically a revolution against tyranny.

Two of the book's essays deal with *Stranger* in a substantial way. Alice Carol Garr's "The Human as Machine Analog: The Big Daddy of Interchangeable Parts in the Fiction of Robert A. Heinlein" (64–82) is followed immediately by Robert Plank's "Omnipotent Cannibals in *Stranger in a Strange Land*" (83–106) The choice of these two essays as the commentary on *Stranger* is quite unfortunate: Garr's essay is barely coherent, and Plank's is the most incompetent Heinlein criticism ever published.

Garr's commentary on *Stranger* is a small section of the essay. She sees Heinlein as personally competing with the universe as a giant, Newtonian machine:

> "It is one thing to regard the human being as a futile creature imprisoned in a
> hostile world, and quite another to see him as part of a system and necessary in kind
> to a cosmic ecology. Possibly this reduction to a component is what is eating at Hei
> nlein's vitals. He has been driven to try to come to terms with it or outdo the
> implied systematic analogy." (65)

Sex is treated by Heinlein as part of an analogy of technology, with interchangeable parts. Mike's Nest is potentially immortal by virtue of its interchangeable sexual parts in a "family" held together—"blessed by association with Mike, by their ritual cannibalism, and by the group sexuality of the love feasts." (77) Sexual attraction is analogical to gravity and magnetism as cosmic forces prompting aggregation. The nuances and "rich variety" of human sex are ignored in favor of the attractive and aggregative power.

Robert Plank begins his essay, "Omnipotent Cannibals in *Stranger in a Strange Land*," by identifying and sifting the novations with which Heinlein has constructed *Stranger*. The structurally important ones he identifies as not the extrapolative novations common to science fiction, but those "in the border areas between sf and fantasy." (84) Mike's psi powers are "the power of achieving any desired change in the real external world by merely wishing it to be so." (85) Immediately, we are in a strange, twilight world of Plank's imagination, related only tangentially to *Stranger*. Heinlein has been quite clear throughout the book that the "psi powers"—many of which are simply yoga—emerge through a combination of correct understanding brought to fruition by intense work—just as the siddhis of Yoga are the result of correct understanding brought to fruition by intense work. We are put on notice that we are reading Plank's imaginative reworking of *Stranger*, and things will only become stranger from this point.

By verbal sleight-of-hand, Mike's innocent preference for nudism becomes "denudative compulsion," which, Plank informs us, is "associated with certain psychotic states." (86) Ben Caxton fled the Nest, not because of moral revulsion, not because of sexual jealousy—not even to provide a convenient opportunity for exposition—but out of "homosexual panic" (86–87). Ben, it appears, was gay all along, though deep in denial (presumably he returns to the Nest to have his denial validated). These random bits of psychoanalytic jargon, forcibly assimilated to the incidents of the book, are pointless, if amusing in their wrongheadedness.

The point of the sexual goings-on in the Nest, Plank then supposes, is to achieve the maximum number of mechanical couplings. "It is surprising," Plank wonders, "that Heinlein allowed this opportunity [of increasing the number of possible combinations by allowing homosexual couplings] to slip through his fingers." (87) This is intended as sarcasm—Plank goes on to derive Caxton's homosexual panic from this exclusion of homosexual pairings in the Nest—but it does illustrate a trope that recurs frequently in Heinlein criticism, though nowhere as densely as it appears here, of a critic exploring the deficiencies of his interpretive or critical schema and imputing the failure to the book—or sometimes to Heinlein personally.

Cannibalism is assigned to a pre-linguistic "oral-aggressive" stage of child development. (97–98) Pointless psychoanalytic jargon is succeeded by pointless anthropology. Plank takes ten pages in exploring two theories of cannibalism in an attempt to determine why *Stranger* was so apparently successful with it—and then spends a part of one paragraph on the third model, which is stated (indirectly) in the text, but which Plank dismisses as "even to think of such a possibility seems absurd." (96)

Plank then returns to the subject of Martian powers, assigning them to the psychoanalytic concept of "omnipotence of thought," (97) which also belongs to a pre-linguistic stage of child development. (98) Although normal people are expected to "grow out of" such a stage, the readers of *Stranger* seem to crave it. How is it possible, Plank wonders, that Heinlein has achieved such an enormous readership? His answer is that the book—a utopian fantasy and not science fiction at all—gives its readers vicarious experience, a vicarious acting out of suppressed power and promiscuity fantasies—not quite as primitive as fantasies of omnipotence. (101) He can make nothing of the necrophagic fantasy. (103)[92]

Stranger works, Plank concludes, as a corruptor:

> "A writer who wants to get a hearing for his embodiment of a primitive fantasy may lull the countervailing forces into inactivity by throwing them the meat of the loftier, more realistic, less primitive aspects of his work. He may say, in substance, to the distrustful superego: Look, I am not pandering to omnipotence or promiscuity. What I really want is to present a picture of the science of the future and of the workings of supranational government, and to demonstrate the shortcomings of Christianity. If I also discuss necrophagy, well, it's an interesting subject and good clean fun, and so remote that it can't do harm! You do not seriously think that I would corrupt your pupil, seeing that he isn't going to become a cannibal whatever I say, is he? This would be the function of the ideological content in works that do not truly want to transcend the fantasies they embody." (105)

This is not a hypothetical statement on Plank's part: "...*Stranger* presents the id with the sweet gratification of its desires, getting license to do so by bribing the superego with pretended interest in nobler thoughts." (106)

The element, of course, that Plank leaves out of his entire approach to *Stranger* is art. In Plank's view, there are no dramatic elements in the work, no purpose other than the didactic—and particularly are there none of the elements of satire, viz, laughter and ridicule. At the very least, this is not a *literary* critique; and in its inability to distinguish between innocence and psychosis, it is not even competent as a psychoanalytic statement.

The almost total collapse of Plank's ability to see *Stranger* as a work of fiction represents an extreme example of what has by now evidenced itself as a "trend" in Heinlein criticism, of critics who look at the work but can see nothing but their own preconceptions, who stand so firmly in their own light that they cannot see Heinlein. Neither Heinlein nor the public has been well served by the critical commentary, especially on *Stranger*.

---

92. Again, an interpretive scheme that fails entirely to address one-third of the elements a critic identifies as important to understanding the book is fatally flawed. At the very least, it needs to be re-thought.

∾

The next substantial commentary to appear was the section (14 pages) devoted to *Stranger* in H. Bruce Franklin's 1980 *Robert A. Heinlein: America as Science Fiction*, written for the Oxford University Press. Series editor Robert Scholes selected Heinlein for treatment as "a major American mythographer," in the structuralist definition of the term in which "myth provides a reconciliation in fictional forms of cultural oppositions too painful to be considered rationally." (*Id.,* viii) Franklin, as a Marxist, is the "ideal critic" to explicate the cultural oppositions Heinlein exemplifies.

> "Heinlein...must be understood as a very representative American because he embodies the contradictions that have been developing in our society ever since the Depression flowed into the Second World War, to understand the phenomenon of Robert Heinlein is finally to understand the culture that is the matrix for ourselves." (6)

Franklin's commentary on *Stranger* is embedded in an extended discussion of the story line, studded with some exaggerations and half-truths that have become traditional in Heinlein criticism, though they have no basis in the text—e.g., Mike is "the most desirable lover in the world" (130), though the text says only that he is devoted and enthusiastic and very good therefor (possibly his Tantric abilities give him an edge); he is "the richest man on earth" (130), though after ceding away his problematical "Larkin rights" (ownership of an entire planet would indeed justify the superlative, but the rights are illusory), he is merely the heir of several not-inconsiderable personal fortunes. Though not insensible to the book's literary or esthetic values, Franklin's concern is with the metaphor of his subtitle, and he concentrates almost exclusively on the *dianoia* ("thought" or thematic philosophy) of the book. He points out structural resonances that constitute technical criticism, between the samples we are given of Jubal Harshaw's commercial writing and his esthetic theory of art that seeks to move the reader to pity or terror (a classical Aristotelian esthetic) or "to divert the tedium of his hours." (326/400) He also notes that the screenplay Jubal is composing as the book ends is titled "A Martian Named Smith," one of the working titles of *Stranger*, so that Heinlein has built in a circular story pattern, ending with the beginning of the story we have just experienced. (133)

Franklin identifies the principal dialectic of the book as the mutual transformation of Mike and Jubal: Mike has been transformed by Jubal, learning how to be a successful huckster with his own brand of popular fiction. Note in this regard that Jubal says of Fosterism that he is "in the same grift"—carnival or half-world argot for a patterned con game—meaning that he sees both pop religion and pop fiction as pragmatically identical in his esthetic evaluation. And Jubal has equally been transformed by Mike—apparently from a popular hack into a serious artist composing a gospel.

Franklin, too, sees Calvinism in Mike's selection of his "disciples" (136), though his comments fit historical Calvinism or historical Puritanism even more poorly than do Slusser's; nor does he seem to grasp the important point that Mike is sifting—not selecting—those who have selected themselves and brought their self-selection to the next stage of their personal evolution. He is acting as a guide and Initiator.

But the book's deepest appeal, Franklin concludes, is in its embodiment of a "quest for community" (137) which will reverse the progress of alienation, narcissism, and solipsism among "free" isolated individuals in the twentieth century. Franklin surveys the nineteenth century American communitarian experiments on which Heinlein draws and concludes, quite correctly, that

> "[t]his yearning for communism[93] restricted to a small elite moves in precisely the opposite direction from the mass revolutionary movements that have characterized our own historical epoch." (138)

This makes Valentine Michael Smith an "ahistorical" and even "anti-historical" figure. It is also "anti-scientific" and "anti-materialistic." (139) This latter quality would generally be regarded as a positive feature of the book; but Franklin's usage is within a conventional framework of Marxist political analysis, in terms of Marx's underlying philosophy of Dialectical Materialism, and they mean something other than what they appear to mean.

In Marxist political theory, history has a strict and deterministic dynamic that leads to the revolution of industrial workers, the establishment of the workers' state, and the classless society, at which point the dialectic ceases and there is an "end of history." This idea exactly corresponds to the Christian notion of the Apocalypse. Mike is "anti-historical" because he comes to rescue us from the inexorable working out of the historical dialectic. In the Christian-Apocalyptic view, this is a good thing because we will enjoy the classless society of Heaven, uniting in adoration of God. In the Marxist-Dialectical Materialist view, this is a bad thing, because it prevents us from enjoying the classless society that will come when the workers' state withers away. It is easy to see why Marxism has been called a Christian (or sometimes Jewish) heresy.

Franklin's factual observations, of an interest in community, are directly on target, though his value-judgments as to their meaning will probably strike most readers as somewhat awry. But his conclusion is also probably something on which most readers may agree:

---

93. The term "communism" was used almost interchangeably with "socialism" in the nineteenth century, before either term had acquired Marxist implications (see, e.g., the quotation from John Humphrey Noyes in Chapter 20). Franklin does not seem to realize that there may be a "yearning for communism" in the American mind which may yet reject Marxism.

"Is there any wonder, then, in the appeal of Michael's message to the dreams of the utopian part of the counterculture, from its origins in the beatnik movement through the flower children and hippies of the 1960s to the cultists of the 1970s." (139)

৵

Anthropologist and H.G. Wells scholar Leon Stover "wrote the book" on Heinlein (literally: *Robert Heinlein*) for *Twayne's United States Authors Series* in 1987. This series consists of general surveys of the careers of various American writers, each written by a prominent scholar. *Robert Heinlein* considers Heinlein as an American writer, and not as a genre writer.

Stover's confessedly conservative approach to Heinlein—though still not an exact fit—yielded the first critical approach to Heinlein that seemed to comprehend at all the kind of person Heinlein was and thus provides, for the first time, a framework for interpretation that shows promise of being able to cope with what sometimes appears to be contradictions in political stances or social attitudes. For all its virtues, however, the book contains a number of errors in description of stories. The errors sometimes do impact the interpretation of individual stories, but one never has the impression that it is some other Heinlein of an alternate and not-quite-parallel universe who is under examination.

Stover approaches *Stranger* as a work of American culture criticism, not as genre product. He notes that "*Stranger* was the first science-fiction novel to place on the national best-seller list published weekly by the Sunday New York *Times*." (*Id.,* 53) In its treatment of sexual matters, *Stranger* falls on a progression from "the extraordinary innocence of Howells' society, through the self-conscious sinning of Dreiser's characters, to the casual promiscuity of Kerouac's beatniks." (53, quoting Nelson Manfred Blake, *Novelists' America: Fiction as History, 1910–1940*. Syracuse, NY: Syracuse University Press, 1969). Heinlein blew the genre-mind by jumping directly from the stage of "Howellsian primness" to Kerouacian promiscuity in one leap—and without adopting "the mainstream's carnal attitude toward sex." (54) Stover's summary of the story line is curiously awry: he has Jubal advising Mike "how to make commercial use of his powers by setting up a profitable religious cult." (55) Stover relates the book's concern with religious hucksterism to Scientology, to Mark Twain's concern about the popular growth of Christian Science, and to Heinlein's own earlier foray into false religion, the 1940 novella "'If This Goes On—'." This illustrates one of the book's real strengths: by converging back on his subject, Stover minimizes the effect of descriptive errors and reinforces his master themes.

Stover addresses the Manson "connection," which, he notes, though it has no factual basis, is accepted as "gospel in the critical literature." (57) The book is no blueprint for murder—or for anything else, for that matter. It stands in a long and distinguished literary tradition:

"To be sure, Valentine Smith is the proverbial Martian, viewing American society from the outside, his cosmic detachment standing for an idealistic viewpoint. He thereby defamiliarizes our accustomed affairs, making them look stranger and stupid, worthy of indictment and fit for radical reform." (57–58)

The culture critique, however, is made by Jubal Harshaw, by way of his tutelage:

"Smith's utopian ideals, then, are derived indirectly from Harshaw, who elicits them point for point against his lessons in culture criticism." (58)

The novel's "real purpose" is to induce "that enhanced sense of American self-awareness." (58)

"The majority of fans, witless hippies aside, sense what Heinlein is doing in his Twain-like watch over their country, as he takes its institutions to task when they make rags of its ideals." (59)

and

"Like Whitman, Twain, and Mencken before him, Heinlein has the confidence to assert the fundamental values of American culture, for all of its failings, on the unabashed premise of its basic superiority. It takes moral courage to uphold that position in these days of cultural relativism." (60)

Questions for Discussion

1. Heinlein criticism seems to be more abuse than literary criticism. Why might this be?

For Further Reading

Blackmore, Tim. "Talking with Strangers: Interrogating the Many Texts That Became Heinlein's *Stranger in a Strange Land.*" *Extrapolation*, Vol. 36, No.2 (Summer 1995), pp. 136–150.

Lawson, John A. "The Strange Flaws in Heinlein's *Stranger in a Strange Land*," *Akos* 1 (May 1969)

McNelly, Willis E. "Linguistic Relativity in Middle High Martian." *Mars, We Love You.* Ed. Jane Hipolito and Willis E. McNelly. New York: Doubleday, 1971

Reno, Shaun. "The Zuni Indian Tribe: A Model for *Stranger in a Strange Land*'s Martian Culture." *Extrapolation*, Vol. 36, No.2 (Summer 1995), pp. 151–158.

Rottensteiner, Franz. "Chewing Gum for the Vulgar." *SF Commentary* 19 (1969)

Samuelson, David N. "Stranger in the Sixties: Model or Mirror?" *Critical Encounters: Writers and Themes in Science Fiction.* Ed. Dick Riley. New York: F. Ungar, 1978.

PART FIVE
"His Happy Destiny"

"Humans are not Martians."

– 22 –
...and Transfiguration:
Stranger as Text

Any book is more than the author's intentions and craft: it is an interaction of the author with the reader, mediated by the text. The author's private subset of the language expresses the first reading of the body of the work that may be partially reconstructed by textual analysis. The author-reading is somewhat—but only slightly—privileged, in the sense that a critic's reading may not *contradict* the superficies of the text—though it may *contain* the text as a special case of a broader interpretive schema—e.g., as the exception that "proves" (meaning "tests") the rule—unless there is good reason to believe the text is not what it appears to be. There is, in fact, a body of modern criticism that proceeds by a process of "falsifying" the superficial reading in order to draw out hidden implications—a process drawn from twentieth century philosophy of science. Deconstruction, also, is intensely interested in the originating text at this stage—not for consideration of the author's deliberate communication, which Derrida calls the *vouloir-dire*, or "command," but for elements unconsciously or undeliberately marginalized or dismissed. Deconstruction seeks to force every work to confront Other. *Stranger* provides an interesting test-case for Deconstruction in that it dismisses and expels itself, all firm opinions being denied and contradicted. In addition, *Stranger* has engendered a number of unique historical readings beyond the *vouloir-dire*. By 1969 the public *Stranger* was capable of surprising its author, of in-coming as other—indeed, as stranger creating its own, strange land.

Public critics often attempt a reconstruction of an author's intentions in order to make value-judgments, particularly about the work and its relations to social norms. This has particularly been the case with *Stranger*. But the real "business" of a work of fiction is the reader's individual interaction with the work—a massively complex set of "moving targets."

A writer may confidently expect to communicate a good deal of his intentions to his contemporaries, who have approximately the same set of public experiences to draw on, and whose private and personal experiences will largely belong in the same ethos or frame of cultural reference. A writer—and most particularly a commercial writer—must first speak to his contemporaries, as Heinlein here says, "to render emotional the reader," moving them to pity and terror (the classical Aristotelian virtues), or at the very least to "divert the tedium of their hours." (326/400)

Most fiction never moves beyond its immediate milieu. Even "stories that will live forever," we have it on Mark Twain's authority, have a lifetime of only about thirty years—the generation of its first readers.

Yet some of Twain's stories are working on their second century and show no sign of losing vital contact with the new audience. New generations of readers continuously recreate the work in contexts wider than the mere monkey recognition of successful or diverting mimesis.

When *Stranger* was released in 1961, it was so far out of the mainstream of genre fiction—or, indeed, of American literature in general—that there was serious doubt it could draw any kind of market. In discussions with his agent before the book was published, Heinlein acknowledged that "it might sell lots of copies" (*Grumbles*, 226) but "I will be unsurprised and only moderately unhappy if it turns out that the result is unsalable." (230) As part of the contract negotiations with Putnam's, Heinlein agreed to allow the book to go early to the Doubleday Science Fiction Book Club, which had a guaranteed minimum sale to its membership and an attractive royalty split between the publishers—though less attractive to the writer. That way, Heinlein reasoned, Putnam's could at least recover costs of printing and distribution. It was, nevertheless, disconcerting to have the Book Club edition issue in June 1961, *before* Putnam's first trade edition (July 1961) (*Grumbles*, 233). Typically, a publisher will want to let the more expensive trade edition have first crack at the market before all other, less expensive editions are allowed to be printed. This was an admission on Putnam's part that they believed *Stranger* would have substantially no audience at all on the general market, though the editor at Putnam's apparently had some confidence in the book.[94]

It sold about as well as science fiction books did sell in 1961—roughly five thousand copies in its initial release: a respectable, if not spectacular sale. It did

---

94. Or at least in the commercial sense of the author. Heinlein had made a legendary amount of money for Scribner's during the 1950s. This confidence was justified when the book went into numerous reprints. Although there are numerous "revised and corrected editions" among other authors, that this book continues to sell in two different editions—the "as published" and the "director's cut"—which compete *successfully* with each other is a fact almost without parallel in modern publishing.

cause some stir in the science fiction community and received the Best Novel Hugo Award for 1961. His last book, *Starship Troopers*, had received the 1959 Best Novel Hugo and generated furious controversy among science fiction readers. No doubt the strength of Heinlein's literary reputation within the genre helped sustain the sales figures in the initial release. The SF Book Club contract ran for two years and then was renewed. In 1963 the book went into paperback.

Science fiction books (and *Stranger* had been marketed as science fiction) tend to have a relatively long shelf-life—though that fact was not yet known to publishers in 1961. *Stranger* completed its initial release. Putnam's made a little money on it, so Heinlein knew it demonstrated that he could write "my own stuff, my own way" and make a living at it. He might never again have the sales and financial stability he had with the Scribner's juvenile series, but he also would not have to fight with librarians and editors over material suitable for young readers. It was a successful book in a minor way. Heinlein moved on to other things. In 1962 he wrote a kind of juvenile for Putnam's (*Podkayne of Mars*), because he knew Putnam's had hoped to take over the commercial strength of the Scribner's juveniles. Then *Glory Road* (1963), a Cabellian comedy in the sword-and-sorcery tradition; *Farnham's Freehold* (1965), and *The Moon Is a Harsh Mistress* (1966), a recapitulation of the American Revolution set on the Moon colonized as a prison. No book was remotely like any of the others. He stabilized financially and even did well enough to move from Colorado Springs, Colorado, and build a house he designed himself among the redwoods outside Santa Cruz, California.

But a seed had been sown with *Stranger*, and the ground was not quite so stony as it first appeared. Heinlein had "thought that the parables in it might take hold, too, at least for some readers" (*Grumbles*, 245), and they gradually did. As early as 1966, it was clear that something quite unusual was happening with *Stranger*:

> "The fan mail on this book has been steadily increasing instead of decreasing and it clearly is enjoying quite a lot of word-of-mouth advertising...I am getting letters from people who insist on looking at me as some sort of a spiritual adviser. (I fight shy of them!) All in all, the ripples are spreading amazingly." (*Grumbles*, 235–236)

By 1967, the ripples had broached America's cultural life. There were new reviews (six years after publication!), invitations to speak about the book, inquiries from Hollywood, a magazine of literary/culture criticism titled *Grok*—the word was even appearing in advertising; university level classes in science fiction were appearing for the first time, teaching from *Stranger*. Demand for the book was increasing instead of decreasing, but Putnam's would not reissue it. Conventional marketing wisdom in the publishing industry had it that you could not make money with a hardcover reissue after the initial sales decline had begun, and that all subsequent income would come from paperback sales. But they were not printing enough paperbacks to satisfy the demand. Figures, images, words from the book were circulating by word of mouth.

"A young woman...asked me where I had gotten the word *grok*—no, she had not read the book, had not been able to lay hands on a copy...but that she knew what it meant as 'everybody uses it now.'" (*Grumbles*, 237)

What on earth—or on Mars!—was going on?

The short answer is that a perennial part of American society was reasserting itself after two decades of suppression. Americans have had a continuous effervescence of communitarian experimentation. The Puritans of new England were only the first in a series of religiously-based intentional communities. The Shakers, still barely hanging on after two hundred years, are another example. During the 1800s, a wave of German Anabaptist immigration—Hutterites, Mennonites, Amish—swept into the country.

Secular and non-Marxist, socialist communities were formed during the 1840s and 1850s: Robert Owens' community, New Harmony; Fourierite Phalanxes; the home-grown and immensely influential Brook Farm;[95] Josiah Warren's Modern Times; Anaheim, California, now the home of Disneyland, was originally formed as an intentional community of German "mechanics" from San Francisco.[96]

The religious and secular trends were combined in the Oneida Colony. Its founder, John Humphrey Noyes, deliberately combined Christianity and Saint-Simonian socialism to come up with the Oneida ideology. Into this mix he tossed in an American strain of sex radicalism that had been started by the Second Great Awakening (revival) of the early nineteenth century, which fed also into Mormonism. The Oneida Colony was not only an intentional community—it was a group marriage.

This trend slowly waned due to persecution, silliness (the community Home, outside Seattle, self-destructed over the issue of skinny-dipping), economics, war, and, finally and fatally, the capture of American radicalism by Marxist-Leninism.[97]

In the years immediately following World War II, American society had taken on "conformism" as a way of coping with the enormous internal social changes going on. Some of those changes were the end result of trends that had been gathering force for decades: World War II was, for example, the end of the period in which America went from being 80% rural to 80% urban. The Great Depression had put an end to one era of sexual experimentation, but the impulses that encouraged liberalization of social mores were just in abeyance. Other changes

---

95. William Channing, Horace Greeley, Ralph Waldo Emerson, Nathaniel Hawthorne, and Charles A. Dana are only a few of the many mid-nineteenth Century American intellectuals who visited or lived at Brook farm.

96. Who says God doesn't have a sense of humor?

97. In one of the greatest ironies of all time, the American Communist Party was founded in the meeting hall of the Industrial Workers of the World. The IWW was, later, effectively killed by the cuckoo it had hatched in its own nest.

came about in response to the conditions of the war: wartime production demands had put America's industrial base on a modern footing. The old tradition that jobs were scarce and hard to find died, and America gained a permanent, critical labor shortage. The post-war world was clearly different from the world of the 1930s.

Highways and automobile transportation made it possible for the middle-class to live outside urban cores, and the suburbanization of America took place, housing developments trying to re-create on a much lower scale the country homes of the wealthy in the early part of the century. However awry it may have gone, the movement to the suburbs was a utopian movement in just the way that the settlement of the Ohio Valley had been 120 years earlier when settlers fled the crowded and banker-dominated cities of the eastern seaboard.

One aspect of the post-war social change that has been fairly thoroughly explored is the oppression of women. At the immediate end of the War, when government and industrialists alike were still operating in the job-scarcity paradigm of the Depression years, there was a major and deliberate effort to get women out of the labor force to make way for returning soldiers. Women were encouraged—by being fired from their positions, by magazine articles and advertising images, and by the perceived desires of their returning men-folk—to turn inward to the home and devote the energies unleashed in industry during the war to transforming Rosie the Riveter into a domestic engineer-*cum*-sex kitten for the nuclear family. And for the first time in American history, the nuclear family now meant the husband and children *only*. The flight to the suburbs had finally broken up the traditional extended family. Now all the "little boxes made of ticky tacky" housed isolated groupings of individuals cut off from their traditional psychological and social support systems. The bizarre and iconic image of Donna Reed or Mrs. Ward Cleaver doing housework in black cocktail dress and pearls expresses the contradictions of the era in its image of itself.

All of these factors fed into conformism, experienced as an unacknowledged psychological pressure. To this date the era of the 1950s is viewed with two very different emotional values: in one picture, the 1950s was an idyllic period (punctuated, it is true, by terror of atomic bombs falling from the sky). In the other picture, the 1950s was a period of alienation, of "The Man in the Gray Flannel Suit" slowly going to pieces amid the accoutrements of wealth and power. Both pictures are "true." The social pressures separated individuals from their extended family setting, forced the marital focus intolerably inward, and reshaped the individual into a cog in a rational social-industrial machine. At first, it was only individuals that opted out of the flow: cranks, misfits, and rebels. A society's cranks and misfits are the miners' canaries that warn of social problems. In our time we have gangs and Goths; in the late 1940s, there were a few bright individuals with nervous energy shuttling back and forth across the new highways, from New York to San Francisco, driven to *do something* but unable to commit themselves to the values of their society. At the core of this social group were two writers with a mutual muse. Jack Kerouac's *On the Road* and Allen Ginsberg's "Howl" perfectly embody the Beat pained rejection of the dominant values of their society and show, by way of opposition, what was felt to be missing. When a social movement becomes pronounced, its polar opposite comes about by a dialectical process of supplying the elements that are left out of the mainstream movement. When *On the Road* was written in 1951 (Kerouac coined the term "Beat Generation" to express a combination of "beaten-down" combined with "beatific"), the stirrings of discontent in the culture at large were too small to need expression; by the time "Howl" (Allen Ginsburg) was published in 1956, followed by *On the Road* in 1957, they expressed feelings that had already been voiceless too long.

The Beat writers (including William S. Burroughs) are noted for developing a highly mannered style that expresses a raw, improvisational quality, deliberately incorporating suppressed and disowned elements of experience—Jazz music, Buddhism, sex, mysticism, and drugs. Science fiction writer Norman Spinrad links this search for and insistence upon the immediacy of experience to the American Transcendentalist movement:

> "Religion has nothing to do with uptight Christian morality and everything to do with Eastern concepts of satoric transcendence, meaning, among other things, that sex, drugs, and yes, jazz and rock and roll, can be functional sacraments of the godhead...

> "Disreputable as it might be, this mystical libidinal anarchism was as American as Mom and Apple Pie, as old as the myth of the West, as the American transcendentalists of the nineteenth century."

Spinrad points out that Robert Heinlein also stands firmly in the same tradition—though the mechanics of his life in his mid-fifties were as far from the Beat Experience as it is possible to imagine.

As the Beat Generation became a media phenomenon, the "Beatnik" became a social norm to which young people gravitated in the late 1950s, the groupings still centered in New York's Greenwich Village and around Lawrence Ferlinghetti's City Lights Bookstore in San Francisco.[98]

On college campuses, the Beat interest in Buddhism was reflected in student interest in Alan Watts' popularizations of Buddhism and in Hermann Hesse's fictionalized life of Gautama Buddha, *Siddhartha*, as supply a missing element in the conventional worldview. Other missing pieces and disowned bits they found in J.R.R. Tolkien's mythopoeic fantasies of Middle Earth, then circulating in pirated paperbacks, the originals having gone long out of print; in Frank Herbert's *Dune*

---

98. It was a youthful ambition of one of the authors to become a Beatnik when he grew up. Fortunately or unfortunately, he never grew up and so failed, unlike a Horatio Alger character, to "make good."

series; in the call of Thoreau's *Walden* to "simplify, simplify, simplify!"; and in *Stranger in a Strange Land*. By the middle of the decade,

> "it had become a cult book popular among students attracted to its counterculture critique of bourgeois social mores, its argument for free love, and its celebration of an altered state of consciousness." (Singleton, 684)

As the college students of the pre-1965 era left the relative cloister of the campus, they turned it over to political activism, and particularly the anti (Vietnam) war movement. But enough of them opted out of the corporate, "gray flannel" track to form a noticeable enclave in San Francisco, where social columnist Herb Caen dubbed them "hippies." Soon there were thousands of hippies gathering in San Francisco and in other cities, forming a counter-economy and finally a counter-culture. "The performance of the text, mediated by language, became the performance of people in the political and social world of the 1960s counterculture." (Blackmore, 141)

In de-emphasizing the competitive, the mechanical, and the hierarchical, the counterculture emphasized instead the personal and the communitarian—for which *Stranger* suggested some useful social rituals. The language of water-sharing spread rapidly throughout the counterculture, shared even by the weekend hippies who lived halfway in the old world of experience and the forming society of innocence. Heinlein found himself positioned, appropriately but quite unintentionally, among those "adult radicals" and "middle class revolutionaries" Theodore Roszak (*The Making of a Counter Culture*, 1969) saw as resembling "the bourgeois intellectual in Marxist theory." (34) Shut out from the self-empowering revolutions happening elsewhere and among other classes, they find:

> "On the other hand, the disaffected middle-class young are at hand, suffering a strange new kind of 'immiseration' that comes of being stranded between a permissive childhood and an obnoxiously conformist adulthood, experimenting desperately with new ways of growing up self-respectfully into a world they despise, calling for help. So the radical adults bid to become gurus to the alienated young or perhaps the young draft them into service." (35)

Heinlein, drafted as a personal guru, refused to serve. But *Stranger* was out in the world and was adopted—not entirely inappropriately—as a powerful voice of the "ethos of disaffiliation" from the conformist, mechanist mainstream, the process Marxist social critic Herbert Marcuse called "the Great Refusal."

These formulations cast the process in terms of negatives, rejections, refusals, but the process is a positive one, of building a lifestyle outside the dampening folkways of the mainstream.

> "So how *do* you grow up? Where is the life-sustaining receptacle that can nourish and protect good citizenship?

"The answer is: you make up a community of those you love and respect, where there can be enduring friendships, children and, by mutual aid, three meals a day scraped together by honorable and enjoyable labor. Nobody knows quite how it is to be done. There are not many reliable models... It will take a deal of improvisation, using whatever examples one can find at hand... And where else can one any longer look for the beginnings of an honest revolution except in such 'pre-revolutionary structure-making' (as Buber calls it [in *Paths in Utopia*])" (Roszak, 203)

Stranger coincidentally provided one such model.

The Flower Power generation brought a powerful and divergent worldview to bear on their shared creation of *Stranger*-as-text, and their reading differs in several critical aspects from the author-reading and the science-fiction community reading, as the quotation above from *America in the Sixties*, an encyclopedic reference work, illustrates. It is difficult, for example, to see how *Stranger* might be viewed as a celebration of "an altered state of consciousness" in reference to psychotropic and hallucinogenic drugs in light of obvious disapproving statements in the book (e.g., Jubal's "I'd rather see Mike smoking marijuana than be converted by Digby." [261/323]). But the readers of the late 1960s incorporated their own life-experience into their reading, the "need of the young for unrestricted joy" (Roszak, 39), identifying the Nest and its spiritual and sexual customs as an idealized image of the qualities they wanted to achieve in their own lives. They "backformed" their reading to incorporate their new cultural experiences. The Flower Children reading of *Stranger* was as a myth of acceptance and affirmation.

This process of backformation is exactly the same thing we do in creating our individual, contemporary reading: we cannot possibly any longer see the endogamous sexual liberalism of the Nest as a call to the barricades, as the Flower Children did; nor can it be "simply" an *epater les bourgeoisie*, as, perhaps, Heinlein viewed it, *vouloir-dire*, when he wrote it in 1959 and 1960. We bring a different set of associations to our reading. That particular revolution is a fact accomplished and abandoned in the light of the harsh realities of STDs including AIDS. A new reader might view that same sexual openness in a rather Wellsian light, as a utopian vision of what might follow on the final technological conquest of AIDS.

In 1969, Berkeley Books brought out a new paperback and sold literally hundreds of thousands of copies—a quarter million copies that year alone. Rock concerts at Woodstock and Altamont demonstrated to the public that the peace-and-love counterculture had a dark underside of parasitism extending beyond the mere "ripoff." As *Stranger* was read as an exemplar of the fair side of the counterculture, so, too, did it come to be read as an exemplar of its dark side.

In August 1969, actress Sharon Tate and four guests at her home in the canyons north of Beverly Hills were butchered in what newspapers headlined as "ritual murders." The killings were gruesome, barbaric—demonic. The words "Helter Skelter" were scrawled in blood on one of the walls. That was the title of a Beatles' song from the *White Album*. The next day a middle-aged couple near

Griffith park, Leno and Rosemary LaBianca, were murdered in similar style, the words "Healter Skelter" [sic] written in blood on the refrigerator. The brutal murder of Sharon Tate made headlines everywhere, but it was particularly shocking to Heinlein, who had just become acquainted with Tate and her husband, director Roman Polanski, when they had been guests together at a film festival in Rio de Janeiro that spring. The Heinleins were a gregarious couple, and they collected new friends everywhere they went. The Polanskis were among their newest friends. But it was not their acquaintance with the Polanskis that formed the connection. The police investigations over the course of several months led to the arrest and eventual trial of Charles Manson and several members of his "Family." One of the girls had appealed to Heinlein in a letter for help with police harassment. She saw Heinlein as a personal guru—a role which he rejected, though he tried to assist.

In January 1970, while Heinlein was hospitalized with a life-threatening case of peritonitis, the San Francisco *Chronicle* ran an unsigned story linking the Tate-LaBianca murders to *Stranger*, saying Manson had murdered "by the book." The story was picked up by *Time* magazine and ran nationally.

Over the years Manson has several times told inquirers that he had never read *Stranger*. He does not in fact read at all for pleasure. When he was in San Francisco, his "girls" had read *Stranger* and had used the jargon of water sharing. He had picked it up from them, though after he moved to Los Angeles in 1967, water-ritual took a backseat to obsessions with Los Angeles death cults, the Beatles *White Album*, and a coming race war coded "Helter Skelter." When the *Time* story broke, the prosecutor's office in Los Angeles, led by Vincent Bugliosi, investigated it and concluded that there was nothing to the story, no more than a coincidental connection with a popular book. It was not made a part of the prosecution case at trial. The index to Bugliosi's exhaustive 1974 book about the trial *Helter Skelter* does not even contain an index entry for Heinlein or for *Stranger* (though it does have an entry for L. Ron Hubbard). An assisting attorney, Deputy District Attorney Steven Kay,[99] disagreed and rushed into print in 1971 with a sensationalist book co-authored with Ed Sanders, *The Family: The Story of Charles Manson's Dune Buggy Attack Battalion*, which built on the *Chronicle* and *Time* stories (though the descriptions of the book sound like third-hand retellings of a book neither Kay nor Sanders had ever read).

Trying to come to terms with this enormity, the traditional Apollonian-demonic orientation of mainstream society reasserted itself in rejection of the

99. In one of history's little ironies, Kay had a more direct connection to The Family than did Heinlein: he had dated one of the Manson girls, Sandra Good—one of the Family members who had written to Heinlein for help.

Dionysian-innocence reading of *Stranger* among the Flower Children. A *pharma-kos*-reading[100] of *Stranger* has come into being: the Tate-LaBianca murders are seen as direct consequences of the philosophy embedded in *Stranger*. The histori-cal events are re-cast in terms of the literary tradition of classical tragedy, making *Stranger*—and in some extreme (and, frankly, unbalanced) readings, Heinlein per-sonally—into a tragic *pharmakos* that can be distanced, rejected, driven out so that society's wounds may heal in tragic catharsis. This reading superimposes on the text a myth of distancing, denial, rejection.

The demonic, *pharmakos*-reading is a symmetrical mirror-image of the Flower Children's myth of acceptance and integration—though necessarily far more dis-torted in terms of its relations to the author's *vouloir-dire*.

These mirror-image readings of *Stranger* as social text—as a song of Dionysian innocence and then of demonic experience—bracket the counterculture of the 1960s. The Tate-LaBianca murders were but an early movement in a dialectical process of social evolution.

Why *Stranger*, and Heinlein individually, was—and is—made a scapegoat for the excesses of the counterculture, is both easy and difficult. First, it was done because it was possible. Making the Beatles, or their *White Album*, or the song "Helter Skelter" the scapegoat would strike too close to home. The Beatles were not only a pop icon, they were central to the era's self-consciousness. If they were rejected, then *everything* had to be rejected—and that prospect couldn't be faced. *Stranger* was "in" enough to be acknowledged, but also far enough "out" to be disowned.

Second, naïve readings of *Stranger* are doubtless earnest and well intended, but they are misinterpretations. In one naïve reading, the nascent Feminist Movement extended its critique of the counterculture sexual subjugation of women to *Stranger*, where it is simply out of place. In this reading, women have no place other than the bedroom; they find their highest value in pleasuring men. Forcing the reading of *Stranger* into this restrictive mold casts off much of the book's most important material.

The most pernicious of the naïve readings of *Stranger* is as "directions for liv-ing" instead of satirical questioning. *Stranger* could not possibly be put into prac-tice, without some real-life equivalent of Martian. Why this reading existed in the first place is a mystery: Heinlein time and again reiterates that the only reason the

---

100. In the traditional poetics of classical tragedy, a *pharmakos* is a tragic victim cast out of soci-ety to purge it of an evil. Sometimes the term is translated "scapegoat," after the Hebrew tradition of symbolically heaping the sins of the community on a sacrificial goat and driv-ing it out of the community and into the desert. The *pharmakos* is the dominant literary and mythic image of Christ's passion: he voluntarily takes on the sins of the world and thus redeems mankind from original sin. He marks the transition from the old law of fear to the new law of love. Valentine Michael Smith preaches to the crowd about fear and concludes his martyrdom with "I love you."

Nest can exist is Mike's knowledge of Martian—but the reading did (and does) flourish. Why *Stranger* is reviled for "being unworkable and utopian" when its basis is impossible—after all, there isn't a Martian/English–English/Martian dictionary—is, well, strange.

Finally, there were those who read it and were repulsed. Heinlein certainly attacked sacred cows, and those with gored oxen felt compelled to retaliate. Everything Heinlein attacked had its defenders, and the defense was loud and shrill. Theologians to atheists, Marxists to Republicans, radical feminists to *Kinder/Kirche/Kuchen*-ists attacked the book, and Heinlein personally, with arguments as diverse as the defenders'.

By 1974, the outer flourishes of the counterculture had disappeared from media attention, mutating into the Human Potential Movement of the 1970s, and contributing to the re-emergence of disciplines such as Cognitive Psychology and Transpersonal Psychology in the 1980s and 1990s. Organizations such as the Church of All Worlds, founded in the early 1970s, still survive, though the dogmatic drift has gone from Gaia to neopaganism in the interim.

So strongly defined, by opposition, was the counterculture that it is tempting to identify *Stranger* exclusively with that period and those ideas. The fact that critics have seized on one book, written years before the fact, to symbolize the hopeful beginning of the counterculture and its monstrous end signifies the robustness of the book, but does not begin to exhaust it.

✍

Stranger in a Strange Land has never been out of print. In 1991, three years after Heinlein's death, in response to a crescendo of reader demand, Virginia Heinlein authorized publication of the as-written, uncut version of *Stranger*, at 220,000 words nearly a third longer than the version that moved so many young people in the 1960s. Despite the fact that there is no startling new material, the uncut version has for ten years been continuously in print, in direct commercial competition with the traditional version—a remarkable phenomenon, almost completely without parallel in literary history.

Stranger continues to "speak to our condition," as may be seen in the readers' comments posted on the Amazon.com website. Amazon.com encourages users to write book reviews, and there are hundreds of reviews of *Stranger*, running from "this book changed my life" to "don't see what the fuss is about" to "worst tripe I've ever read."

It can only be that, as Heinlein had hoped, some of the parables did take hold, with some people. *Stranger* speaks to that perennial part of the American mind that values community and love and affirms the rightness of the unacknowledged pain we numb ourselves to in the practice of hypocrisy. In the perspective of history, it may be argued that the counterculture's adoration of *Stranger* was an aberration—too much acceptance, too uncritical, too fast—and only now is *Stranger in a Strange Land* settling into the permanent role Heinlein had hoped for it from the start: an asker of hard questions—a deliberate provoker of outrage—a moment of illumination about us and our society frozen in time for examination and for grokking. There is no likelihood that it will date and become irrelevant, for it addresses hypocrisy, which is with us ever.

Never thirst.

"My God, what some people will do for money!"

Questions for Discussion

1. What do you think of the living arrangements described for Mike's Nest? Would you like to try something like that one day?

2. Would you keep some of the rituals and language of *Stranger*, even if you don't want to live in a Nest?

3. Now talk about grok. Do you grok grok?

For Further Reading

Roszak, Theodore. The Making of A Counter Culture: Reflections on the Technocratic Society and Its Youthful Opposition. Garden City, New York: Doubleday & Co., Inc., 1969

Blackmore, Tim. "Talking with Strangers: Interrogating the many texts of *Stranger in a Strange Land.*" *Extrapolation* (June 1995)

Appendix:
The Significance of Names in *Stranger*

Heinlein always chose his characters' names with care. Sometimes the names are allegorical descriptions of something going on in the story. In *The Number of the Beast* (1980), for example, he plays Cabellian anagram games with versions of his own name for the villains, showing that the author is the Beast. In one memorable instance—*The Moon Is a Harsh Mistress*—the names of the principal characters contain a capsule description of the entire story. Bernardo is the St. Bernard who preached the crusades of the twelfth century; this new preacher who "professes" the lunar crusade of the twenty-first century is also the professor of the peace ("Paz" means "peace" in Spanish). The response of the Loonies is initially lukewarm but tending to "Wye Knott," a joke made explicitly in the book. Their conspiracy is carried out by the "hand" of Manuel (from the Latin "manus" meaning "hand"), and almost the first thing Manny does in the book is to change from his "social arm" to his "working arm." Manny lost his arm in a mining accident years before the story started, and his prosthetics are machines. His most important prosthetic/machine "arm" is the computer Mycroft H.O.L.M.E.S.—Mycroft Holmes being Sherlock Holmes' smarter brother who solved mysteries by pure cogitation, never venturing out of his club. Like Mycroft Holmes, Mycroft H.O.L.M.E.S. was a fair dinkum thinkum.[101]

The character names of *Stranger in a Strange Land* were also chosen carefully, functioning to bring in many associations, to build richness of subtext into the

---

101. And yet another Michael (Mike) "who is like God."

book. Tracing out the associations referenced by names leads one into many strange byways and illuminates the rich landscape of Heinlein's mind. They bring home forcefully just how *artistic* an artist Heinlein could be.[102]

Valentine Michael Smith

Valentine Michael Smith's name looks superficially like one of Heinlein's common-man/historical figure combinations, like Woodrow Wilson Smith or Andrew Jackson Libby. Certainly the family name "Smith" is probably intended to stand for or symbolically represent everyman—though it equally may refer to Joseph Smith, founder of the Church of Jesus Christ of the Latter-Day Saints (Mormons). But there is no historical Valentine Michael to complete Heinlein's universal-with-particular combination. These two names (Valentine and Michael) are joined together for their religious associations.

The name "Michael" is a Hebrew phrase of praise and wonder: "who is like God!" meaning no one is like God: He surpasses everyone. In terms of the satire, the phrase is inverted to mean that Valentine Michael is not only *like* God, he *is* God. Thou, in fact, art God.

Valentine Michael Smith is also the Archangel Michael. Milton's *Paradise Lost* dramatizes a war in heaven that takes place at the beginning of time, among the angelic forces of Lucifer and the forces of God. Before the war, Lucifer is the most favored of God's creations, ruling all the cosmos jointly with Gabriel and Michael. But he rebels against the divine authority, saying *non serviam*—"I will not serve." He loses the war and is cast out of Heaven. Michael led the Heavenly forces and is therefore the emblem of the (Christian) Church Militant, the church orthodox and in defense of conservative social values.

The name "Valentine" gives an obvious association with St. Valentine's Day and therefore with erotic love. The cupids of Valentine's Day cards, in fact, are the Roman version of the Greek god Eros. Read together, the names Valentine and Michael encapsulate the two satiric subjects of the book, sex and religion. Valentine, however, has other historical associations particularly appropriate for *Stranger*.

There are at least eight Saints Valentine of the early Christian church listed in *The Catholic Encyclopedia*. One was a candidate for the bishopric of Rome in 189 C.E., losing to Pope Victor. At that time, the See of Rome was not the head of the universal ("catholic" means "universal") Christian church—just one bishopric among many, most of them in Asia Minor. Before about 200 C.E., there were essentially three different Christian churches: the orthodox Nazarenes, among

102. Special acknowledgment and thanks must be extended to the efforts of the Internet Heinlein Readers Group, and in particular to its leader, David Silver, for their concerted efforts in 2000 to turn up fresh information and fresh viewpoints on the question of character names.

whom were the descendants of Jesus' immediate family, kept to the Mosaic law and were therefore excluded from Roman civic life. A branch of the Nazarenes gave up the Mosaic law in order to enter the mainstream of Roman public life. This branch eventually hooked up with the churches founded in Greece and Rome and eventually became the Roman Catholic and Greek Orthodox Churches.

The third Christian church has come to be called "gnostic." By the third century C.E., the Gnostic Christian church was followed by about a third of all Christians. The name of Valentine is associated with the Gnostic-Christian church.

The core gnostic teaching is of knowledge by direct experience (*gnosis*). Christ is alive in each individual and can be directly experienced. Gnostics practiced the equality of women, and some Gnostic-Christian congregations may have practiced a group-marriage form of communism perhaps somewhat like the Oneida colony of the mid-nineteenth century. It is probably for this reason that they were labeled orgiasts and libertines by the more conservative branches of Christianity. It is difficult to determine what Gnostic-Christian social practices might actually have been because their history was later wiped out. Certainly, they assimilated Christian teachings to the predominant mystic traditions of the Hellenistic world, including the teachings of Mani, which had become the heretical philosophy of Manichaeanism. As the See of Rome, with its assimilationist Nazarene bias, gained ascendency after about 200 C.E., Gnosticism was declared heretical. St. Valentine's Day was named for the most prominent of the gnostic leaders of the third century C.E.—a martyr killed on February 14, 269, C.E. by Emperor Claudius II for secretly marrying Roman soldiers forbidden to marry. Valentine's final message to his lover was signed "from your Valentine"—a phrase that was to become very familiar in the twentieth century.)

The Christian church we recognize in its historical place dominating the Middle Ages did not come into existence until the 4th century C.E.—specifically with the Council of Nicea (325 C.E.), and the enunciation of the Nicene Creed.

Valentine Michael Smith contains within everyman (Smith) both the radical/heterodox (Valentine) and the orthodox/conservative (Michael)—but the sexual/gnostic Valentine comes first.

Jubal Harshaw

Jubal Harshaw is one of the deepest characters Heinlein ever created, and there are layers upon layers of meaning in his name, with no indication we are anywhere near a complete understanding of what goes into him. What follows is just a light scratch on the surface of some rather surprising material. Jubal starts where *Candide* leaves off; we find him cultivating his garden.

No one has proposed any significance to the Harshaw last name. The interesting material relates to the name "Jubal."

Two lines of research have turned up bits of information. The first is Biblical references in *Genesis*. Jubal is the "father of all who know music," and he is traditionally referred to as a patron of makers of musical instruments. Hence the references in the book to "father Jubal." Music is a Dionysian art, so this is a hint that Jubal contains the Dionysian within him, as well as his obvious Apollonianism and appreciation of the Apollonian art of sculpture.

The ethos of music has been taken over in our time by fiction, and a maker of musical instruments would translate to a maker of printing equipment. It is quite possible that Jubal is an indirect evocation of one of Heinlein's particular literary heroes, Mark Twain. Twain was a printer in his earliest job and later a successful publisher of subscription books. He nearly bankrupted himself underwriting the Paige typesetting machine. This would be very circumstantial if it were not for other details—e.g., Twain famously dictated much of his writing after 1905 to a succession of three typists, for instance.

However, Twain is not the model for Jubal's physical appearance. Jubal is described as bald and pot-bellied with scrawny limbs, which is a physical type Heinlein has used over and over for his wisdom figures. It is probably an approving portrait of Alfred Korzybski—though there is a remote possibility that it refers to Aleister Crowley.[103] It is implied that Jubal is in his nineties or late eighties at the time of *Stranger*; both Korzybski and Crowley were born in the late 1870s and would, therefore, have been in the same age range around the time of the publication of *Stranger* (if they had not both already died).

Heinlein's own work notes for *Stranger* show that the character was built up from that of Kettle Belly Baldwin in "Gulf," combined with the sybaritic lifestyle of Erle Stanley Gardner (author of the Perry Mason mysteries)—in particular the "hot and cold running secretaries" of Jubal's Poconos house is taken from the reportage about Gardner's menage in the national magazines.

The other line of research develops out of the Biblical and leads toward Freemasonry. Jubal in *Genesis* is the brother of Tubal-cain. Tubal-cain is a name that is said to appear once in a Masonic ritual, but there seems to be no significance in *Stranger* to this fact. In *The White Goddess*, Robert Graves mentions Tubal-cain as a Kettian goat-god. The Masonic reference is confusingly associated with a reference to Hiram Abiff, the traditional architect of the Temple of Solomon. These characters would have lived centuries apart.

Heinlein is known to have been interested in Freemasonry as a young man, though no application he may have submitted has been found to have been finalized. Mrs. Heinlein has said that by the time he was able to afford to become a Mason he had moved on to other things. But it was clearly a subject of some

---

103. According to some traditions, Aleister Crowley is the most important magic-worker of the twentieth century. His principal affiliations were with nineteenth century hermetic groups such as the Order of the Golden Dawn and Order of the Silver Star, but in 1909 he founded the separate religion of Thelema ("great soul"). Crowley in his public persona took great delight in twitting Christians, and he sarcastically billed himself for newspaper reporters as "the wickedest man alive."

interest to him at one time, as references to Freemasonry appear in several of his early stories (e.g., Prof. Frost's mention of "The Great Architect" in "Elsewhen" and the important role a Masonic lodge plays in "If This Goes On—"). However, a great deal of Masonic ceremonial has been published and is widely available, so there is no particular implication that Heinlein was privy to secret information.

An essay titled "Whence Came the Stranger: Tracking the MetaPattern of *Stranger in a Strange Land*" by Adam Walks Between Worlds, however, makes an interesting connection of Jubal with Freemasonry by way of the Knights Templar. The essay was originally published by the neo-pagan Church of All Worlds magazine *Green Egg*, but is available online through www.wegrokit.com.

There is no actual evidence that European Freemasonry was ever connected with Templarism, but a highly romantic mythology was created in the nineteenth century linking them, which has become part of the pop mythology of Freemasonry. Briefly, the Knights Templar were a crusading order created in the twelfth century to collect assets in Europe for a crusade to take and hold the Holy Land, particularly Jerusalem, from the Moslems—a project they were briefly successful in doing. When the Moslems retook the Kingdom of Jerusalem (1291) the Order continued its existence, collecting money for a return engagement (which never materialized). They also did a brisk business in holy relics, pieces of the True Cross, etc. They used the money from their various collections and ventures to underwrite banking activities, heavily subsidizing the French throne until Philip the Fair got the idea to get out from under the debt by having the order disbanded and confiscating their assets. On one Friday (the thirteenth of October 1314—which is how the Friday the 13th legend got started) he ordered the arrest of all the 2,000 Templars in France and started a witch hunt against the order, accusing them of satanic and heathen practices. At the time, the Papacy was under the thumb of the French throne, and all of Christendom was ordered to comply with the persecution, though other countries were notably lukewarm to what they saw as bullying by France and never extracted any of the confessions gotten by torture and publicized in France. There are three historical treatments of the trials, all French, the latest of which mixes the Templars up with the violent anti-Cathar crusade a hundred years before the Templars were disbanded. The Cathars (Albigensians) were heretics, incidentally, in the south of France who revived a lot of St. Valentine's gnostic-antinomian doctrines. They were massacred in 1224 in a famous incident in which they were herded into their church and it was burned to the ground. It was pointed out that not everybody in the church was a heretic. "Kill them all," the leader of the crusade, Simon de Montfort, is reported to have said: "God will know His own."

One of the heathen practices of which the Templars were accused was that they worshiped in the Jerusalem chapter house a floating head, or a picture of a head, Baphomet, that represented Satan. In terms of the heresy trials of the Templars, the practical effect is somewhat reminiscent of the Russian Gulag experience of

178 – *Appendix: The Significance of Names in Stranger*   Patterson & Thornton

the twentieth century: the Templars in Jerusalem were accused of being "contaminated" by displaying a Sufi relic. A television documentary on the Shroud of Turin a few years ago suggested that the head was actually the face part of the Shroud, with the rest folded back and the whole put in a display case. There seems to be no authority for this speculation. Later commentators (an essay on this point can be found at http://intranet.ca/~magicworks/knights/solved.html) have decided that the head probably existed and probably was a relic of a Sufi martyr, Husayn ibn Mansur al-Hallaj (d. 922 C.E.) and the name "Baphomet" was a corrupted phonetic transliteration of "abufihamet," the head's nickname ("father of understanding" or "father of all wisdom" in Arabic—hence father of all=Jubal). To make things even more interesting, al-Hallaj (and the Sufi order of The Builders) has been identified with Hiram Abiff, and we are back to Freemasonry.

In support of this identification, Adam Walks Between Worlds offers the observation that the only ornament in the Nest was a stereographic bust of Jubal Harshal—a disembodied head. The rationale given for Jubal's special status in the Nest is that Jubal was the only human to grok in fullness without learning Martian.

This seems a bit far-fetched, but Heinlein did grow up with the romantic mythology of Templarism: when Heinlein was fourteen years old, the Order of DeMolay was founded in his home town of Kansas City, for boys aged (then) 14–21, and this is a direct reference to the Templars. Jacques DeMolay was the last Grand Master of the Order of Templars, and with two lieutenants, after he confessed under torture then repudiated his confession, was burnt to death by Philip on an island used regularly for the purpose of such executions in the middle of the Seine in Paris. Complete records of membership in the early DeMolay chapters is not available, so it cannot be determined whether Heinlein was a member—but in any case he was positioned to pick up anything that was "in the air" at the time, and Templarism was in the air in Kansas City while Heinlein was in high school.

Adam Walks Between Worlds makes more of the character, connecting him with the "preternatural spirit" Aiwass who dictated Aleister Crowley's *Book of the Law* in 1904, because Jubal, like the *Book of the Law*, was "born on three successive days." This seems a minor coincidence—but it may be a more fruitful line of research than it may appear on the surface, for the three "laws" of Thelema, the religion Crowley founded based on the *Book of the Law* are:

1. Do what Thou Wilt shall be the whole of the Law;

2. Love is the Law, Love under Will;

3. Every person is a Star.

In a sense, *Stranger* appears to be entirely devoted to and formed by these laws. In fact the third law is a restatement of "Thou art God." *The Book of the Law* is one of the many "oddities" Mike is mentioned as reading during his seeking phase.

Of this mass of material, what did Heinlein *really* mean? It's impossible to say—certainly some of it; possibly a lot of it. It may—or may not—be coincidental that Father Jubal Harshaw's name is assonant with and has the same metrical values as *abufi-hamet*, "father of Wisdom."

Ben Caxton

"Benjamin" is a Hebrew name that means "Son of my right hand," and "Caxton" is the first printer of English, best known for his English edition of *The Bible*. The connection of a printer to Caxton's profession of journalism seems clear enough. Perhaps the combined names indicate that Caxton is to be a journalistic tool for Mike and for Jubal, the "right hand" being the good hand for making or doing. Certainly, Caxton plays this function at more than one point in the book. He set up the process that will free Mike from the Federation and later he reports on Mike's adult activities to Jubal.[104]

Gillian Boardman

The name "Gillian" or "Jillian" means simply "youthful" or "fresh." She is most often called "Jill," which is associated with the "Jack and Jill" of a children's rhyme, who went down a hill to fetch a pail of water. Jill and Mike did go down the slippery slope of religious seeking to fetch the water of life to humanity. However, her function in the novel is to be parent (mother) and consort to Mike, and this is reflected in the series of "Magna mater" deities she portrays at a service of the Church of All Worlds when Jubal visits the Nest: Cybele, Isis, Frigg (Freya), Ge (Gaia), Devi, Ishtar (Isis by another name, also Hastur and Astaroth, the consort-goddess of Jahweh), Maryam, Mother Eve.

The Secretaries

The names of the three secretaries present a special problem; over the years several schemes have been suggested to interpret them, but without success. They "almost" hang together in several ways, but the key to the coherence that can be sensed remains elusive. It is possible that they hold the master key for interpreting the entire book.

"Miriam" is "Maryam" is "Mary," the mother of Christ, or perhaps Mary Magdalene, traditionally a reformed prostitute who ministered to Christ's personal needs. Since no mention of a relationship between Miriam and Anne is made in *Stranger*, the reference may be to Mary Magdalene.

---

104. In his article, "Linguistic Relativity in Middle High Martian," Willis McNelly makes a sly reference to a forthcoming Martian/English dictionary by Jubal Harshaw, to be printed by Caxton Press.

St. **Anne** is the mother of Mary, and therefore the grandmother of Christ. According to tradition, St. Anne (or in Hebrew, Hannah) was barren. She prayed for a child, and she became pregnant with Mary at quite an advanced age. The story is an obvious typology of Abraham and Sarah, which places Mary and Christ in line to fulfill Old Testament prophecies.

Robert Graves discusses Anna as a generalized name for the Great Goddess prior to the patriarchial Olympian gods of the Achaeans, becoming the Queen of Heaven, a role taken over in Christianity by Mary (Miriam) the mother of Jesus. By a stroke of etymological legerdemain, Graves also derives Miriam from Anna, reinforcing the St. Anne–Virgin Mary connection in Christianity and showing the connection of the Christ story to the older mythology. As Mary is the Mother of God, Anna is, to Christian mystics, the Grandmother of God.

"Dorcas" means "doe," a deer, a female deer. Re: a drop of golden—no, wait, wrong work of fiction. The most prominent Biblical story concerning a Dorcas is the charity of a seamstress who took care of widows and orphans. Dorcas herself is a widow and she has a son. Her son is a "widow's son"—in fact, the emblematic widow's son of the best-known of the Masonic pass signs: "who will help the widow's son?"

If the third name in this sequence could be connected also to Anna, or to Miriam, there would be good reason to think there is some specifically Christian meaning being keyed by them. If not specifically Christian, they may nonetheless be aspects of the Triple Goddess or Her Erato derivative aspects of the muses (originally three, expanded later to nine), so there is a female trinity to complement the male Trinity implicit in a Christian reading. Graves' *The White Goddess* was published in 1948 and is eminently the kind of thing Heinlein would have been interested in, though there is no definite evidence of influence in *Stranger*. But the third name cannot be fitted within this frame of reference, and so some other interpretive scheme must be sought.

There are two oddities about the secretaries, and one is rather well remarked upon in the critical literature: their characterization in Jubal's household is almost interchangeable, except for slight differences in speech patterns. Several critics hastened to conclude that they are there merely as interchangeable sexual machines, imposing an alien anti-feminist reading on the book. This generates the absurdity, tiresomely repeated, that Mike travels around the country with a harem of willing sex-slaves—a figure found nowhere in the book.[105]

When we see the secretaries later, in the Nest, they are individualized in the same way that other characters are portrayed. This is puzzling and much more interesting than the harem—though it does not validate anyone's prejudices. It

---

105. Heinlein criticism has been seriously crippled by the degree of superficiality and self-indulgence his critics have permitted themselves.

signals to us that there is something going on and that they may be part of a deeper structure tying the book together.

The other peculiarity about the secretaries is that they are not given family names at all—which seems significant; it appears that they are to be interpreted allegorically and possibly together rather than as individual, novelistic characters.

Of the several schemes that have been proposed to interpret them, none seems to work out properly in terms of the symbolism. The scheme that seems to have the most promise is that the five "servants" in Jubal's household represent the five modes of Yoga. This interpretation is suggested by a remark by Anne: when called to witness to the color of a house on a hill, she remarks "it's white on this side," and Jubal points out it wouldn't occur to her, because of her Fair Witness training, to assume it was white all over. This unwillingness to make the assumption marks Anne as representing Jnana Yoga. Dorcas and Miriam may represent Hatha Yoga and Bhakti-Yoga, and Duke and Larry may represent Raga-Yoga and Karma-Yoga—or some other combination. Although this scheme has at least the virtues of (a) hanging together, and (b) being extensible to Mike's Martian powers (since most of them are Yogic demonstrations and not supernatural at all), there just isn't any strong evidence to support or contradict it. If it's a true schema, Heinlein may not have been interested in revealing the fact to make a point, just using it to organize the figures.

Anne is the most highly characterized of the three, the only one for whom there is any significant personal detail. She is a "blonde Valkyrie" from Dallas—a Fair Witness, an unusual figure that may have been suggested by a remark in Korzybski's *Science and Sanity*, but is also an indirect reference to Samuel Renshaw, as she has apparently been trained by Renshaw's methods. The Fair Witness is in Heinlein's earliest set of notes about the book and dates from the same brainstorming session in November or December of 1948 that gave rise to "Gulf," another story that uses Renshaw concepts from a three-part article that appeared in 1948. Perhaps Anne shows us another typology in action in the book: as a Fair Witness, Anne is the world's memory of important documents and events of the past—wills and contracts (note that Mnemosyne—memory—is the mother of the muses, so it might be possible to connect Anne, with her white cloak of office, to the White Goddess after all); Jubal is knowledge and living memory of the present culture; and Mike is the knowledge of new culture to come.]

However the relatively blank characterization at the start and developed characterization at the end suggest that the secretaries may be involved in the typological progression from Martian Heaven to Human Heaven. In Jubal's household, the secretaries are counterparts of the Martian Adults—hewers of wood (Larry, Duke) and drawers of water (the secretaries). They are laborers in this context, because Jubal's is a tragic heaven, barricaded from the world; Mike's Nest, however, is a comic-apocalyptic heaven, where the individual spirit is released to flourish. Mike inhabits, serially, all three—tragic, comic, and apocalyptic heavens, just as he has been in the comic earth-paradise (NeoPlatonic) Mars, the tragic earth of the Federation, and the apocalyptic earth of the Nest. In the tragic heaven of Jubal's household, the world of man is excluded, while the Nest is actively engaged in embracing such of the world of men as is ready to join them: this is the traditional distinction between tragedy (separation, isolation) and comedy (integration, community).

Thus, the problem of the secretaries can be "resolved" in a single sentence (which nevertheless has all the inadequacies of single-sentence resolutions): The individuality of the secretaries is suppressed at the start of the book so that it can flower at the end and establish a contrast between Jubal's household, as a tragic Heaven, and Mike's Nest, as a comic Heaven.

Agnes Douglas

"Agnes" means "lamb," as in sacrificial animal, and Agnes Douglas' professional role as an angelic operative is to be martyred—so long as the role is essentially virginal. This apparently throw-away comment reveals the inner significance of Agnes Douglas to the book. [106]

St. Agnes was an early Christian martyr identified with virginity. She would not renounce Christianity, and her holiness was such that her torturer-rapist was permanently paralyzed. She became the patron saint of young girls and would grant her charges visions of their future husbands if they would perform certain rites on the eve of her feast day, January 20. John Keats' "The Eve of St. Agnes" (1820) contains many oblique references to enchantment and fortunes, and these references may have wound up in *Stranger* in the somewhat unusual relationship between Agnes Douglas and Becky Vesey, *q.v.*

Joseph Douglas

The Secretary General's name seems at first glance unremarkable, but it gains meaning in combination with his wife's name. St. Joseph is the human father of Jesus, as the Virgin Mary was his mother.

Alexandra Vesant/Becky Vesey

"Madame Alexandra Vesant (Becky Vesey)" seems to evoke Annie Wood Besant—socialist firebrand at the center of the family planning trials of the 1870s.

---

106. The character of Agnes Douglas essentially disappears from the book about halfway through. It is interesting to note that when she resurfaces, in a brief mental aside by Archangel Foster, it is as "Alice Douglas" (299/370). Consistency errors are rare in Heinlein's work. How this error could remain in a book as thoroughly and repeatedly edited as *Stranger* is a mystery.

When Madame Helena Blavatsky died in 1904 (a very crucial year), Besant assumed leadership of the Theosophical Society, a Buddhist-influenced quasi-religious organization that was to have, at its peak, a membership of over 20 million adherents. She ultimately (1920) moved the Headquarters of the Society to India and hailed her adoptive son, Krishnamurti, as the new Messiah, avatar of Horus. Krishnamurti politely declined the honor, and the membership of the Theosophical Society thereafter declined, though it is still around today. In "Lost Legacy," Heinlein had showed a thorough (though probably not an insider's) acquaintance with Theosophy, which he apparently picked up from his second wife's mother, Skipper (Florence Gleeson) MacDonald, the only Theosophist known to have been in his immediate acquaintance. A "Vessy" is also a French culinary term for the caul of fat in which roasts may be wrapped so that they are both protected and basted during the cooking process. It might be possible to spin an analogy based on this meaning, but it's probably coincidental.

Becky Vesey's deceased husband had a stage name of Professor Simon Magus, and there are some interesting associations in that name. Simon Magus was a Samaritan magician who after converting to Christianity (*Acts* 8:9-25) offered to purchase from the Apostles Peter and John the power of the Holy Spirit. From his name comes the sin "Simony," the purchase of sacred offices or implements.

There are several legends surrounding Simon Magus. One says that he was an incarnation of Zeus (the way Christ was an incarnation of Jehovah). Another attributes the founding of Gnosticism to him. A third says that he became a false messiah in that very messianic time and confronted Sts. Peter and Paul in Rome, performing magic before the Emperor Nero. Yet another looks to him as a founder of the medieval alchemical tradition. There were Simons in abundance in the ancient near east, and it was a time for messiahs, so it is possible that several different Simons could have been conflated in the popular memory.

Professor Simon Magus is dead during the entire time frame of *Stranger*, so it's unlike any of these associations were intended to be shown as working in Mike's life on earth. But it is interesting that he was a friend of Jubal's during his carny days and the name refers to a failed messiah. Jubal is also a failed messiah in the sense that he groks but can't use the knowledge to revitalize the world.

Patty Paiwonski

The character of Patty Paiwonski—not the name, but the character—can be traced to the character of the landlady in the Clifton/Riley *They'd Rather Be Right*, a 1954 Dianetics novel that won the Hugo. The landlady was the first person to be "cleared" by the computer they build in the book. The name "Patricia" is the feminine complement of Patrick, both of which mean "aristocrat" or "patrician." The Greek equivalent would be "Aristocles," which is Plato's name.

The Next Generation

At the end of the book, all three of the secretaries are pregnant with children of Mike. Anne's child is to be **Abigail Zenobia**. "Abigail" comes from the Hebrew "abigayil," literally "father is rejoicing." It also used to be an English slang term for a lady's maid, from the Beaumount & Fletcher character in *The Scornful Lady* (1616), though it is not likely this association is intended. Zenobia, however, has an interesting set of associations. Anne went from "Abigail" to "Zenobia" in deciding what to name her and wound up with both. The significance of this set of names is particularly remarked by Jubal—he wonders if Mommy knows how very appropriate indeed they are. Besides "A" to "Z" in the Alpha to Omega sense, what does it mean?

Zenobia was a desert Arab Queen of Palmyra from 267 or 268 to 272 C.E. who led a revolution against Rome in 275 C.E. She had some alarming (from the Roman's point of view) success, capturing Egypt before being put down. She died the next year, in 276. "Zenobia" is a Romanized form of the Queen's real name, which is rendered variously by the Library of Congress' index as Septimia Bathzabbai, Zineubyea, Zaneybya, Zaynab al-Zabbea, Septimia Zenobia, Bat Zabbai, Bath Zabbeay, Zabbea, Settinia Zenobia, Septemia Zenobia, Sebaste, and Sebaste Septimia Zenobia.

At any rate, Zenobia was associated with the downfall of the Gnostic Christian church. Until her rebellion, the gnostic bishops had more or less avoided currying temporal recognition from the governors of Roman empire. Gibbon hints and others tell us that Zenobia favored one particular Gnostic bishop over orthodox ones holding sway in the East during her reign, and she elevated him over the orthodox before she was conquered by the Emperor Aurelian (270–275) in 273. But she fell. Shortly following that, in 276 C.E., persecution by orthodox Christians of what by then was known as the Manichaean heresy (with which the Gnostics had been associated) began in the Eastern areas of the Empire and the then leader Mani, who gave the heresy his name, was crucified. Following the persecutions of Diocletian, which fell on all brands of Christians indiscriminately, there were not many Gnostics left to enjoy the offical toleration Constantine instituted in 313 C.E.

Miriam's daughter, **Fatima Michele** is named after Michael and Mohammed's daughter, probably indicating that Mahmoud, whose name is a slight orthographic variation of Mohammed, intends to raise the child as his own.

Dorcas will indeed also have a son (Michael has grokked it will be a boy), to be named Dennis and, as he will be born posthumously to Mike, she will be a "widow" with a "widow's son." We may therefore be somewhat confident that the Masonic implications of the Dorcas name were intended.

"Dennis" is Denis is Dionysos—a third century martyr and patron Saint of France as well as the Greek god of wine and the dark mysteries. He is also, significantly, the patron of the Greek satyr plays, which many scholars say form one of the two principal roots of the satiric tradition (the other being the Roman *lanx satura* literary model named after an overflowing tray of mixed fruits).

℞

These are the major name associations within the book, though other minor characters have names packed with meaning as well. Saul and Ruth, for example, are quintessentially Jewish names for the two most prominent Jews in the Nest.

It remains certain that we will still be trying to grasp Heinlein's intention with these names for years to come.

Bibliography

Adam Walks Between Worlds. "Whence Came the Stranger: Tracking the Metapatterns of *Stranger In a Strange Land*."
http://www.wegrokit.com

Aldiss, Brian. *The Trillion Year Spree*. New York: Atheneum Press, 1986

Allen, James B. and Glen M. Leonard. *The Story of the Latter-Day Saints*, 2nd ed. Salt Lake City, Utah: Deseret Book Co., 1992

Amis, Kingsley. *New Maps of Hell*. New York: Ballantine Books, 1960

Armstrong, A.H. *Introduction to Ancient Philosophy*. 3rd Ed. Totowa, New Jersey: Littlefield, Adams, & Co., 1957.

Armstrong, Karen. *A History of God: The 4,000-Year Quest of Judaism, Christianity and Islam*. New York: Alfred A. Knopf, Inc., 1993

Aristotle. *The Poetics*. Trans. Theodore Buckley. Buffalo, New York: Prometheus Books, 1992

Asimov, Isaac. *I, Asimov*. New York: Doubleday & Co., 1979

Asimov, Isaac. *In Memory Yet Green*. New York: Doubleday & Co. 1977

M.M. Bakhtin. *The Dialogical Imagination*. Austin, TX. University of Texas Press, 1981.

Benedict, Ruth. *Patterns of Culture*. New York: New American Library (Mentor), 1934

Blackmore, Tim. "Talking with Strangers: Interrogating the Many Texts That Became Heinlein's *Stranger in a Strange Land.*" *Extrapolation*, Vol. 36, No.2 (Summer 1995), pp. 136–150.

Blish, James (writing as "William Atheling, Jr."). *The Issue At Hand*. Chicago: Avent: Publishers, 1964

Cabell, James Branch. *Beyond Life: Dizain des Démiurges*. New York: Robert M. McBride & Co., 1919, 1927 (Storisende edition)

Cabell, James Branch. *Figures of Earth: A Comedy of Appearances*. New York: Robert M. McBride & Co., 1921

Cabell, James Branch. *The High Place: A Comedy of Disenchantment*. New York: Robert M. McBride & Co., 1924

Cabell, James Branch. *Jurgen: A Comedy of Justice*. New York: Grossett & Dunlap, 1919, 1927

Cabell, James Branch. *The Rivet in Grandfather's Neck: A Comedy of Limitations*. New York: Robert M. McBride & Co., 1915, 1921

Cabell, James Branch. *Something About Eve: A Comedy of Fig-Leaves*. New York: Robert M. McBride & Co., 1927

Campbell, Joseph. *The Hero With a Thousand Faces*. 2nd ed. Princeton, New Jersey: Princeton University Press, 1968

Cavanaugh, Jack. *The Puritans*. Wheaton, Ill.: Victor Books, 1994

Eliade, Mircea. *Myth and Reality.* London: Allen & Unwin, 1964

Eliade, Mircea. *The Sacred and the Profane*. New York: Harper & Row, 1961

Emerson, Ralph Waldo. *The Selected Writings of Ralpha Waldo Emerson*. Ed. Brooks Atkinson. New York: The Modern Library, 1992

Foster, John Burt, Jr. *Heirs to Dionysus: A Nietzsche Current in Literary Modernism*. Princeton, N.J.: Princeton University Press. 1981

Franklin, H. Bruce. *Robert A. Heinlein: America as Science Fiction*. New York: Oxford University Press, 1980

Frazer, Sir James George. *The Golden Bough: A Study in Magic and Religion* (1 vol. abridged) New York: The MacMillan Co., 1958

Frye, Northrup.* *Anatomy of Criticism.* Princeton, New Jersey: Princeton University Press, 1957

Frye, Northrup. *Fables of Identity: Studies in Poetic Mythology.* San Diego, California: Harcourt, Brace, Jovanovich, Publishers: 1963

Frye, Northrup. *The Double Vision: Language and Meaning in Religion.* Toronto, Canada: University of Toronto Press: 1991

Frye, Northrup. *The Great Code: The Bible and Literature.* San Diego, Calif.: Harcourt, Brace Publishing Co., 1981

Funk, Robert W., trans. and commentary, with Hoover, Roy W. and The Jesus Seminar. *The Five Gospels.* New York: MacMillan & Co., 1993

Garr, Alice Carol. "The Human as Machine Analog: The Big Daddy of Interchangeable Parts in the Fiction of Robert A. Heinlein." *Robert A. Heinlein.* Eds. Joseph D. Olander and Martin Harry Greenberg. New York: Taplinger Publishing Co., 1978, pp. 64–82

Gifford, James. *Robert A. Heinlein: A Reader's Companion.* Sacramento, Calif.: Nitrosyncretic Press, 2000

Graves, Robert. *The White Goddess: A Historical Grammar of Poetic Myth.* (2nd ed.) New York: David Farrar, 1966

Greeley, Andrew. *Thy Brother's Wife.* New York: Warner Books, 1982

Greeley, Andrew. *An Occasion of Sin.* New York: G.P. Putnam's Sons, 1991

Griffin, Dustin. *Satire: A Critical Reintroduction.* Lexington, Kentucky: University Press of Kentucky, 1994

Guillamont, A.; Puech, H.C.; Quispel, G, and 'Abd al Masih, Y. *The Gospel According to Thomas.* Leiden, Netherlands: E.G. Brill/ Collins/Harper, 1959

Heimert, Alan and Andrew Delbanco, eds. *The Puritans in America: A Narrative Anthology.* Cambridge, Mass.: Harvard University Press, 1985

Heinlein, Robert A. *Assignment in Eternity* (1953). New York: Baen Books, 2000

Heinlein, Robert A. *Expanded Universe.* New York: G.P. Putnam's Sons, 1980

---

* Frye's name, confusingly, is spelled both "Northrup" or "Northrop" in his various books.

Heinlein, Robert A. *Have Space Suit—Will Travel.* New York: Charles Scribner's Sons, 1958

Heinlein, Robert A. *The Past Through Tomorrow.* New York: G.P. Putnam's Sons, 1967

Heinlein, Robert A. *Red Planet.* New York: Charles Scribner's Sons, 1948

Heinlein, Robert A. *Starship Troopers.* New York: G.P. Putnam's Sons, 1959

Heinlein, Robert A. *Stranger in a Strange Land.* New York: G.P. Putnam's Sons, 1961

Heinlein, Robert A. *Stranger in a Strange Land* (Original, uncut). New York, Ace Books, 1991

Heinlein, Virginia, ed. *Grumbles From the Grave.*

Huxley, Aldous. *The Perennial Philosophy.* New York: Harper & Brothers Publishers, 1945

Jung, Carl G. *Alchemical Studies.* Vol. 13 of The Collected Works of C.G. Jung (Bollingen Series XX). Trans. R.F.C. Hull. Princeton, New Jersey: Princeton University Press, 1967

Kondo, Yoji, ed. *Requiem: New Collected Works by Robert A. Heinlein and Tributes to the Grand Master.* New York: Tor Books, 1992

Korzybski, Alfred. *Manhood of Humanity: The Science and Art of Human Engineering.* New York: E.P. Dutton & Co., 1921

Korzybski, Alfred. *Science and Sanity: An Introduction to Non-Aristotelian Systems and General Semantics.* Lakeville, Connecticut: The International Non-Aristotelian Library Publishing Company, 1933 (4th ed. 1958)

Lévi-Strauss, Claude. *Structural Anthropology.* Trans. C. Jacobson and D.G. Schoepf. New York: Basic Books, 1963

Mead, Margaret, ed. *Writings of Ruth Benedict: Anthropologist at Work.* New York: Atherton Press, 1966.

Moskowitz, Sam. *Seekers of Tomorrow: Masters of Modern Science Fiction.* Cleveland, Ohio: The World Publishing Co., 1966

Nietzsche, Friedrich W. *The Birth of Tragedy.* Trans. Walter Kaufmann. New York: Random House, 1967

Nietzsche, Friedrich W. *Froeliche Wissenschaft.* Trans. Walter Kaufmann as *The Gay Science.* New York: Vintage Books, 1974

Nietzsche, Friedrich W. *Thus Spoke Zarathustra.* Trans. Walter Kaufmann. New York: Penguin Books, 1966

Noyes, John Humphrey. *History of American Socialisms* (1869). New York: Dover Publications, 1966

Otto, Rudolph. *Das Heilige.* Trans. John W. Harvey *The Idea of the Holy.* London: Oxford University Press, 1958

Ouspensky, Petr Demianovich. *A New Model of the Universe,* 2nd Edition. New York: Vintage Books., 1930, 1934

Ouspensky, Petr Demianovich. *Tertium Organum* (1912). Trans. Nicholas Bessaraboff and Claude Bragdon. London: Manas Press, 1922

Owenby, Phillip H. "Robert A. Heinlein: Popular Adult Educator and Philosopher of Education." Unpublished Doctoral Dissertation, 1996

Panshin, Alexei. *Heinlein in Dimension.* Chicago: Advent: Publishers, Inc., 1968.

Panshin, Alexei and Cory Panshin. *Science Fiction in Dimension.* Chicago: Advent: Publishers, Inc., 1976

Parker, Patricia. "Anagogic Metaphor: Breaking Down the Wall of Partition." *Centre and Labyrinth: Essays in Honour of Northrup Frye.* Toronto: University of Toronto Press, 1983

Patterson, Bill. "Early Chronology of *Stranger.*" *The Heinlein Journal,* No. 6 (January 2000), pp. 4–6.

Patterson, Bill. "The Heir of James Branch Cabell: The Biography of the Life of the Biography of the Life of Manuel (A Comedy of Inheritances)." 2000 Cabell Prize; Virginia Commonwealth University: http://www.library.vcu.edu/jbc/speccoll/exhibit/cabell/prize3.html

Patterson, Bill. "The Hermetic Heinlein." *The Heinlein Journal.* No. 1 (July 1997), pp. 15–25

Patterson, Bill. "Robert A. Heinlein: A Biographical Sketch." *The Heinlein Journal,* No. 5 (July 1999) pp. 7–36.

Patterson, Bill. "A Study of 'Misfit'" *The Heinlein Journal,* No. 3 (July 1998), pp. 24-34

Plank, Robert. "Omnipotent Cannibals in *Stranger In a Strange Land.*" *Robert A. Heinlein.* Eds. Joseph D. Olander and Martin Harry Greenberg. New York: Taplinger Publishing Co., 1978, pp. 83–106

Plato. *The Republic and Other Works.* Trans. B. Jowett. New York: Anchor Books, 1973

Rand, Ayn. *Atlas Shrugged.* New York: Random House, 1957

Reno, Shaun. "The Zuni Indian Tribe: A Model for *Stranger in a Strange Land's* Martian Culture." *Extrapolation*, Vol. 36, No.2 (Summer 1995), pp. 151–158

Ricoeur, Paul. "'Anatomy of Criticism' or the Order of Paradigms." *Centre and Labyrinth: Essays in Honour of Northrup Frye.* Toronto: University of Toronto Press, 1983

Roszak, Theodore. *The Making of A Counter Culture: Reflections on the Technocratic Society and Its Youthful Opposition.* Garden City, New York: Doubleday & Co., Inc., 1969

Samuelson, David N. "Stranger in the Sixties: Model or Mirror?" *Critical Encounters: Writers and Themes in Science Fiction.* Ed. Dick Riley. New York: F. Ungar, 1978

Sears, Hal D. *The Sex Radicals: Free Love in High Victorian America.* Lawrence, Kansas: The Regents Press of Kansas, 1977.

Singleton, Carl. ed. *The Sixties in America*, Vol. 3. Pasadena, Calif.: Salem Press, 1999

Slusser, George Edgar. *Classic Years of Robert A. Heinlein.* Riverside, Calif.: Borgo Press, 1976

Slusser, George Edgar. *Robert A. Heinlein: Stranger In His Own Land.* Riverside, Calif.: Borgo Press, 1975

Smith, E.E., Ph.D. *Gray Lensman.* Reading, Penn.: Fantasy Press, 1951

Spinrad, Norman. "SF/Beat: Les Slans de Van Vogt et les Clochards célestes de Kerouac sont des frères littéraires tout comme le héros de *Dune* et Timothy Leary." *Magazine Litteraire*, October 1992, pp. 47–51.

Stover, Leon. *Robert Heinlein.* New York: Twayne United States Authors Series, 1987.

Strenski, Ivan. *Four Theories of Myth in Twentieth-Century History: Cassirer, Eliade, Lévi-Strauss and Malinowski*. Iowa City, Iowa: University of Iowa Press, 1987

Swift, Jonathan. *A Modest Proposal*. New York: Grossman, 1969

Tarrant, Desmond. *James Branch Cabell: The Dream and the Reality*. Norman, OK: University of Oklahoma Press, 1967

Thornton, Andrew. "Mythos and Logos: The Influence of P.D. Ouspensky in the Fiction of Robert A. Heinlein," Part 1: "Foundations Laid in 'Elsewhen.' *The Heinlein Journal*, No. 1 (July 1997), pp. 9–14; Part 2: "Ouspenskyan Ideas in *Stranger in a Strange Land*." *The Heinlein Journal*, No. 2 (January 1998), pp. 8–16; and Part 3: "*Glory Road* and the World As Myth Books." *The Heinlein Journal*, No. 3 (July 1998), pp. 13–18.

Twain, Mark. "Captain Stormfield's Visit to Heaven." *The Bible According to Mark Twain: Irreverent Writings on Eden, Heaven, and the Flood by America's Master Satirist*. Howard G. Baetzhold and Joseph B. McCullough, eds. New York: Simon & Schuster, 1995

Twain, Mark. *Letters From the Earth: Uncensored Writings by Mark Twain*. Ed. Bernard DeVoto. New York: Harper & Row, 1962

Twain, Mark. *The Mysterious Stranger & Other Stories*. New York: New American Library, 1984

Twain, Mark. *What is Man?* New York: Oxford University Press, 1996

Vlastos, Gregory. *Socrates: Ironist and Moral Philosopher*. Ithaca, NY: Cornell University Press, 1991

Voltaire, *Candide*. Trans. Tobias Smollett. Franklin Center, Penn.: Franklin Library, 1979

Wells, Arvin. *Jesting Moses: A Study of Cabellian Comedy*. Gainesville, Florida: University of Florida Press, 1962.

Wells, H.G. *A Modern Utopia* (1905). Lincoln, Nebraska. University of Nebraska Press, 1967.

Wells, H.G. *The War of the Worlds: A Critical Text of the 1898 London First Edition, with an Introduction, Illustrations and Appendices*. Ed., Leon Stover. Jefferson, North Carolina: McFarland & Company, Inc., 2001

Wittels, David G. "You're Not as Smart as You Could Be" *The Saturday Evening Post*, 220: 42, 43, 44 (April 17, 24 and May 1, 1948)

Glossary

Agape

Generally, unselfish "intellectual" love without sexual connotations; love that wishes the highest and the best for the beloved. Also the love of God or Jesus for humanity, and the echoing love of Christians for others. *Cf.* Eros.

Allegory, Allegorical

A method of metaphor or polysemous (*q.v.*) interpretation by which the literary figure is an analogy of the material being referenced (rather than being referenced by direct substitution, as in symbol, *q.v.*) An example of allegory at this level would be to view the Mosaic wandering of the Israelites in the Sinai Desert as an analogy of the wandering of the soul in confusion before its moment of enlightenment. The term is also used casually as a synonym for myth.

Anagnorisis

A Greek term, meaning "recognition." In poetics, anagnorsis is the moment in which an important character "recognizes" the nature of his (or her) situation or of the relationships important to the story situation. For example, in *Oedipus Rex*, the anagnorisis comes at the moment when Oedipus recognizes that Jocasta, his wife, is also his mother and that he has fulfilled the prophecy and killed his father.

Anagogy

In multi-leveled, "polysemous" interpretation of literature, anagogy is the exploration of the aspect of the story that concerns humanity's relation to the divine—or, as Frye has it, to the total order of literature. The most common "movement" identified with anagogy is separation or union with the divine.

Apollonian

Briefly (and roughly), "Apollonian" (from the Greek god Apollo) stands for the linear, rational, orderly, thinking impulse in humans. See also *Apollonian-Dionysian Dichotomy.*

Apollonian-Dionysian Dichotomy

Heinlein introduces the Apollonian-Dionysian dichotomy, a metaphor borrowed from F.W. Nietzsche (*q.v.*) and Ruth Benedict, as the controlling dynamic of *Stranger*. Any individual and any society tends more toward one of these "poles" of experience than to the other, but they have to be combined together or synthesized to make a whole person. The task of Valentine Michael Smith's Church of All Worlds is to bring the separated Apollonian and Dionysian elements together and make whole, healed human beings. Heinlein makes varied and extensive use of the metaphor, ringing change after change throughout the book. See also *Apollonian, Dionysian.*

Ascetic, asceticism

The idea that self-denial is a route to spiritual progress.

Cabell, James Branch (1879–1957)

James Branch Cabell was, during the 1920s, the most famous or infamous writer in the English language. His 1919 *Jurgen: A Comedy of Justice* was suppressed under the censorship laws. The resulting trial marshalled literary opinion around the world in his favor and resulted in the abandonment of the attempt to censor literature. He was also one of Heinlein's most important literary influences. He was introduced to *Jurgen* in 1929, at the very end of Cabell's most productive period. In retrospect, Cabell turns out to have been a "transitional" writer between the nineteenth and the twentieth century styles of literature. His popularity faded away after about 1930, though he continued to write and publish almost to the end of his life in 1957.

Catharsis

A term from Aristotle's *Poetics* describing the "purging" or sense of emotional relief that takes place in Greek tragedy and other dramatic forms. It might be said that catharsis is the sensation brought about in the audience by its recognition that a tragic fate is both terrible and just. Comic catharsis was implied, but never explored.

Crowley, Aleister (1888–1947)

Aleister Crowley is a pivotal figure in many different occult and esoteric traditions of the twentieth century. His method of studying several mystical traditions together—e.g., symbology of the tarot together with kaballah—set the style for twentieth century magical traditions, which he named "magick" to distinguish them from stage magic. Crowley entered the Order of the Golden Dawn as a young man, becoming the head of the Order early in the twentieth century, then founding an offshoot, the Ordo Templo Orientalis (O.T.O.), which is still active. In 1904 he received the highly poetic *The Book of the Law* by dictation of a "preternatural spirit" and in 1909 founded the religion of Thelema based on *The Book of the Law.* Crowley was fanatically anti-Christian and took for newspaper publicity the sarcastic motto that he was the "wickedest man in the world." He even had himself photographed crucifying a frog. The adverse publicity has been something of a thorn in the side of his followers, who have since tried to legitimatize his religions, with little success.

Dionysian
Briefly (and roughly), "Dionysian" (from the Greek god Dionysos) stands for the feeling, nonlinear, arational or anti-rational and disorderly impulse in humans. See also *Apollonian-Dionysian Dichotomy.*

Emerson, Ralph Waldo (1803–1882)
American essayist and philosopher, leading figure of the Transcendentalist school. Emerson trained as a Congregationalist minister but left the church in 1835. He adopted NeoPlatonic transcendentalist ideas and discussed them in England and Scotland with influential transcendentalists such as Carlyle. His two series of essays (1841 and 1844) were very widely read and extraordinarily influential on American intellectual life until well into the twentieth century. "Self-Reliance" is still found in a number of contemporary anthologies for high school literature classes. He was also a friend and patron of Henry David Thoreau, of "Walden" and "Civil Disobedience" fame.

Eros
Physical, usually sexual love. *Cf.* Agape.

Epistemology
The branch of philosophy that deals with knowledge—what we can know and how we can know what we know.

Frazer, Sir James (1854–1941)
See *The Golden Bough.*

General Semantics
General Semantics is a discipline invented by Alfred Korzybski to apply the insights of Russell and Whitehead in mathematical logic to linguistic theory. General Semantics was regarded as "cutting edge" intellectual technology

before World War II, but semantics developed away from that foundation work, keeping only slogans such as "the map is not the territory."

Golden Bough, The

By the end of the nineteenth century, some very significant academic work had been done in the theory of myth and magic. Sir James George Frazer's 12-volume study, *The Golden Bough: A Study of Magic and Myth*, comprehensively collected and analyzed dozens of ritual survivals in (mostly) European folklore, showing their relationship to each other and to neolithic agricultural rituals.

Graves, Robert (1895–1985)

See *The White Goddess*

Hellenism

The cultural combination of Roman law and government with Greek learning that characterized the Roman empire.

Heterodoxy

"Other"+"teaching." An opinion differing from and possible contrary to an acknowledged standard doctrine. *Cf.* Orthodoxy.

Irony

Irony is a figure of speech in which the referent is indicated by something other than a direct description, most commonly by the opposite of what is meant.

Korzybski, Alfred (1879–1950)

Founder of General Semantics, *q.v.*

Literal (interpretation)

A level of polysemous interpretation, *q.v.*, in which the events of the story are regarded as an imitation of real life or an analogy of history.

NeoPlatonism

NeoPlatonism is a philosophical tradition very important in the history of western civilization. The teachings of Plato were assimilated by Plotinus, among others, to hellenstic intellectual issues of the late Roman empire. St. Augustine thereafter assimilated NeoPlatonism to Christianity, where it was carried forward, at the same time as secular NeoPlatonism continued to develop outside the Church. A nineteenth century revival of interest in non-Christian NeoPlatonic ideas brought the basic idea of a cosmos filled with intelligences on many levels back into prominence, and they were adopted into American Transcendentalism (*q.v.*) through Ralph Waldo Emerson (*q.v.*)

Nietzsche, F. W. (1844–1900)

German philologist-philosopher. His highly original philosophical writings from about 1870 to 1885 were extraordinarily influential on the intellectual life of the west well into the early 20th century. After Nietzsche's death, his literary estate passed into the control of his sister, who slanted his work to conform to the racist agenda of her husband, and in the U.S. H.L. Mencken enthusiastically presented him as a Social Darwinist, by strip-quoting and falsifying the context of what he wrote. The corrupted Nietzsche was adopted as a patron-philosopher of Adolph Hitler's Nazism and he became unfashionable as a dialog partner in the liberal west. Heinlein was educated at the time of Nietzsche's greatest intellectual influence and shows many signs of thoughtful dialog with Nietzsche's ideas throughout his career and particularly in *Stranger in a Strange Land.*

Noumenal

In NeoPlatonic thought, the Nous is the mind of God, the eternal and unchanging reality of which phenomenal reality is a broken reflection in Plato's teachings. Rudolph Otto suggests that all religion is rooted in the experience of the noumenal.

Orthodoxy

"Correct"+"teaching." A standard of opinion or frame of reference. *Cf.* Heterodoxy.

Orthopraxis

Literally "correct" "action"—the conventionally correct way of doing things, esp. of religions. See also *Orthodoxy.*

Over-Soul

In Ralph Waldo Emerson's Transcendentalist writings, particularly the essay "The Over-Soul," the Over-Soul is the one true reality (see, Noumenal) of which everything we can see or experience is a small part—a tendril of the Over-Soul intruded into time (the Over-Soul as a whole stands outside of time), so that the separateness we can see is an illusion. We are actually all parts of the same whole being.

Platonism

The philosophy of Plato as expressed in the Dialogs and *The Republic.* See, NeoPlatonism.

Polyamory

This new word compounded of Greek ("poly" meaning "many") and Latin ("amor" meaning "love") roots was devised as a neutral term for group marriages of any composition, replacing gender-specific words such as "polyandry" (marriage of one woman with multiple husbands—"andros" for man) and "polygyny" (marriage of one man with multiple women—"gunos" for "woman"—the same root from which "gynecology" is derived). ("Polygamy" is many "marriages" simultaneously; "bigamy" is two ("bi-") marriages simultaneously.)

Polysemy

Literally "many meanings." Many-leveled. A mode of interpretation in which the "meaning" is simultaneously carried on four levels: literal, symbolic, allegorical, and anagogic, each of which, *q.v.*

Positivism / Positivist Materialism

A philosophy invented by Auguste Comte in the 1830s as "Logical Positivism," to the effect that scientific observation of natural phenomena replaces metaphysics and theology as ways of knowing. As Logical Positivism became widely accepted around the turn of the twentieth century, Positivists became more dogmatically materialist, assimilating reductionism to Positivism, so that, for example, every scientific discipline is viewed as being reducible to the principles of physics—which seems to have worked well for physical chemistry, less well for biochemistry, and not very well at all for disciplines such as psychology.

Semantics

The study of meaning as it is embodied in language and linguistic patterns.

Symbol(ic)

The level of polysemous interpretation in which a literary figure is taken for something else, by direct substitution, as in: when a white carnation—or snow—appears in the story, death is meant to be thought of.

Syncretism

A combination or fusion of practices or beliefs from several different systems, without the implication of integration or synthesis. In languages, verbs may have different tenses or other forms taken from different languages or different dialects (as in "go" "went") or as some verbs in Russian have entirely different roots for different tenses. In religions, rites or dogma from different systems accumulate without being transformed. The hellenistic mid-winter festival (Saturnalia) has been assimilated into Christianity as Christmas, but the Christmas Tree has not been given a Christian overlay of meaning—and similarly the hellenistic spring fertility rite has become Christianized as Easter, but the Easter Bunny has not been given a specifically Christian meaning. So both synthesis and syncretism is going on in Christianity.

Transcendentalism

A NeoPlatonic philosophy created in the nineteenth century principally by Ralph Waldo Emerson, to the effect that humans are more than (i.e., transcend) the phenomenal world, that all the universe is a single living, conscious being, and that we are all parts of this being, and everything that exists is part of us.

White Brotherhood

A society of illuminated individuals who work together for the betterment or protection of mankind, or specifically for its spiritual evolution or advancement. The corresponding notion in the Hindu tradition is the Society of Mahatmas.

The White Goddess

In 1948 the poet Robert Graves published a long study of the roots of northern mythic and poetic imagery, which he traced back to a pan-neolithic agricultural cult of The White Goddess. A certain amount of care must be taken when making use of Graves' anthropology, because he relies on his poetic intuition for it. However, his discussion of the working of the mind of a poet is rare and useful.

Index

This book was produced using FrameMaker
on a Windows-based publication system.

The Adobe Garamond font family
has been used throughout,
with titling in Hiroshige
and text accents in Stone Sans.

nitrosyncretic
press

Printed by Thomson-Shore, Dexter, Michigan